Edited by Nick Pulford

Contributors

Richard Birch
Andrew Dietz
Joe Eccles
David Jennings

Paul Kealy
Richard Lowther
Tyrone Molloy
Kevin Morley

Justin O'Hanlon
Dave Orton
Jonny Pearson
Graeme Rodway

Stefan Searle
Tom Segal
Craig Thake
Nick Watts

Designed by David Dew
Cover artwork by Duncan Olner

Published in 2025 by Pitch Publishing on behalf of Racing Post, 9 Donnington Park, 85 Birdham Road, Chichester, West Sussex, PO20 7AJ. www.pitchpublishing.co.uk info@pitchpublishing.co.uk.

ISBN 978-1801509466

Printed by Short Run Press

VIEWS FROM THE SPECIALISTS

4

The Racing Post's top tipsters and form experts, along with the major bookies, pick their fancies and debate the big issues

RACE-BY-RACE GUIDE

114

In-depth form guide to the main contenders by Racing Post top tipster Paul Kealy, with all the key trends

WELCOME to the Racing Post Cheltenham Festival Guide – and once again we have a bumper 208 pages packed with essential information and advice for the biggest week in the jump racing calendar.

Twenty years ago there was a festival revolution with the increase from three days to four and this is another year of change. Perhaps not as seismic as 2005, but significant nonetheless.

The alterations to the racing programme are detailed on page 14 and hopefully they will bring a more competitive and exciting festival. Terrestrial television viewers will get to watch more of the action, with an extra race each day on ITV, while racegoers should see the benefits of the Jockey Club's efforts to improve the on-course experience at Cheltenham.

If the stars align – and by 'stars' many will think first of Galopin Des Champs and Constitution Hill – this could be a vintage festival.

As usual we have aimed to provide a wide range of expert opinion and insight in this comprehensive festival preview. The first half of the book features the views of tipsters and bookmakers, Racing Post Ratings, analysis of the key formlines, the lowdown on the Irish challenge and trainer pointers.

In the second half of the book, Racing Post top tipster Paul Kealy provides his race-by-race guide with forthright opinions and profiles of more than 100 of the top horses, along with key trends from Kevin Morley.

We hope you enjoy this guide and have a festival to remember.

NICK PULFORD, EDITOR

THE SPECIALISTS

The Racing Post's team of experts reveal their festival fancies and the major bookmakers discuss the big issues in our Q&A

Final Demand can pay off

Richard Birch

IRELAND'S domination of the Cheltenham Festival will continue this year and Willie Mullins' runners will sweep many before them once again. You only needed to watch the Dublin Racing Festival to realise that.

Mullins has the best horses, the most powerful owners with the deepest pockets, and is clearly training his top-notchers to peak at the spring festivals.

Galopin Des Champs will be the Mullins headline horse by joining the greats in winning a third Cheltenham Gold Cup. He raised the roof at Leopardstown when netting a hat-trick of Irish Gold Cups and looks better than ever. The manner in which he pulled clear on the run-in was a joy to watch.

However, he's likely to be around 1-2 favourite for chasing's most sought-after prize

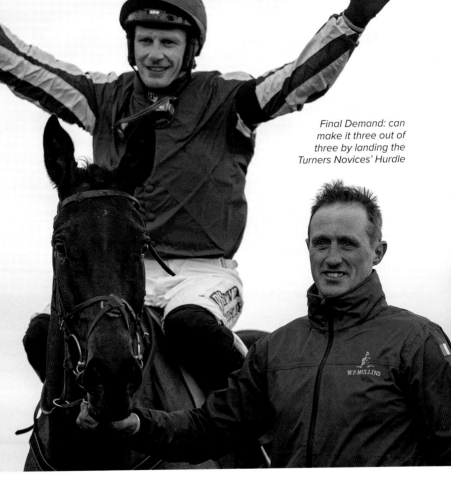

Final Demand: can make it three out of three by landing the Turners Novices' Hurdle

and a better bet is stablemate **Final Demand**, who makes maximum punting appeal in the Turners Novices' Hurdle.

Unbeaten in two starts, the six-year-old took the step up from maiden to Grade 1 company in his mighty stride when simply strolling through the 2m6f Nathaniel Lacy & Partners Solicitors Novice Hurdle at Leopardstown.

He jumped beautifully and barely came out of cruise control to slam the 140-rated Wingmen by 12 lengths. It was the performance of a potentially outstanding youngster and had 'Cheltenham winner for the next three years' written all over it.

Cheltenham Festival form is one of my key requirements in assessing races at the meeting and my other three selections all possess it.

Ballyburn looked to have the world at his feet when romping home by 13 lengths at last year's festival in what is now the Turners Novices' Hurdle.

His performance at Cheltenham earned him the honour of fourth-highest-rated novice hurdler – behind Constitution Hill, Iris's Gift and The New One – since the Anglo-Irish Jumps Classifications were introduced in the 1999-2000 season.

The seven-year-old looked special that day and, while it's fair to say he hasn't yet quite recreated that aura in three runs over fences, it's still early days.

He was far from spectacular when landing Leopardstown's Ladbrokes Novice Chase, but you get the impression he's being brought along steadily to peak on the Wednesday of the festival again, this time in the Brown Advisory Novices' Chase.

The presence of his stablemate Dancing City, an out-and-out stayer, makes it likely punters will be able to get a better price about Ballyburn than you could have dared to imagine 12 months ago.

He'll simply outclass and outspeed Dancing City up the hill and be promoted to second favourite behind Galopin Des Champs for the 2026 Gold Cup.

The time to back Constitution Hill was at 11-8 on December 24 for the Christmas Hurdle

at Kempton when he trailed Lossiemouth in the market.

I wrote an article last November saying that Nicky Henderson would never run Constitution Hill in any race apart from the Champion Hurdle if there was even the remotest thought in his mind that racing's biggest superstar would be beaten.

Preserving his unbeaten record is crucial if Constitution Hill is to go down in history as jump racing's best-ever horse.

Constitution Hill duly won at Kempton and then stretched his unbeaten tally to ten when surviving a last-flight scare in Cheltenham's International Hurdle.

It's likely that all his famed ability remains, but it's not totally proven and the air of invincibility Constitution Hill once carried no longer remains after his year off the track with health issues.

State Man, who benefited from Constitution Hill's absence to land last year's Champion Hurdle, boasts a formidable strike-rate in his own right, having landed 13 of his 18 starts.

The departure of Lossiemouth in the Irish Champion Hurdle meant State Man had no more than an exercise gallop, a perfect prep for the defence of his Cheltenham crown.

Odds of 6-1 about State Man represent outstanding each-way value. If the best version of Constitution Hill turns up, you'll make a slight profit on the bet. However, with that lingering doubt in my mind, it would be no shock if State Man turned over Constitution Hill.

Cheltenham is far too big to be all about one man, so I'll sidestep Closutton for my fourth tip.

Springwell Bay, winner of seven of his 15 races, is entered in the Arkle, Brown Advisory and Ryanair but Jonjo and AJ O'Neill will surely go for one of the handicaps, the Ultima or the Plate.

It's interesting that three of his four runs over fences have been at Cheltenham and he was an impressive nine-length winner from Marble Sands over 2m4½f on New Year's Day.

He's up to a career-high mark of 154 but there looks to be plenty more to come.

Surely it's got to be Better

David Jennings

THE more things change, the more they stay the same. The Cheltenham Festival has gone under the knife but, even after all the surgery has been done, Willie Mullins looks guaranteed to dominate yet again.

Prior to the Dublin Racing Festival there were question marks hanging over the novice hurdling team from Closutton. Not anymore. Kopek Des Bordes was awesome and is now impossible to oppose in the Supreme Novices' Hurdle, while Final Demand is also unbeaten and could easily give Mullins a record-extending eighth win in the Turners Novices' Hurdle.

Another race where Mullins appears to have a stranglehold is the Brown Advisory Novices' Chase, with Ballyburn and Dancing City topping the market. However, both could be vulnerable to 2024 festival winner **Better Days Ahead**, who looks cracking each-way value at 10-1.

Stamina is his strong suit – as you saw in

Better Days Ahead: rates cracking each-way value in the Brown Advisory

last year's Martin Pipe Handicap Hurdle when he hit a high of 33-1 in running on Betfair before powering up the hill to beat Waterford Whispers – and he really should be unbeaten over fences for Gordon Elliott.

All he needed was another stride against Croke Park at Leopardstown over Christmas in a slowly run, small-field Grade 1. He wants a proper end-to-end gallop and he should get that at Cheltenham.

I fancy him to upset Ballyburn, who doesn't look as though he's going to be better over fences than he was over hurdles. In contrast, Better Days Ahead looks like he will be.

Elliott has trained five winners of the Cross Country Chase, the same number as Enda Bolger, but he could be out on his own after this year's race as **Delta Work** is fancied to land the unique spectacle for a third time.

It might be a handicap this year, in contrast to when he won it in 2022 and 2023 off level weights, but he's likely to be running off a mark of 157, which is 14lb shy of his peak rating.

I'm not sure he has regressed that much and his eyecatching fourth in the Cotswold Chase suggests the engine is still working well enough to win a race of this nature. He's been trained with spring in mind and should be favourite.

Maughreen impressed me on her jumping debut at Punchestown. She was 4-11 and entitled to win easily, but she looked a natural most of the way and just seemed to blow up approaching the final flight. You can forgive her that, given she hadn't seen a racecourse in more than a year, and I think she'll take the world of beating in the Mares' Novices' Hurdle.

One of the most surprising festival stats is that Mullins hasn't won any of the last four runnings of this race. His last victory was with Concertista in 2020, but win number six could

be coming his way thanks to Maughreen. I think she'll take care of Sixandahalf.

You could argue that Elliott's **American Mike** has been one of the most disappointing chasers in training over the last couple of years. He beat Fact To File at Navan in November 2023 but has done little since that impressive chasing debut, apart from a Grade 2 win at Navan last season over 3m.

The Grand Annual looks right up his street and he'll go there fresh, so he could be worth a few quid each-way at around 33-1. That seems to be the race that is being targeted from listening to connections.

He's been running reasonably well of late since being dropped in trip, especially two starts ago at Fairyhouse, and a strong gallop combined with the uphill climb to the line should bring out the best in him. He looks overpriced if you're able to forgive him a host of underwhelming efforts.

Finally, a sneaky one. Joseph O'Brien has won the Martin Pipe Handicap Hurdle for conditional jockeys twice since 2019 thanks to Early Doors and Banbridge and he could be worth siding with again.

Comfort Zone *(above)* will be one of my strongest fancies of the week wherever he shows up. I have a feeling that will be the Martin Pipe, given his Irish mark of 133. It looks the perfect fit for him, especially as he already has winning form on the New course from when he was a juvenile hurdler.

O'Brien has kept him fresh for the festival, a wise move, and his Irish hurdles mark looks very tasty indeed. He ran a cracker off 131 over Christmas and his last start on the Flat saw him land a big premier handicap at Naas off a mark of 86 in great style.

He's rated 94 on the Flat now, which makes his 133 over hurdles look on the lenient side. He's unexposed and has loads more to offer off his mark.

Warrior to fight back again

Graeme Rodway

ONE of the disappointments at the Dublin Racing Festival was Willie Mullins' **Gaelic Warrior**. He never got going when finishing 14 lengths behind Solness in the Dublin Chase but wasn't given a hard time to stay in touch and kept on for a distant third.

He has now been beaten at odds of 4-7, 13-8 and 6-4 on his three starts over fences at Leopardstown and his one win at the track was off a mark of just 143 in a handicap over hurdles, when he didn't need to be at his best. Maybe he simply doesn't like that course.

Gaelic Warrior was running a dismal race behind Fact To File before he unseated Paul Townend at last year's DRF, but turned up at Cheltenham a different horse when coming away with the Arkle. He looks like he could do the same in this season's Queen Mother Champion Chase.

The seven-year-old has a much better record at Cheltenham than he does at Leopardstown, having finished runner-up in the Fred Winter

Gaelic Warrior: Cheltenham can bring out his best again in the Champion Chase

and what is now the Turners over hurdles before his victory at last year's festival, and a reproduction of his Arkle form should be good enough.

He had smart rivals like Found A Fifty and Il Etait Temps a long way behind him in that race and might have too much for Jonbon around this course. That rival is clearly a superstar away from Cheltenham, but he's vulnerable at this track and three defeats from five prove it.

Dan Skelton was the British trainer who took it to the Irish when saddling four winners at last year's Cheltenham Festival and he can break Ireland's grip on the Turners Novices' Hurdle with **The New Lion**, who is considered to be among the best Skelton has trained.

It's eight years since this race was last won by a British-trained horse in Willoughby Court, but The New Lion *(right)* looks as good as any that the home side have sent to the contest since. He comes in with an unbeaten record of four wins from four, one in a bumper and three over hurdles.

The six-year-old has improved steadily with each of those runs and produced a stunning visual display when landing the Grade 1 Challow Novices' Hurdle at Newbury over Christmas.

He travelled strongly through that race and Harry Skelton was even able to manoeuvre him from inside to out on the run to the last. The response was instant when Skelton asked him to go and The New Lion sauntered clear without having to be ridden, winning easily.

It wasn't just a good performance on the eye, it was a solid one on the clock too and The New Lion recorded a Topspeed figure of 132. That's 3lb better than Final Demand and 1lb higher than Kopek Des Bordes, who both won at the DRF and are the Irish star novices.

That leaves little doubt The New Lion is something special and he should be capable of running even faster times when he's ridden out right to the line. That's an exciting prospect.

On to the Triumph Hurdle and one who definitely loves Cheltenham is **East India Dock**. He's won on his two starts at the course by a combined distance of 28 lengths and has a good chance to lower Lulamba's colours in Friday's opener.

East India Dock is a throwback to the days when smart, up-and-coming Flat performers regularly went jumping. He was rated 89 on the Flat but is already a better hurdler and his victory over course and distance in January was achieved in a good time.

He's a slick jumper who'll be well suited by the demands of this race and is taken to become the first British-trained Triumph winner since Pentland Hills in 2019.

The Albert Bartlett Novices' Hurdle is the other big race for novices on Friday and course form could again be key because **Jet Blue**, a Cheltenham winner in December, has a huge chance.

Jet Blue went clear in that Grade 2 novice hurdle over course and distance and was going away at the line, proving he stays this far well enough for such a test.

Stamina has always been the most important factor for Albert Bartlett winners and it was a good effort from Jet Blue to win on that debut for David Cottin, which was his first run beyond 2m2f. He's unexposed and open to plenty of further improvement, both at this trip and for his new stable.

Owner Caroline Tisdall said the plan was to come back in March after that win and there's every chance Jet Blue can be a rare French-trained festival hero.

Diamond can sparkle

Nick Watts

WHILE it's generally accepted that Willie Mullins will play a huge role in the Grade 1 events at Cheltenham, his grip on the handicaps is generally much weaker – except in the County Hurdle.

He has won that race seven times in the last 15 years and has some strong contenders again this year, including **Ethical Diamond**.

In five hurdles starts the five-year-old has been unplaced in four and won only a fairly nondescript maiden at Punchestown last time when odds-on favourite.

That doesn't sound too promising, but dig a little deeper and tipping him makes more sense. He was beaten only a shade over five lengths in a Grade 1 won by Kargese at the Dublin Racing Festival last year and ran better than his position of tenth suggested in the Triumph Hurdle after that.

Then last summer, when switching codes, he was a narrowly beaten runner-up in a 1m2f Leopardstown handicap before running well again when fourth at Royal Ascot in the Duke of Edinburgh.

A bit free on both occasions, he now wears a hood and, while his last-time-out win didn't prove an awful lot, it will have been good for his confidence. A big-field handicap should help him settle and he could do some damage off his current mark in the spring, granted better ground.

Gavin Cromwell's **Sixandahalf** can make a splash in the mares' novice hurdle. She's another who has useful Flat form from last summer, in her case a win in a Newmarket handicap followed by a placed effort in the Irish Cesarewitch behind The Euphrates.

This January she made an immediate impact over hurdles, thrashing the much more experienced Qualimita by a double-digit margin. The runner-up has since run a great race at the Dublin Racing Festival, finishing third behind Vischio, so it was a good performance by Sixandahalf that was

Ethical Diamond: good handicap prospect for Willie Mullins

characterised by good jumping and strong travelling.

Inexperience is an obvious issue, but it's encouraging she won on her only start in Britain and I have no doubt she has the ability to win. It's just a question of whether she can hold it together at the jumps and on the evidence of her hurdles debut you would hope she can.

Cromwell also has an excellent chance of taking the Cross Country Chase with both Vanillier and Stumptown in his corner.

Vanillier can be very good, as he was last time at Punchestown, and he's a previous festival winner too, but he isn't the most consistent and my preference is for **Stumptown**.

Narrowly beaten in the 2023 Kim Muir, he has made a stunning transition to banks racing, winning his last three races in that sphere – two at Punchestown and the other at Cheltenham last time out.

On the latter occasion he beat perennial bridesmaid Mister Coffey by a length, with Latenightpass back in third, but the winning margin didn't do any justice to his superiority. Keith Donoghue didn't have to get remotely serious with him as he strolled up the Cheltenham hill in complete control.

That came off a mark of 149 and he'll inevitably have to race off a higher rating in March, but such is his current form I can see him dealing with it and bringing up his four-timer.

There's conjecture about where **James's Gate** might end up as Martin Brassil has entered him in the Supreme and Turners but could opt for the Coral Cup.

Graded company might be flying too high and it's the Coral Cup where I'd like to see him, a race for which he's around 12-1.

Brassil has a small stable but is a brilliant target trainer who has festival runners only if he's confident they'll go well.

James's Gate has already been placed at the festival – third in the 2022 Champion Bumper when with Willie Mullins – and, although he's on the fragile side, two wins from two starts for Brassil this season highlight that he's in a good place right now.

Last time he beat the Mullins-trained C'Est Ta Chance by three-quarters of a length over 2m, which is short of his optimum, and before that he took a 2m3f maiden hurdle at Punchestown comfortably.

That form had substance to it with Dublin Racing Festival winner McLaurey well held in third and the fourth, Joystick, also a winner since.

A RAFT of changes to the Cheltenham Festival was announced by the Jockey Club last September following a wide-ranging review of the showpiece event. The review was a response to growing criticism of the competitiveness of the race programme and the festival experience for racegoers, particularly in terms of value for money.

Six key changes have been made to the festival race programme, with alterations made to the conditions of five individual races as well as new requirements for horses running in non-novice handicaps.

Particular emphasis was placed on the festival's four novice chases, in recognition of unsatisfactory field sizes in recent years. As a result, the 2m4f Golden Miller Novices' Chase, run most recently as the Turners, has been axed, in the belief that potential runners will instead tackle the 2m Arkle or 3m Broadway, which is sponsored by Brown Advisory.

In place of the Golden Miller, the Jockey Club has revived the 2m4f novice handicap chase, last run in 2020 but now reintroduced as a Grade 2 limited handicap. The marathon National Hunt Novices' Chase – which has had an average field size of 7.7 across the last three years – will now be open to professional riders and scheduled as a 0-145 handicap, having most recently been a Grade 2 prize.

Opening the National Hunt Chase to professionals was one of the most controversial moves, although both the Fulke Walwyn Kim Muir Handicap Chase and St James's Place Festival Hunters' Chase will continue to be restricted to amateurs only.

KEY CHANGES

Golden Miller (Turners) replaced with handicap The 2m4f Golden Miller, introduced as a Grade 2 in 2011 before attaining Grade 1 status three years later, has been discontinued in a bid to strengthen the 2m Arkle and 3m Broadway. Taking the Golden Miller's place is a Grade 2 2m4f novice limited handicap chase, an adaptation of the contest held at the festival until 2020, after which it was moved to Sandown.

NH Chase, a novice handicap open to pros Used to be confined to horses who had been maidens at the start of the season and has most recently been a 3m6f Grade 2. After poor numerical turnouts, the marathon has been downgraded to a 0-145 novice handicap. The traditional stipulation that only amateur jockeys can ride in the race has been removed.

Cross Country turns into limited handicap The Cross Country became a conditions race in 2016, having initially been staged as a handicap. It will revert to its old handicap status, although now with a 19lb weight range in an effort to attract high-quality chasers.

Winners of Pertemps qualifiers get final slot The previous change was that horses had to finish in the first four in one of the 22 qualifiers. That requirement remains but qualifier winners will now receive protection from elimination in the final, provided they are within the handicap at declaration stage.

Experience tweak for non-novice handicaps In 2022 the experience criteria for the festival's non-novice handicaps was amended to three chase runs and four hurdle runs. That becomes four chase runs and five hurdle runs, the intention being to make handicaps more competitive and direct potential top-class novices into the festival's championship races.

Penalties gone from Mares' Novices' Hurdle Winners of a Class 1 or 2 race have been required to carry a 3lb penalty, with winners of a Class 1 weight-for-age race forced to shoulder a 5lb burden. That is thought to have reduced the number of times some mares ran in the lead-up to the festival. No penalties will now be applied.

Paul Townend and Willie Mullins

TOP TRAINERS

Festival award winners
2024 Willie Mullins 9
2023 Willie Mullins 6
2022 Willie Mullins 10
2021 Willie Mullins 6
2020 Willie Mullins 7
2019 Willie Mullins 4
2018 Gordon Elliott 8
2017 Gordon Elliott 6
2016 Willie Mullins 7
2015 Willie Mullins 8

Total festival winners
Willie Mullins 103
Nicky Henderson 73
Paul Nicholls 49
Gordon Elliott 40
Jonjo O'Neill 27
Henry de Bromhead 23
Philip Hobbs 20
Edward O'Grady 18

TOP JOCKEYS

Festival award winners
2024 Paul Townend 6
2023 Paul Townend 5
2022 Paul Townend 5
2021 Rachael Blackmore 6
2020 Paul Townend 5
2019 Nico de Boinville 3
2018 Davy Russell 4
2017 Ruby Walsh 4
2016 Ruby Walsh 7
2015 Ruby Walsh 4

Total festival winners
Paul Townend 34
Rachael Blackmore 16
Nico de Boinville 16
Jack Kennedy 11
Mark Walsh 10
Patrick Mullins 9
Harry Skelton 9

Tuesday, March 11

1.20 Sky Bet Supreme Novices' Hurdle ITV/RTV
2.00 My Pension Expert Arkle Novices' Chase ITV/RTV
2.40 Ultima Handicap Chase ITV/RTV
3.20 Close Brothers Mares' Hurdle ITV/RTV
4.00 Unibet Champion Hurdle ITV/RTV
4.40 Fred Winter Juvenile Handicap Hurdle ITV/RTV
5.20 National Hunt Chase (novice handicap) RTV

Wednesday, March 12

1.20 Turners Novices' Hurdle ITV/RTV
2.00 Brown Advisory Novices' Chase ITV/RTV
2.40 Coral Cup (handicap hurdle) ITV/RTV
3.20 Glenfarclas Cross Country Chase (handicap) ITV/RTV
4.00 BetMGM Queen Mother Champion Chase ITV/RTV
4.40 Grand Annual Handicap Chase ITV/RTV
5.20 Weatherbys Champion Bumper RTV

Thursday, March 13

1.20 Ryanair Mares' Novices' Hurdle ITV/RTV
2.00 Jack Richards Novices' Handicap Chase ITV/RTV
2.40 Pertemps Network Final (handicap hurdle) ITV/RTV
3.20 Ryanair Chase ITV/RTV
4.00 Paddy Power Stayers' Hurdle ITV/RTV
4.40 TrustATrader Plate (handicap chase) ITV/RTV
5.20 Fulke Walwyn Kim Muir Handicap Chase RTV

Friday, March 14

1.20 JCB Triumph Hurdle ITV/RTV
2.00 William Hill County Handicap Hurdle ITV/RTV
2.40 Mrs Paddy Power Mares' Chase ITV/RTV
3.20 Albert Bartlett Novices' Hurdle ITV/RTV
4.00 Boodles Cheltenham Gold Cup ITV/RTV
4.40 St James's Place Festival Hunters' Chase ITV/RTV
5.20 Martin Pipe Conditional Jockeys' Handicap Hurdle RTV

ALONGSIDE changes to the race programme, this year will bring enhanced ITV coverage of the festival with an extra race added to each day's live programme.

The first six races will now be shown live on ITV, with just the final event on the seven-race cards on Racing TV only. The extended live racing show on ITV will run from 12.45pm to 5pm.

Another significant change is that the feature race each day has been moved to fifth on the card, due off at 4.00. Previously the main race was fourth at 3.30. The Jockey Club said the change was aimed at "allowing the sense of excitement and anticipation to build through the afternoon".

The most extensive reshuffling of the running order is on the final two days. Thursday will start with the Ryanair Mares' Novices' Hurdle (up from sixth on the card), followed by the newly introduced Jack Richards Novices' Handicap Chase. The next four races all move down a place, with the Fulke Walwyn Kim Muir Handicap Chase remaining as the last event.

On Friday the Mrs Paddy Power Mares' Chase is up to race three (from sixth) and the next three races all move down a place. The festival will finish again with the Martin Pipe Conditional Jockeys' Handicap Hurdle.

Once again there will be an Opening Show programme on ITV4 each morning, running from 9am to 10am.

Racing TV will show all 28 festival races live and there will be a live preview show from Cheltenham every morning until racing starts.

'Jonbon has to be taken on'

Who do you fancy for the Gold Cup?

Richard Birch This was supposed to be the season when a multitude of richly talented Irish-trained chasers ganged up to topple Galopin Des Champs. It hasn't worked out that way and he looks a certainty. His Irish Gold Cup win suggested he's better than ever at the age of nine.

David Jennings I have Specsavers on speed dial, so give me a shout if you don't fancy Galopin Des Champs. He's bulletproof. If Inothewayurthinkin is supplemented, he could be placed. If not, I'd go for Corbetts Cross to run a big race as I have a feeling he's better suited to smaller fields. He'll get that here.

Graeme Rodway It's very hard to see beyond Galopin Des Champs. He has looked at least as good as ever at Leopardstown on his last two starts and we know he can run fast over course and distance because he has won the race twice already. At double-figure odds it wouldn't surprise me if Corbetts Cross ran well and he makes some appeal for an each-way play.

Nick Watts It's impossible to come up with any logical reason as to why it won't be three in a row for Galopin Des Champs. Judged on his performances this season he appears to be better than ever. Corbetts Cross could reach the places but he's not in the same class.

Who's your pick for the Champion Hurdle?

Richard Birch Constitution Hill is no longer an invincible force after his well-publicised health issues. It's a bold statement, but one I believe.

According to Racing Post Ratings he was well below his extraordinary best when winning at Kempton and Cheltenham. An each-way bet on State Man makes plenty of sense.

David Jennings Just about Constitution Hill. I'm not sure he's regressed as much as people think. Brighterdaysahead adds an extra layer of intrigue to the race. King Of Kingsfield will presumably set a brisk tempo and his more esteemed stablemate will track him every step of the way, just like at Leopardstown. Can the mare beat the best hurdler I've ever seen? I'm not so sure.

Graeme Rodway I can't have Constitution Hill and will be taking him on provided the opposition is strong enough. Lossiemouth did everything wrong when finishing only

Gaelic Warrior: last year's Arkle winner is one of the chief dangers to Jonbon in the Champion Chase

two and a half lengths behind him in the Christmas Hurdle at Kempton and is fancied to reverse the form at this course, where she's three from three and has recorded two of her four highest RPRs.

Nick Watts I believe Constitution Hill will win, although it might not be straightforward if Brighterdaysahead gets the green light to run, as she should. We still don't know if she'll go for the Mares' Hurdle instead, and the same goes for Lossiemouth, so it's hard to pinpoint the biggest danger with any clarity.

What do you make of the Champion Chase?

Richard Birch I tipped Jonbon at 10-1 immediately after Cheltenham last year when the generally held view was that he'd

be aimed at the Ryanair. He's done nothing wrong since and looks very much the complete two-miler now. I'll be surprised, albeit not totally shocked, if he's beaten.

David Jennings If the ground were proper soft, Gaelic Warrior would be a big player, but surely this is the year Jonbon finally gets rid of his Cheltenham demons. He's had the perfect season and seems to be getting better with age. If Il Est Francais ran here, he'd scare me if I were a Jonbon backer.

Graeme Rodway Jonbon has to be taken on. He's a superstar away from Cheltenham but his record shows he's vulnerable at this track. He's been beaten more times than he has won here with a record of 2-5, compared with 15-15 elsewhere. Gaelic Warrior has the ability to turn over the favourite, granted soft ground. He was good when winning last year's Arkle over course and distance.

Nick Watts It's a confusing picture. Jonbon might not be at his best around Cheltenham and the obvious one to beat him, Gaelic Warrior, has been moderate in his two starts this season. If the ground is reasonable Marine Nationale comes into the equation, but I really hope Il Est Francais goes for it. He's a superb jumper and could make them all go at his best.

What's your view on the Stayers' Hurdle?

Richard Birch It's hard to go against Teahupoo in a staying division lacking quality in numbers. Gordon Elliott's star was a dominant winner last year and has been given a similar preparation. As a result he remains lightly raced and it's by no means inconceivable the best is yet to come.

David Jennings It looks an even weaker race than the one Teahupoo won last year. His Hatton's Grace defeat was every bit as encouraging as his win in the race last season and it would be foolish to oppose him. On decent ground the unpredictable Langer Dan might be his biggest danger.

Graeme Rodway I'm not keen on Teahupoo. He's still the most likely winner and will be dangerous if the race isn't strongly run, like when he won last year. However, he didn't finish off that well when faced with a faster pace the previous season and might be vulnerable in a real test of stamina. It's really difficult to find something against him, though.

Nick Watts I like Teahupoo, partly on form and partly because nothing else has really come through in this division to challenge him. Going to the Hatton's Grace and then straight on to Cheltenham worked last season and he can't really be blamed for losing out to a faster horse in Lossiemouth at Fairyhouse in December. Mystical Power is quite interesting – he has looked dreadful in two starts this term but maybe a massive hike in trip will help him.

Marine Nationale: decent ground would aid his bid for the Champion Chase

'I could see him giving the favourite plenty to think about'

Who do you fancy for the Gold Cup?

Bet365 Pat Cooney It looks a straightforward task for Galopin Des Champs. He's by far the best in the race, so he can keep it simple, jump off in front and outclass and outstay all of them. Monty's Star appeals in the each-way and 'betting without' markets, having run with credit behind the favourite last time.

Betfair Barry Orr Not a staying chaser alive has the ability, determination or talent to topple a fully fit Galopin Des Champs. His body of work is second to none and he deserves to be mentioned in the same breath as the chasing greats. Winning a third Gold Cup will ensure that happens.

Coral Andrew Lobo It's hard to oppose Galopin Des Champs given the consistency he's shown this season. I'm not writing off Monty's Star for a place. Henry de Bromhead's horses weren't in the best of form after Christmas but I'm sure they'll come good in March and Monty's Star could be each-way value on the day if he runs to the level of his placed form in the Brown Advisory last year.

Ladbrokes John Priddey If conditions come up on the quick side, Banbridge will be a big threat. He jumped beautifully in a frenetic King George and is still unexposed at the distance.

Chasing Gold: Monty's Star and (inset) Banbridge

State Man (left) and Lossiemouth: could clash again in the Champion Hurdle

Paddy Power Paul Binfield Galopin Des Champs is an even bigger certainty this year. I adored the way Paul Townend landed the Paddy Power Irish Gold Cup on him without giving him a hard time at all and I think that'll assist him not only in retaining his crown at Cheltenham but going on to prevail at Punchestown this year.

Tote Jamie Benson It's impossible to look past Galopin Des Champs. Looking for one at an each-way price, I'll side with Monty's Star. Henry de Bromhead's lightly raced second-season chaser can progress into contention.

William Hill Jamie McBride It's hard to see past Galopin Des Champs but if the ground is deemed suitable I could see Banbridge giving him plenty to think about. I don't think the form of his King George win puts him too far behind the favourite, although his stamina would have to be taken on trust.

Who's your pick for the Champion Hurdle?

Bet365 Pat Cooney It's hard to pick holes in a horse who's unbeaten in ten hurdles races, so it has to be Constitution Hill. It looks as though there may be several front-runners in opposition and that'll suit him. My only concern is that he's too fast and slick over his hurdles. Remember even the mighty Istabraq fell twice over hurdles.

Betfair Barry Orr It all depends what the two mares do. If both Brighterdaysahead and Lossiemouth take on Constitution Hill, the race will have a very different complexion and I'll be laying him on the Betfair Exchange. If they go elsewhere, he'll take a lot of beating as State Man looks regressive and the rest are a moderate bunch.

Coral Andrew Lobo If Lossiemouth was 4-1 or 5-1 on the day I'd chance her to turn around the Christmas Hurdle form with Constitution Hill. With State Man we know roughly what

his best level is, but we still don't quite know how good Lossiemouth could be. Her defeat at Kempton was fairly excusable with the way the race unfolded and her fall last time was out of character.

Ladbrokes John Priddey Constitution Hill looks stronger than ever, while State Man and Lossiemouth have arguably regressed. The 'how far' lines will arguably be more interesting puzzles than the main market on the day.

Paddy Power Paul Binfield I know Constitution Hill beat Lossiemouth in the Christmas Hurdle, but the mare was dropping to the minimum trip having been running over 2m4f. She got taken off her feet a little that day, but both she and connections will have learned a lot. Admittedly she has to bounce back from a tumble in the Irish Champion Hurdle but I think she can reverse the Kempton form.

Tote Jamie Benson Constitution Hill should win if he gets there sound. He'll come on again for his win on Trials day and it's tough to see anything being able to live with him.

William Hill Jamie McBride Despite things not going to plan on her last couple of starts I'll still be siding with Lossiemouth at the likely prices. Coming here off a fall is far from ideal but I thought she was the one to beat at the start of the season and my belief in her just about remains intact.

What do you make of the Champion Chase?

Bet365 Pat Cooney Jonbon has won 17 of his 20 races but all three defeats have been at Cheltenham, which stops me thinking he should be odds-on to win this. He's probably better round right-handed Sandown, where he's five from five. That said, he has looked unstoppable this season and would be a worthy winner.

Betfair Barry Orr Jonbon is the only contender who comes into the race undefeated this

Energumene: hat-trick bid in the Champion Chase

season and it's difficult to see what's going to trouble him. I don't put any stock in the theory that he isn't at his best around Cheltenham. He goes on all ground and sets a high standard.

Coral Andrew Lobo Jonbon feels like a solid favourite. Energumene is my idea of the main danger. The level he was running at two years ago would put him right there if his master trainer can bring him to his peak on the big day.

Ladbrokes John Priddey The Champion Chase is always such a pressure cooker where one mistake can be crucial, as shown by the number of surprise results in the past few years. You'd be brave to steam into any horse at odds-on. Nothing stands out among the opposition but a top-two lay of Jonbon could be a cheap interest bet on the day.

Paddy Power Paul Binfield Jonbon's price puts me off a bit for a Cheltenham championship race, but he'll be a definite in my multiples. It's not just that he's been winning this season, it's the manner of those successes that has impressed me so much. I struggle to make a case for why any of his potential rivals can topple him at Cheltenham.

Tote Jamie Benson It's a fascinating race. I wonder if Jonbon might be taken off his feet slightly with the amount of pace that looks likely. I'll be with Marine Nationale, who has improved with each run this season and should be able to cruise off whatever pace is set. He can make it two out of two in Grade 1s at Cheltenham.

William Hill Jamie McBride Jonbon's occasionally erratic jumping and his record at Cheltenham offer bookmakers some hope we can get him beat, but this isn't a division with lots of depth. At a big price I could see Matata again enjoying the demands of the Old course and hitting the frame.

What's your view on the Stayers' Hurdle?

Bet365 Pat Cooney Teahupoo is the most likely winner provided it's soft ground. The going on the day will determine both his price and

chance more accurately, as he's much better on an easy surface. Home By The Lee has done well this season and is the main danger in theory, but he has been beaten in this race in all three attempts. On good ground Lucky Place would be interesting.

Betfair Barry Orr Teahupoo is a worthy favourite despite not really capturing the imagination, given that he isn't seen much due to his inclination to being at his best when fresh. Home By The Lee ran a blinder in the race last year and has been rock solid in his two defeats of Bob Olinger this season, making him an attractive alternative to the favourite.

Coral Andrew Lobo It's been a weak division for a while. If they skip the Pertemps with The Wallpark, I'll take the hint and go with him each-way. He was fairly eyecatching in the Long Walk at Ascot before Christmas and is young enough to be improving.

Ladbrokes John Priddey Teahupoo remains a notch better than the rest in a poor division. He was a cosy winner last year and this season's crop doesn't look any stronger.

Paddy Power Paul Binfield It wouldn't take a massive stretch of the imagination to see all four championship races going to the favourites. Teahupoo couldn't live with Lossiemouth in the Hatton's Grace Hurdle but he's better over a longer trip. He was the best staying hurdler last season and he'll take an awful lot of beating back at three miles.

Tote Jamie Benson Teahupoo is a rock-solid favourite but it's a race that can throw up a big-priced winner, so I'll chance Hiddenvalley Lake. He didn't give his running last time at Gowran, but prior to that he looked a highly progressive staying hurdler and a return to form for Henry de Bromhead's yard could see him run a big race.

William Hill Jamie McBride Teahupoo looks hard to beat but I've backed Gold Tweet at big prices in the hope he comes here and can repeat the level of form from his Cleeve Hurdle win in early 2023. That would give him every chance of hitting the frame.

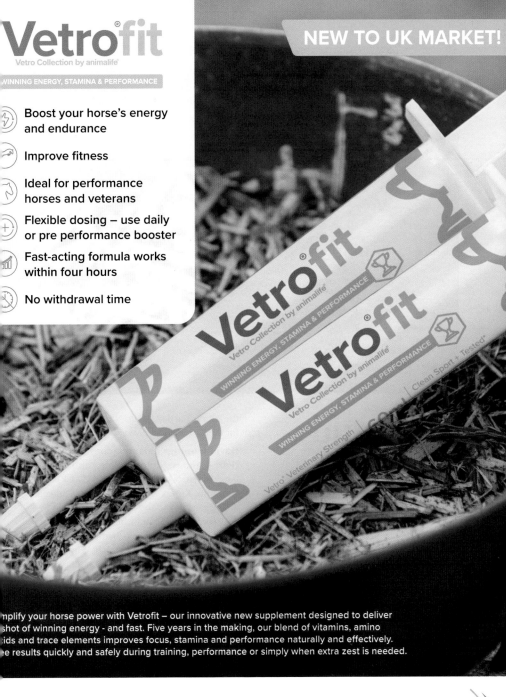

Lulamba: hot fancy for the Triumph

'He could be a big improver over further'

Who do you fancy for the novice hurdles?

Richard Birch Kopek Des Bordes looked an absolute monster at Leopardstown and is banker material in the Supreme. Final Demand created a similar impression in his prep run for the Turners and rates a tremendous bet at odds-against. It says it all that I believe Wingmen, who finished 12 lengths behind Final Demand at Leopardstown, could win the Albert Bartlett. Hello Neighbour appeals for the Triumph.

David Jennings Lulamba does everything right – settles, jumps, gallops and stays. I fancy him to take down East India Dock in the Triumph. Kopek Des Bordes looked special at Leopardstown and will probably win the Supreme, but I'd rather be a watcher than a backer at odds-on. Potters Charm should outrun his odds in the Turners, as might Wingmen in the Albert Bartlett. The latter is settling much better now and could be hard to catch.

Graeme Rodway Kopek Des Bordes should win the Supreme and the Turners looks set to be a cracking race between Final Demand and The New Lion, who are both top-class novices. Preference is for The New Lion, who looked a superstar when winning the Challow at Newbury and is my idea of the 2026 Champion Hurdle winner. I prefer East India Dock over Lulamba in the Triumph.

Nick Watts Kopek Des Bordes has to be top of the Supreme list after his demolition job

questrian
irectsurfaces

Best in Class
Riding Surfaces

Perfect for new and
topping up surfaces

ENVIRONMENTALLY APPROVED SURFACES

★★★★★
**5 STAR RATED
CUSTOMER SERVICE**

LEADING THE FIELD
30+
FOR OVER 30 YEARS

We have over 30 years of experience in helping equestrian enthusiasts with all types of riding surface matters. From your first surface to commercial facilities, we offer a friendly, professional and practical service that is second to none.

ot sure what surface you need? Contact Equestrian Direct today to arrange a site visit in your local area.
01564 794 020 | www.equestriandirectltd.co.uk

at the Dublin Racing Festival. Kawaboomga has form that ties in with him and could be a big improver over further, so he gets the vote in the Turners. The Albert Bartlett is one of the hardest puzzles of the week to solve but maybe Argento Boy can go well at a price. East India Dock has the edge over Lulamba in the Triumph for me. Salvator Mundi is one to take on. He doesn't look easy and is unlikely to have the assistance of Paul Townend.

Which novice chasers stand out?

Richard Birch Majborough has the Arkle at his mercy following the defection of Sir Gino. He boasts Cheltenham Festival-winning form, having landed the Triumph last year, and clearly has an abundance of class. Even though his main rival at Leopardstown last time, Ile Atlantique, ran no sort of race, he looked in a different league to the rest. Ballyburn is a confident choice to outclass his Brown Advisory rivals. He's a potential superstar.

David Jennings Majborough doesn't have Sir Gino to worry about anymore and the Arkle looks his for the taking. I'm taking on Ballyburn in the Brown Advisory with Better Days Ahead, who'll relish the uphill climb to the line and is already a festival winner having landed the Martin Pipe last year. He's cracking each-way value at 10-1.

Graeme Rodway Majborough has the Arkle at his mercy after Sir Gino was ruled out and Ballyburn is the right favourite for the Brown Advisory, although I wouldn't be as certain about him winning. Springwell Bay is an interesting one at big odds and he's in both races.

Nick Watts The Arkle should really go to Majborough barring mishaps. He got close to a few at Leopardstown last time but never looked like falling and has a huge engine. The Brown Advisory looks another one for Willie Mullins after The Jukebox Man's season-ending injury. Ballyburn has the most natural ability but Dancing City is a strong stayer who jumps well. I'll take Ballyburn to edge it.

Argento Boy: one to consider in the Albert Bartlett

World Horse Welfare is the only equine welfare charity that actively supports the responsible involvement of horses in sport.

With racehorse welfare under the spotlight like never before, we provide independent advice to British racing to help them meet the high expectations of everyone in the sport and outside of it.

Please give £3 a month to help support our work.

Scan the QR code to donate today.

www.worldhorsewelfare.org
Registered charity no. 206658 and SC038384

Anne Colvin House, Snetterton, Norfolk, NR16 2LR, UK

Registered with
FUNDRAISING
REGULATOR

The Big Westerner (left):
Albert Bartlett contender
for Henry de Bromhead

'He'll love the strong gallop in the Supreme'

Who do you fancy for the novice hurdles?

Bet365 Pat Cooney Kopek Des Bordes and Final Demand are both bankers for their races. Lulamba is the most likely winner of the Triumph but is no value, and I'll go for The Big Westerner in the Albert Bartlett. Take care in that race, though, as it often throws up a big-priced winner and has regularly been a bookmakers' benefit.

Betfair Barry Orr Hello Neighbour looks a bet for me in the Triumph. He's done absolutely nothing wrong in his two wins and looks like he'll relish the Cheltenham hill when others will be crying enough. I like The Big Westerner in the Albert Bartlett. She stepped up considerably from her debut when winning a Grade 2 at Limerick and it looks like the 3m here will be right up her alley. The New Lion looked smart in the Challow and will go well in the Turners. It's hard to see past Kopek Des Bordes in the Supreme. He looked very special at the Dublin Racing Festival.

Coral Andrew Lobo I'll follow the obvious form line of Kopek Des Bordes and Kawaboomga for the Supreme and Turners respectively. The Triumph might feel like hype versus form book but I favour Lulamba at the prices. The Nicky Henderson yard have an excellent record at knowing their good ones and his debut win at Ascot did nothing to suggest they were wrong. The Albert Bartlett often goes to an outsider and I'd always be happy to oppose the obvious form horses, but I'll wait until closer to the day when we'll have more idea of who's running.

Ladbrokes John Priddey Recent years have shown that the key Dublin Racing Festival novice hurdles are way ahead of the main British races and Kopek Des Bordes and Final Demand look daunting favourites. The Albert Bartlett is much more open and I think Jacob's Ladder will give you a run for your money at a huge price.

Paddy Power Paul Binfield There are the usual difficulties of knowing who's going where but I'll go for Kopek Des Bordes (Supreme), Kawaboomga (Turners), Derryhassen Paddy (Albert Bartlett) and East India Dock (Triumph). The one I'm particularly keen on is East India Dock as he strikes me as the type you'd want on your side in a bar-room brawl. Derryhassen Paddy improved hugely when stepped up to three miles last time and is a massive price.

Tote Jamie Benson Anyone for a game of Willie Mullins bingo? It's hard to look past his favourites, but in the search for some value I'll chance a couple at bigger prices. William Munny will love the strong gallop in the Supreme and can stay on late to hit the frame, while Wingmen looks to have been crying out for a trip and getting a nice lead in the Albert Bartlett can see him to best effect.

William Hill Jamie McBride I've been hugely impressed by Kopek Des Bordes in both starts this season and I'm in no hurry to oppose him. I was also impressed by Final Demand at Leopardstown but I think the Albert Bartlett would be a better fit than the Turners. The lack of emphasis on jumping late on in the Albert Bartlett could help Jasmin De Vaux and he could run well at a price.

Which novice chasers stand out?

Bet365 Pat Cooney Majborough is far from the finished article jumping-wise but is way ahead of his Arkle rivals on form. Ballyburn is the best horse in the Brown Advisory, but it's open to question whether he can settle well enough to get 3m here. I'll probably back a few proven stayers, albeit with a lower level of form, against him each-way.

*William Munny and (inset)
Derryhassen Paddy*

Jango Baie: Grade 1 form for Nicky Henderson

Betfair Barry Orr I fancied Majborough even when Sir Gino was still in the Arkle. He'll have learned so much from Leopardstown and his jump at the last ditch, when Paul Townend really saw a stride and asked him up, was beautiful. That gives me the belief that he not only has considerable ability but loads of scope to go with it. Considering he was headed jumping the last, Ballyburn hit the line strongly in the Grade 1 novice chase at Leopardstown. He's another Willie Mullins hotpot who's difficult to see past.

Coral Andrew Lobo I've long been sweet on Majborough for the Arkle. There are enough reasons to take on Ballyburn at short odds in the Brown Advisory. The novice hurdle he won last year wasn't much of a race in hindsight and on form he still has to prove he's top class. I thought Croke Park had his measure at one point at Leopardstown. Although Ballyburn pulled out more, he now has to prove himself going up to 3m for the first time.

Ladbrokes John Priddey I'm beginning to be converted to Ballyburn as a staying chaser. There are many likeable and solid horses in the Brown Advisory but they feel like potential good handicappers, whereas Ballyburn has that extra class. Sadly we lost the big Arkle clash, leaving Majborough as the clear favourite.

Paddy Power Paul Binfield I fancied Majborough for the Arkle even before the Sir Gino news, although he's a short price now. I'll opt for Jango Baie in the Brown Advisory. He just failed to collar Handstands in the Scilly Isles at Sandown but the all-important extra half-mile will play to his strengths.

Tote Jamie Benson The Arkle is at Majborough's mercy but I'd like Firefox if he were to turn up – he'd be the one for the Exacta. In the Brown Advisory I wouldn't rule out Croke Park, who could benefit from a greater staying test here and run Ballyburn close.

William Hill Jamie McBride The Arkle has sadly become a lot less interesting with the defection of Sir Gino and Majborough looks hard to beat. In the Brown Advisory I think Dancing City will be a rock-solid each-way bet against his more vaunted stablemate Ballyburn, whose jumping is a little ponderous for my liking.

'The race he won was full of fancied horses from strong yards'

What's your best festival bet?

Bet365 Pat Cooney Sixandahalf appeals in the Mares' Novices' Hurdle. She impressed in winning on her hurdles debut and has had plenty of racecourse experience, having won a bumper and been placed in the Irish Cesarewitch on the Flat. Maughreen is an obvious threat but Sixandahalf has achieved more.

Betfair Barry Orr The Big Westerner in the Albert Bartlett. She showed she could quicken and stay well at Limerick over Christmas. It wasn't a great race but she was impressive and will improve again, as she'll need to. Henry de Bromhead won this race with Minella Indo and hopefully he'll do the same with this mare.

Coral Andrew Lobo Copacabana in the Champion Bumper for Willie Mullins in what could be a weakish year. The race he won recently at Navan *(above)* was full of well-fancied horses from strong yards and he was sent off favourite. I could see him being clear favourite on the day.

Ladbrokes John Priddey Jacob's Ladder is interesting for Gordon Elliott at a big price in the Albert Bartlett.

Paddy Power Paul Binfield Derryhassen Paddy each-way in the Albert Bartlett, although I'd advise non-runner no bet as I imagine Lucinda Russell will also consider Aintree for this likeable individual. He's the winner of a three-mile point and I can't wait to see him engage with fences in the future.

Tote Jamie Benson The Placepot. We've seen some huge dividends at Cheltenham over the years (£14k and £24k in 2023) and, with all of these short-priced favourites, all you need is one to be unplaced and the dividend can skyrocket. For a single bet, Nine Graces in the Kim Muir.

William Hill Jamie McBride I think Gold Tweet will be underrated in the market if coming over for the Stayers' Hurdle. Teahupoo is a tough nut to crack but the French raider could offer value in each-way and 'betting without' markets.

COOKE

ATTENTION TO DETAIL IS STANDARD

SPECIALISING IN ALL HGV'S 26T 18T 16T 12T & 7.5T

Celebrating our

50TH

ANNIVERSARY
ESTABLISHED IN 1974

TEL 01270 588598 • COOKECOACHBUILDERS.COM •

Hat-trick on the cards

Jonny Pearson

GOLD CUP

In both of the past two runnings Galopin Des Champs has achieved a Racing Post Rating of 183, the highest figure in the past decade. Now he stands on the verge of becoming the first since Best Mate in 2004 to complete a coveted Gold Cup hat-trick.

The manner of his first success – by seven lengths from Bravemansgame – was more visually impressive but the level of performance was undiminished last year even if the margin of victory was halved as he was chased home by Gerri Colombe.

The Willie Mullins-trained nine-year-old has had an identical build-up as last season. First there was defeat in the John Durkan at Punchestown over a trip short of his optimum. Then came a restorative powerhouse display

Galopin Des Champs is the centre of attention after his Irish Gold Cup win

in the Savills Chase at Leopardstown over Christmas, backed up by a solid victory in the Irish Gold Cup there in February.

It is highly likely that the pattern will continue with a repeat success at Cheltenham.

The most realistic challenger is Banbridge, who was an impressive winner of the King George VI Chase at Kempton in December when stepped up to three miles for the first time. An RPR of 174 for that success puts him second to Galopin Des Champs among this year's contenders.

The King George was run on officially good ground and Banbridge's best form has come

on a sounder surface. Soft ground would be difficult for him, but on good he would be the most likely candidate to thwart the hat-trick bid.

Fact To File has strong claims too, having beaten Galopin Des Champs in the John Durkan. However, he had to settle for second and third behind his illustrious stablemate in the Savills Chase and Irish Gold Cup respectively. His top RPR of 171 was achieved in the Savills, but he was beaten seven and a half lengths on that occasion and that mark puts him 12lb below the Gold Cup-winning standard set by Galopin Des Champs in the last two years.

With Gerri Colombe out for the season, fourth-placed L'Homme Presse is the most credible challenger left from last year's race. He has come back in good form this season, staying on well when third in the King George before going on to win the Cotswold Chase at Cheltenham, although he was then pulled up in the Ascot Chase.

GOLD CUP

This year's top rated	RPR
Galopin Des Champs	183
Banbridge *(right)*	174
Fact To File	171
Hewick	170
L'Homme Presse	170
Corbetts Cross	169
Grey Dawning	168
Grangeclare West	165
Jungle Boogie	163
Monty's Star	162

How the past ten winners rated

Year	Winner	Win RPR	Pre-race RPR
2024	Galopin Des Champs	183	184
2023	Galopin Des Champs	183	177
2022	A Plus Tard	181	180
2021	Minella Indo	179	170
2020	Al Boum Photo	172	178
2019	Al Boum Photo	178	171
2018	Native River	177	174
2017	Sizing John	171	168
2016	Don Cossack	182	181
2015	Coneygree	178	168

10yr winning average Racing Post Rating: 178

Constitution challenged

Jonny Pearson

CHAMPION HURDLE

This division still revolves around Constitution Hill, albeit with less certainty than when he achieved his best RPR of 177 in winning the 2023 Champion Hurdle.

After an early-season setback he came back from a year off to win the Christmas Hurdle at Kempton and the International Hurdle at Cheltenham. For these victories he achieved RPRs of 162 and 150, considerably below his best.

The International victory looked particularly disappointing compared with his past achievements and many question if he still has his old top-end ability. However, he was simply much better than his rivals in that race. Fils D'Oudairies, who finished fourth, had the next-best RPR in the field at just 155.

State Man won the Champion Hurdle in the absence of Constitution Hill last season, running to an RPR of 160. He has achieved his career-high 168 on five occasions, although his best this season is 166. That is not world-beating form and he has looked vulnerable this season.

First time out he suffered a narrow defeat against Brighterdaysahead, but then the mare beat him by more than 30 lengths at Leopardstown over Christmas. He went some way to rebuilding his reputation with a third victory in the Irish Champion Hurdle, although

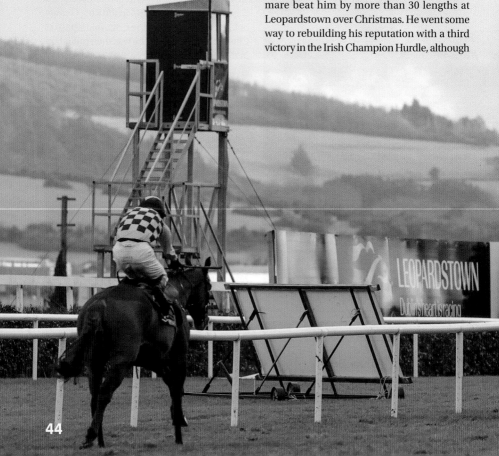

Lossiemouth's fall made the race something of a non-event and his RPR was only 162.

The best hurdling performance of the season came from Brighterdaysahead with an RPR of 165 in that wide-margin Christmas success at Leopardstown in the Neville Hotels Hurdle.

If she ran in the Champion Hurdle she would be in receipt of a 7lb mares' allowance, effectively putting her on 172 at her best and considerably ahead of the marks achieved by Constitution Hill and State Man this season.

Mares have a good record in the Champion Hurdle, with four wins in the last nine runnings, and the best mare we have seen over hurdles in recent times is the 2016 winner Annie Power. If Brighterdaysahead were able to match that mare's best RPR of 170, she would effectively be in line with the level Constitution Hill has achieved in the past.

Lossiemouth is an intended runner for the same connections as Annie Power, but on all form she would need a significant career-best performance to be challenging Constitution Hill, State Man and Brighterdaysahead.

CHAMPION HURDLE

This year's top rated		RPR
Constitution Hill		177
Brighterdaysahead *(right)*		172*
State Man		168
Lossiemouth		163*
Burdett Road		155
Winter Fog		154
Golden Ace		146*
Senecia	*Includes	146
Brentford Hope	7lb mares'	144
King Of Kingsfield	allowance	144

How the past ten winners rated

Year	Winner	Win RPR	Pre-race RPR
2024	State Man	160	168
2023	Constitution Hill	177	176
2022	Honeysuckle	159	166
2021	Honeysuckle	165	163
2020	Epatante	162	158
2019	Espoir D'Allen	171	164
2018	Buveur D'Air	165	171
2017	Buveur D'Air	170	159
2016	Annie Power	162	164
2015	Faugheen	170	169

10yr winning average Racing Post Rating: 166

State Man cruises home in the Irish Champion Hurdle

Jonbon's big

Jonny Pearson

CHAMPION CHASE

Only two of the past ten runnings have had a double-figure field but the quality remains high. The average winning RPR is the second best of the championship races, bettered only by the Gold Cup.

El Fabiolo went off at 2-9 last season but got no further than the fifth fence, where he was pulled up, and Captain Guinness took the winning opportunity. His RPR of 168 made it the second-lowest winning performance in the past decade, and the lowest if you factor in the mares' allowance for Put The Kettle On's success in 2021.

This year's strong favourite is Jonbon *(left)*, who is three from three this season. His latest victory in the Clarence House Chase at Ascot earned him a career-best RPR of 177, a figure good enough to have won eight of the past ten Champion Chases and above the average winning RPR for the race.

The doubters will say his form at Cheltenham is below what he has achieved elsewhere, but he has won there this season and we haven't seen a huge amount from his potential challengers.

Energumene, winner of this race in 2022 and 2023, has been below his best and was comfortably held by Jonbon in the Clarence House. Last year's Arkle winner Gaelic Warrior was seen as the biggest threat for a while but has disappointed on both starts this season, while El Fabiolo fell at the second fence on his only outing.

The biggest threat to Jonbon could be the French-trained Il Est Francais if he is given

chance for festival glory

the go-ahead. He runs hot and cold but his front-running performance at Kempton in the King George VI Chase this season took him to an RPR of 173. He would be a real threat to Jonbon if getting his own way from the front over this much shorter trip.

Competition for the lead would be likely, however, with Solness in the field. His front-running style has been seen to great effect in his two Grade 1 wins at Leopardstown this season.

Marine Nationale was a close second to Solness in the Dublin Chase last time but will have to improve again if he is to get close to winning here.

RYANAIR CHASE

The Ryanair Chase typically has a muddling look until close to raceday, with many of the better contenders also entered in other races. Fact To File is a possible Gold Cup runner, while El Fabiolo and Gaelic Warrior are in the Champion Chase mix.

One we know is likely to run is last year's winner Protektorat. He recorded an RPR of 170 then, which would have been good enough to win only three of the last ten runnings. He bettered that mark last time out, however, when winning the Fleur de Lys Chase at Windsor with an RPR of 172. In that form he would have a strong chance of a repeat success here.

Spillane's Tower was a close second to Fact To File in the John Durkan Memorial Chase, although his RPR there was only 166 and he disappointed over 3m in the King George next time.

The form of the John Durkan remains some of the best on offer this season, however. Fact To File continues to frank the form and he will be Ryanair favourite if connections choose to come here rather than the Gold Cup.

CHAMPION CHASE

This year's top rated	RPR
Energumene	179
El Fabiolo *(right)*	178
Jonbon	177
Banbridge	174
Il Est Francais	173
Gaelic Warrior	172
Matata	166
Solness	166
Found A Fifty	165
Master Chewy	164
Marine Nationale	163
Libberty Hunter	160

How the past ten winners rated

Year	Winner	Win RPR	Pre-race RPR
2024	Captain Guinness	168	165
2023	Energumene	179	177
2022	Energumene	177	179
2021	Put The Kettle On	162	160
2020	Politologue	173	173
2019	Altior	173	183
2018	Altior	183	177
2017	Special Tiara	170	170
2016	Sprinter Sacre	176	173
2015	Dodging Bullets	169	173

10yr winning average Racing Post Rating: 173

RYANAIR CHASE

This year's top rated	RPR
Energumene *(right)*	179
El Fabiolo	178
Banbridge	174
Il Est Francais	173
Gaelic Warrior	172
Protektorat	172
Fact To File	171
Djelo	169
Spillane's Tower	166
Found A Fifty	165
Jungle Boogie	163

10yr winning average Racing Post Rating: 173

Teahupoo sets standard

Jonny Pearson

STAYERS' HURDLE

On Racing Post Ratings this race takes less winning than Cheltenham's other championships, with only Thistlecrack recording a mark in the 170s in the past decade.

Last year Teahupoo won with an RPR of 165, which is close to the race average, and he is the one to beat again. His Cheltenham mark wasn't a personal best for him but it was a good performance nevertheless and his rivals here have yet to go to that level.

Trainer Gordon Elliott, who will be attempting to win the Stayers' Hurdle for the third year in a row, has followed the same plan as last season for Teahupoo, giving him just one run in December's Hatton's Grace Hurdle and then keeping him fresh until the festival. While he didn't win the Hatton's Grace this time, Teahupoo gives Elliott a strong chance of the hat-trick.

The biggest challenge is likely to come from Home By The Lee, impressive when winning the Grade 1 Savills Hurdle at Leopardstown in December with an RPR of 159.

Joseph O'Brien's ten-year-old has achieved a personal-best of 163 twice, including when fifth in the 2023 Stayers'. However, he finished behind Teahupoo (third that year) on that occasion and again when moving up to third in last year's race.

Elliott holds another good chance with the progressive The Wallpark. The seven-year-old was only fourth in the Long Walk Hurdle at Ascot in December on his first run in Grade 1 company, but he was an eyecatcher with a strong finish after being too far back. Against him is that his best RPR of 152, achieved there and in handicap victory at Cheltenham the time before, is far below Teahupoo's 168.

Perhaps Nicky Henderson's Lucky Place has the best chance of an upset from the home team. He won the Grade 2 Relkeel Hurdle over 2m4½f at the track on New Year's Day, although he will probably have to improve significantly again from his career-best RPR of 152 there.

The ground is likely to be a key factor. Teahupoo is clearly at his best when racing on a softer surface and he could be vulnerable if it comes up on the quicker side. The going being faster than ideal for him was one of the excuses given for his defeat in 2023.

Of those who might benefit most from a quicker surface, The Wallpark has to rank highly. His Cheltenham win in October came on good ground, albeit on the Old course.

STAYERS' HURDLE

This year's top rated	RPR
Teahupoo	168
Home By The Lee (right)	163
Langer Dan	159
Crambo	156
Hiddenvalley Lake	154
Mystical Power	153
Lucky Place	152
The Wallpark	152
Rocky's Diamond	149
Gowel Road	145

How the past ten winners rated

Year	Winner	Win RPR	Pre-race RPR
2024	Teahupoo	165	168
2023	Sire Du Berlais	164	162
2022	Flooring Porter	166	169
2021	Flooring Porter	168	167
2020	Lisnagar Oscar	158	151
2019	Paisley Park	168	172
2018	Penhill	162	158
2017	Nichols Canyon	164	166
2016	Thistlecrack	176	172
2015	Cole Harden	168	158

10yr winning average Racing Post Rating: 166

Erika Peciulyte with last year's Stayers' winner Teahupoo

Strong hand for Mullins

Jonny Pearson

NOVICE CHASERS

The novice chase division has had a shake-up for this year's festival with the removal of the 2m4f Grade 1 in favour of a handicap chase. The aim was to make the 2m Arkle and the 3m Brown Advisory more competitive by reducing the number of top-level options, but it has not worked out so well in the shorter race.

The Arkle has long had an odds-on ante-post favourite. First it was Sir Gino who deservedly headed the market after recording an RPR of 166 on his chase debut at Kempton in December, and now it is Majborough after Sir Gino was ruled out of the race.

Majborough: last year's Triumph winner is well set for the Arkle

Last year's Triumph Hurdle winner has looked much the best of the Irish novice chasers and he moved close to Sir Gino's level with an RPR of 164 for his impressive win in the Grade 1 Irish Arkle at the Dublin Racing Festival.

A higher RPR is typically required to win Cheltenham's Arkle, but Majborough is likely to improve in a better race against a higher standard of opposition. On the form we have seen, the Arkle looks to be his for the taking.

On paper the Brown Advisory is much more competitive, with several in the field having won impressively on their way to Cheltenham.

Top in the market and the ratings is Ballyburn. Last season's standout novice hurdler, having won the 2m5f Grade 1 at the festival, started his chase career with a win but then was somewhat disappointing in defeat at Kempton over Christmas when he was dropped to 2m to take on Sir Gino. Stepped back up in trip to 2m5½f at the Dublin Racing Festival, he was once again impressive and achieved an RPR of 160.

If there is a chink in Ballyburn's armour, it is likely to be his jumping. He isn't always the most fluent over a fence and can take longer to go from one side to the other compared with some of his rivals. His high level of ability shines through, however, even when he does make a mistake.

As well as Ballyburn, Willie Mullins has a number of other fancied runners for the race, including second favourite Dancing City.

He was third in the Albert Bartlett Novices' Hurdle last season before going on to finish his hurdles campaign with Grade 1 victories at Aintree and Punchestown. He has kept the winning run going in his two chase starts, although he has merited an RPR of only 149.

That mark is 2lb below his best level over hurdles and 11lb behind Ballyburn over fences. Like many in the entries, he is open to improvement but will have his work cut out to get the better of his stablemate.

Lecky Watson is the third Mullins horse with strong claims and on Racing Post Ratings he has achieved more than the better fancied Dancing City. His Grade 3 win at Punchestown in January, when comfortably seeing off Down Memory Lane, was given an RPR of 154.

Gordon Elliott's Stellar Story and Better Days Ahead both have good chances but again are likely to need significant improvement. They met in a Grade 2 at Naas in February and Better Days Ahead won by a neck, although Stellar Story was conceding 5lb and came out with the better RPR of 153. The winner was given 148 there, although he had previously achieved an RPR of 152.

Britain's best hopes look to be Jango Baie and L'Eau Du Sud. Nicky Henderson's Jango Baie has impressed on both chase starts, achieving an RPR of 158, and both the Arkle and Brown Advisory are options. It is likely he would have to improve to win either race but is the closest challenger to the two favourites on RPRs.

L'Eau Du Sud (155) is going to the Arkle and, although he has won all four starts over fences, still has a bit to find with the favourite.

Ballyburn after his victory at the Dublin Racing Festival

NOVICE CHASERS	
Top rated	RPR
Majborough	164
Ballyburn	160
Jango Baie	158
L'Eau Du Sud	155
Gidleigh Park	154
Lecky Watson	154
Stellar Story	153
Better Days Ahead	152
Croke Park	152
Touch Me Not	151
Dancing City	149
Firefox	149
Arkle 10yr av 168	
Brown 10yr av 168	

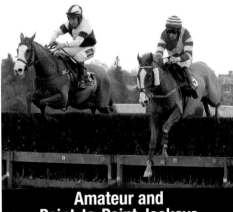

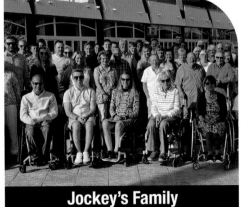

Demand high after big show

Jonny Pearson

NOVICE HURDLERS

It is fair to say that this season doesn't look to have produced the strongest group of novice hurdlers. A few performances have stood out, however, and it is no surprise to find these winners at the head of the ante-post markets for the festival.

Willie Mullins looks to hold the aces again

Kopek Des Bordes:
Supreme top-rated

Despite what our name suggests we deal with much more than injured jockeys.

- We are here to help riders with personal crises whether medical, financial or psychological.
- We have a support team who provide a prompt professional response to potential beneficiaries.
- We have employed a physiotherapist and nutritionist to provide services to jockeys both at the IIJ Facility in RACE and also at the Racecourses.
- In conjunction with HRI/Equuip we have implemented a Financial Literacy course for riders.
- We also have schemes for payment of bursaries to assist jockeys upskill/study for alternative careers when riders finish racing.

All our funding comes from fundraising and donations. Our aim is to make a difference to the lives and welfare of jockeys past and present, and their families by effective use of these funds.

across the division, most notably in the Supreme Novices' Hurdle with Kopek Des Bordes and the Turners Novices' Hurdle with Final Demand. Both were impressive winners at the Dublin Racing Festival.

Final Demand achieved the best RPR in the division this season with his 154 in the 2m6f Grade 1 at the DRF. With the Turners his likely destination, that race has the potential to be the best of the novice hurdles at this year's festival. That has been the case for the past two seasons, both won by Mullins with his successful runners going into the 160s.

The Closutton trainer, in fact, is going for four in a row in the Turners and he will be hard to stop.

The Dan Skelton-trained The New Lion looks to pose the biggest threat. He won the Grade 1 Challow Hurdle at Newbury virtually on the bridle and his ceiling is still unknown.

The Challow form isn't the strongest but he probably could have won by a much greater distance if he had been pushed by Harry Skelton. His RPR of 152 for his near five-length win puts him just 2lb shy of Final Demand and their clash looks one to savour.

The Yellow Clay and Potters Charm are capable of going well, having achieved RPRs of 148 and 146 respectively. A course-and-distance win in November should stand Potters Charm in good stead.

In the last two years the Supreme has taken less winning than has often been the case, with Slade Steel's RPR of 149 last year the lowest recorded in victory in the past decade. Kopek Des Bordes has achieved an RPR of 153 already and, with the potential of much more to come, looks well set to win what looks an ordinary Supreme.

Of his potential challengers, last season's Champion Bumper runner-up Romeo Coolio ranks highly, having achieved an RPR of 149 for his Grade 1 victory at Leopardstown over Christmas.

Next best on RPRs among the likely runners is Salvator Mundi with 146. While he is another Mullins novice to be taken seriously, he has to find improvement to finish ahead of his top-rated stablemate.

The Albert Bartlett is usually the weakest of the festival's Grade 1s for novice hurdlers. No winner has achieved an RPR in the 160s and that looks unlikely to change this year.

The Yellow Clay's 148 looks likely to make him the top-rated, assuming he goes here and Final Demand heads for the Turners. Looking a little further down the list, the fancied Jet Blue has managed an RPR of only 141.

The Triumph Hurdle seems to offer the most likely route to a Grade 1 success for the British novices. While Nicky Henderson's Lulamba heads the betting, it is the James Owen-trained East India Dock who is well clear on achievement. His RPR of 143 in the Triumph Trial puts him 11lb ahead of Lulamba.

East India Dock is proven over the course and distance and should be favourite based on what we have seen out on the track.

Lulamba was impressive on his hurdling debut at Ascot, but it was difficult to rate highly due to the low quality of opposition. As with many novices, he can improve significantly in a better race.

Hello Neighbour and Galileo Dame rate the best Irish chances. Their one-two in the Grade 1 juvenile hurdle at the Dublin Racing Festival is the strongest form on offer among the raiding party. Murcia could also run well, with her second place behind Bacchanalian at Naas being a good formline.

NOVICE HURDLERS		JUVENILE HURDLERS	
Top rated	RPR	Top rated	RPR
Final Demand	154	East India Dock	143
Kopek Des Bordes	153	Murcia	*135
The New Lion	152	Lulamba	132
Romeo Coolio	149	Galileo Dame	*132
The Yellow Clay	148	Hello Neighbour	132
Potters Charm	146	Bacchanalian	129
Salvator Mundi	146	Lady Vega Allen	*129
Sixmilebridge	145	Sainte Lucie	*127
Jet Blue	141	Charlus	117
Workahead	141	Mondo Man	114
Supreme 10yr av 161		*Includes 7lb fillies' allowance	
Turners 10yr av 158			
A Bartlett 10yr av 154		**Triumph 10yr av 149**	

MOORCROFT

Equine Rehabilitation Centre
Charity No: 1076278

Here at the centre in West Sussex, we have over 20 years' experience at retraining ex-racehorses, and we have difference schemes available depending on your needs or your horse's needs. We would love to help, and we do a very thorough caring job with great results. Please come and visit us or call Mary on 0792 666408 for more information and/or to discuss how we can help

www.moorcroftracehorse.org.uk

Huntingrove Stud, Slinfold, West Sussex RH13 0RB   Tel:07929 666408

SUPREME NOVICES' HURDLE

Romeo Coolio (advised at 6-1)
It might be worth sticking to the obvious and opting for Romeo Coolio, a Grade 1 winner who also has Cheltenham Festival form. Gordon Elliott's six-year-old hit the line hard when winning the Future Champions Novice Hurdle at Christmas and nothing travelled better than him in the Champion Bumper last season.

While that might not have been the best edition of the bumper, it doesn't look like being the best Supreme either. Romeo Coolio might not end up too much shorter than 6-1 on the day, but he's the one I want on my side as things stand.

QUEEN MOTHER CHAMPION CHASE

Il Est Francais (advised at 9-1)
I think Noel George and Amanda Zetterholm, trainers of Il Est Francais, will opt for the Champion Chase for their stable star because it's likely to be a small field and the race that provides him with the best chance of winning.

Last time he looked brilliant for nine-tenths of the King George, but according to his jockey he was getting tired coming to the last and couldn't withstand the late challenge of Banbridge.

I'm a firm believer that horses are much more versatile than many believe and that top-class performers can be effective over a

variety of trips. Il Est Francais showed more than enough pace at Kempton to suggest he would have no problem dropping back to 2m.

TURNERS NOVICES' HURDLE

Kawaboomga (advised at 12-1)
Kawaboomga stayed on strongly on his debut for Willie Mullins to be second to Kopek Des Bordes over 2m and the winner clearly improved massively next time, but the selection allowed him first run and

certainly wasn't losing any ground close home.

Since then Kawaboomga has gone on to win a Fairyhouse maiden hurdle, easily beating two horses who had run well in good races previously, and again he stayed on well. Both runs strongly suggest he'll improve a good deal for the step up to 2m5f at Cheltenham and there's probably not as much between him and stablemate Final Demand as the market would have you believe.

On Racing Post Ratings,

Pricewise fancies: (main)
The Wallpark; (inset from
top) Il Est Francais, Romeo
Coolio and Protektorat

STAYERS' HURDLE

The Wallpark (advised at 16-1)
The Wallpark looks more
than capable of taking the
step up into the big league.

The Gordon Elliott-trained
seven-year-old has been a big
improver all season and by far
his best performance came
when winning a Pertemps
qualifier on the Old course at
Cheltenham in October. On
that occasion he easily gave
4lb to Cleeve Hurdle winner
Gowel Road and the best
part of his race was the last
bit when he stayed on really
strongly up the hill.

The stiffer New course will
suit The Wallpark even better
and he showed he could cut
it at the top level when fourth
in a slowly run Long Walk
Hurdle at Ascot in December.
That was the first time Mark
Walsh had ridden him and his
mount got too far back after
a few sloppy jumps but still
finished off much the best of
the whole field. The jockey
will know a lot more about
him now.

The Wallpark will need a
strongly run race to win – and
there's obviously a chance he
could go for the Pertemps
instead – but there aren't
many who can be fancied in
the Stayers' Hurdle and very
few with his upside.

Kawaboomga's maiden hurdle
win was at least as good as
those of Final Demand and
The New Lion, and he hasn't
had the chance to show how
good he is in a Graded race
yet. Come March he could
easily prove himself at least
their equal, if not better.

RYANAIR CHASE

Protektorat (advised at 8-1)
Perhaps Protektorat has
always been underestimated
because he loses lots of races,
but it shouldn't be forgotten
he's won three Grade 1s
and been placed in a Gold

Cup. He's a ten-year-old
but there was no sign of any
deterioration at Windsor in
January. In fact, he looked as
good as ever and we know
what he's going to do in the
Ryanair.

Dan Skelton's contender is
going to go hard from an early
stage, he's going to jump well
and he'll stay on strongly up
the hill. If one of the flashier,
younger horses can get past
him then so be it, but at this
stage he looks the safest
option in a race where there
are so many question marks.

IRELAND beat Britain 18-9 at last year's festival and one of the key questions is whether there will be a fightback from the home team this time.

At the top level over fences, Britain still lacks strength in depth. After the first scratchings stage in early February, there was no British contender left in the Cheltenham Gold Cup shorter than 20-1. In the Queen Mother Champion Chase the favourite Jonbon, a top-priced 10-11, was the only home-trained horse not quoted at 33-1 or bigger in places, while Protektorat was a best-priced 7-1 to repeat last year's victory in the Ryanair Chase, for which every other British contender was 40-1 or longer.

Yet there are more positive signs among the younger ranks, as Protektorat's trainer Dan Skelton pointed out. "It's changing," he said. "If you look at the British novice chasers this season, we've got some good ones."

As well as leading two-miler L'Eau Du Sud from his own yard, Skelton cited Ben Pauling's Grade 1 Scilly Isles winner Handstands, adding: "At three miles hopefully The Jukebox Man will come back next season."

Skelton continued: "Our novice hurdlers are quite good as well. Looking two years down the line, hopefully we're building it all back up. But as we all said when the dominance happened, it won't just be overnight, it will take a bit of time."

'He's on a competitive mark and acts at the track'

How real is the British fightback? And who might lead the way? Tipsters and bookmakers give their views on this year's contenders . . .

Richard Birch I don't understand why some people think Britain will fare better this year. I just can't find any evidence to back up their assertion. Jonbon is my British banker.

David Jennings I'll go for 16-12 to Ireland. Jonbon and Lulamba will be the home bankers for many, but I'm really keen on Caldwell Potter in the new Jack Richards Novices' Handicap Chase. He gets a hard time because of his huge price tag, but he needs at least two and a half miles on soft ground and I think he's really well treated in the mid-140s. He's one of my strongest fancies of the week.

Graeme Rodway This year's home team looks the strongest for a long time and The New Lion could be the star who helps to even things up, both this year and in future.

Nick Watts East India Dock looks like being one for the Brits in the Triumph – and even if he misfires Lulamba offers strong back-up.

Bet365 Pat Cooney I'll go for Ireland by 18-10. Lately the Champion Bumper has been an automatic win for the Irish, but perhaps David Pipe's impressive Ascot winner Windbeneathmywings can change that this time.

Betfair Barry Orr Britain should get into double figures. The New Lion has been really well placed by Dan Skelton and his Challow win was

The New Lion: potential flagbearer for Britain in the Turners Novices' Hurdle

impressive. He'll take all the beating in the Turners.

Coral Andrew Lobo I think it'll end up around the same sort of superiority for the Irish as last year, especially after the loss of Sir Gino from the British team. Hopefully Lulamba can do the business for the same connections in the Triumph to provide some compensation.

Ladbrokes John Priddey Sadly we lost Sir Gino but, with even average luck in the handicaps, I think Team GB will narrow the gap a little. Constitution Hill

should get one in the onion bag on day one.

Paddy Power Paul Binfield It's a massive ask again for British stables versus the Irish powerhouses. Jango Baie is one I'm looking forward to cheering on for the home team.

Tote Jamie Benson I'd be expecting a similar scoreline as last year, especially as the Willie Mullins and Henry de Bromhead strings haven't been quite right at various points this season. That could lead to some well-handicapped horses to

complement the Grade 1 class they have. For Britain I'd give a chance to Ga Law in the Ultima. He's on a competitive mark and the longer trip should see him jump better, plus he acts at the track.

William Hill Jamie McBride One I like for Britain is Telepathique for Lucy Wadham in the Mares' Chase. She could improve again going back left-handed and because of her connections she could be slightly overlooked in the market.

EAST INDIA DOCK

Trainer: James Owen
Won JCB Triumph Trial Juvenile Hurdle, 2m1f, Cheltenham, January 25

Mark Brown, analyst East India Dock made it 3-3 over hurdles in some style. He's now won two Grade 2 events at the course and his blend of speed and stamina, combined with an uncomplicated nature, will make him a more appealing festival bet than current favourite Lulamba. His half-brother Burdett Road was defeated by Sir Gino in last year's race but he's a more nimble version and looks a rock-solid Triumph candidate.

James Owen, trainer "He jumped so economically and quickly. He doesn't need to lead but Sam [Twiston-Davies] wanted to control the race. He handled the ground fine and he's exciting. I wouldn't swap him for any other horse [in the Triumph]. What I like about him is he stays well and he's uncomplicated. He's got a huge future."

HAITI COULEURS

Trainer: Rebecca Curtis
Won Josh Wyke Birthday Novices' Limited Handicap Chase, 3m1½f, Cheltenham, December 14

Mark Brown, analyst This looks good handicap form. Haiti Couleurs looked to have been let in light, up just 5lb for his impressive Aintree win in a small field, and he

Here's what connections and Racing Post analysts said about four strong British contenders . . .

confirmed himself to be a chaser firmly on the up, again impressing deeply with his jumping. The National Hunt Chase, now it's a handicap, or the Ultima look made for him.

Rebecca Curtis, trainer "The National Hunt Chase is the plan. I think it'll be the perfect race for him because I think the further he goes the better he'll be. He's a really exciting horse as he keeps improving and is such a good jumper. He goes out in front, jumps aggressively and other horses find it hard to keep up. He's the best chaser we've had in a while."

JAGWAR

Trainers: Oliver Greenall and Josh Guerriero
Won Timeform Novices' Handicap Chase, 2m4½f, Cheltenham, January 25

Richard Lowther, analyst This is traditionally a good handicap that often has a bearing on the festival, with five of the last six winners going on to finish first or second in March, in three different contests. It was another solid renewal, with two Greenall/Guerriero runners and one other finishing clear.

Jagwar, whose two most

Great British hopes: Windbeneathmywings (above) and East India Dock

WINDBENEATHMYWINGS

Trainer: David Pipe

Won King Edward VII Ascot Membership bumper, 1m7½f, Ascot, December 20

Mark Brown, analyst

Windbeneathmywings, who had won two of his three starts in Ireland for Pat Flynn, had since changed hands and couldn't have been more impressive on this British debut, providing his trainer with a fourth win in this Listed bumper since 2013. He was cut to 8-1 for the Champion Bumper by Paddy Power and it'll presumably be straight to the festival from here.

Jack Tudor, jockey "His Irish form was good and he's clearly stepped forward a hell of a lot. He gives you a nice feeling at home, nothing flashy, but he's shown he's a fair horse there. I was able to get a few breathers in and rounding for home I knew he would keep galloping. He put the race to bed and saw it out well."

recent runs came in races that have worked out particularly well, was produced to collar his front-running stablemate Billytherealbigred on the run-in to win for the third time in four starts over fences. His jumping was assured and he's likely to be back here for the resurrected novice handicap in March.

Oliver Greenall, joint-trainer "It was a reasonably small field but we wanted to go to Cheltenham to see if he would handle it, which he seemed to do pretty well and it was the best he's jumped. Jonjo [O'Neill Jr] was very happy and felt he still has some improvement in him."

GOLD CUP
KEY FORM RACE

Galopin Des Champs slammed his rivals to land the **Irish Gold Cup** for the third successive year. Old foe Fact Or File had more of a go than was the case over Christmas at Leopardstown in the Savills Chase but ultimately paid for those exertions by losing second to Grangeclare West.

This latest win highlighted just what a talented staying chaser Galopin Des Champs has become. The form is rock solid and he's bang on course to emulate some of the greats by landing a third Gold Cup.

SOLID PERFORMER

L'Homme Presse rarely puts a foot wrong. Venetia Williams' ten-year-old was a solid third on his comeback in the King George VI Chase at Kempton on Boxing Day and the following month returned to winning ways with a game victory over Stage Star in the Cotswold Chase at Cheltenham, the pair drawing well clear of the remainder.

His sole defeat at Cheltenham came when a tiring fourth in last year's Gold Cup, but he's capable of getting closer this time with more patient tactics.

DARK HORSE

We know a lot about **Banbridge** and yet he remains unexposed as a staying chaser, even after his victory in the King George.

The Kempton form puts him bang in the mix and he's already a festival winner. If the ground isn't too soft, Joseph O'Brien's hardy nine-year-old will have his best chance to prove himself a true stayer.

VERDICT

It's probably folly to try to get **Galopin Des Champs** beaten. Granted a clear round, Willie Mullins' top-class chaser should write himself into the history books with a third straight Gold Cup. If there's a fly in the ointment it's likely to be **Banbridge**, who isn't fully tested as a stayer by any means.

DAVE ORTON

History beckons for super Galopin

Galopin Des Champs brings up his hat-trick in the Irish Gold Cup

Constitution can make up for lost year

CHAMPION HURDLE
KEY FORM RACE

After his win in the 2023 Christmas Hurdle no-one would have thought it would be a whole 12 months before Constitution Hill appeared in public again, but following his well-documented tribulations he had something to prove when he lined up against star mare Lossiemouth in this year's **Christmas Hurdle** at Kempton.

He silenced the doubters with a cosy victory that blew away the cobwebs and proved the engine is still intact. True, the two and a half lengths he had to spare over Lossiemouth was the shortest winning margin of his career, but he did all that was asked of him.

SOLID PERFORMER

Dependable was **State Man**'s middle name until he ran a shocker at Leopardstown over Christmas, trailing in more than 30 lengths behind Brighterdaysahead, with the unheralded Winter Fog beating him too.

He bounced back in February to land his third consecutive Irish Champion Hurdle, albeit having been left with a simple job when Lossiemouth fell four out, and that was his 11th Grade 1 win in a stellar career. No doubt the 2024 Champion Hurdle hero won't give up his crown without a fight.

DARK HORSE

Runners are going to be thin on the ground, with only ten left in the race after the scratchings stage in early February. A few will run for minor prize-money, which goes down to eighth, but it will be a major shock if more than three or four are involved at the sharp end.

VERDICT

Brighterdaysahead will be a worthy adversary if she takes part in this rather than the Mares' Hurdle and **State Man** looks sure to run his race, but **Constitution Hill** is one of the greats and a confident selection to regain his title.

RICHARD LOWTHER

*Constitution Hill and
Nico de Boinville*

CHAMPION CHASE
KEY FORM RACE

The long-established **Clarence House Chase** at Ascot is famous for big clashes and we were treated to another this January when Jonbon lined up against dual Champion Chase winner Energumene.

Jonbon justified heavy support with a clear-cut victory over his older rival, who had come back with success in the Hilly Way at Cork the previous month.

That made it 2-2 around Ascot for Jonbon, but the manner in which he tended to jump out to his left only further enhanced his obvious chance of landing the big one back around Cheltenham in March.

Jonbon: third shot at festival success

SOLID PERFORMER

Solness hasn't had much of a break since coming up short in the Grand Annual at the festival last March. Joseph O'Brien's seven-year-old has had nine runs since but is thriving on racing and comes back this year in the form of his life having broken through at the top level on his last two starts.

Success at 28-1 in the Paddy's Rewards Club Chase at Leopardstown's Christmas meeting proved to be no fluke when the front-runner repeated the feat back there in the Dublin Chase in February, winning with similar authority.

DARK HORSE

It's been a long road back for **Marine Nationale** since suffering an injury after a flop at last year's Dublin Racing Festival. The 2023 Supreme Novices' Hurdle winner has yet to win since resuming this term but recorded a personal best when chasing home Solness back at Leopardstown in February. He looks to have been trained with the Champion Chase in mind and should have a big say granted a sounder surface this time.

VERDICT

Everything looks in place for **Jonbon** to land a deserved first festival win, having finished runner-up to Constitution Hill and El Fabiolo in the Supreme and Arkle respectively. He's 3-3 this season and is the standout form pick. **Marine Nationale** might give him the most trouble.
DAVE ORTON

Jonbon in top form for moment of truth

Teahupoo: set to turn up fresh and well for his repeat bid

Teahupoo solid – but look out for Diamond

STAYERS' HURDLE
KEY FORM RACE
Last year's **Stayers' Hurdle** is the place to start. Gordon Elliott's Teahupoo justified his short price in a race dominated by Irish runners, with the three British representatives finishing eighth, ninth and tenth.

Since then only Nicky Henderson's Lucky Place has emerged as a credible contender from the home team. Last year's Coral Cup fourth is potentially open to improvement over 3m.

However, it's hard to see beyond another Irish-controlled finish. Teahupoo will turn up fresh and well having not raced since Fairyhouse in December, the same route to the festival he took last year.

SOLID PERFORMER
Home By The Lee was third to Teahupoo last year, when he would have benefited from a more stringent test of stamina, and will turn up in better form than 12 months ago.

He won at Navan first time out and then, with his usual blinkers back in place, followed up in a Grade 1 at Leopardstown over Christmas. Joseph O'Brien seems sure to have him just right for the big occasion and, although the gelding is ten now, he should do himself proud again.

DARK HORSE
Few had heard of **Rocky's Diamond** before his cracking third to Home By The Lee and Bob Olinger at Leopardstown's festive fixture, but he emerged as a genuine Stayers' contender when landing the Galmoy Hurdle at Gowran Park in January.

Trained by Declan Queally, who has never had a winner in Britain, he's run just six times in his life and the limit to his potential has yet to be reached. He'd be the first five-year-old to win the Stayers' since Whim II in 1951, when it was known as the Spa Hurdle, although none from his age group has run in the race since 2015.

VERDICT
A winter break worked in favour of **Teahupoo** last season and he'll arrive at Cheltenham with just one run behind him again, a commendable second to Lossiemouth over an inadequate trip. Irish stables should dominate again and **Rocky's Diamond** and **Home By The Lee** can follow him home.
RICHARD LOWTHER

Djelo looks best value

RYANAIR CHASE
KEY FORM RACE

With Galopin Des Champs back in third, the form of Fact To File's spirited success from Spillane's Tower makes the **John Durkan Memorial Chase** the strongest guide to this year's Ryanair Chase.

Fact To File, last year's Brown Advisory winner, overcame some trouble around three out on his return at Punchestown and showed a cracking attitude to come out on top in his first race in open company.

He was subsequently outstayed twice by Galopin Des Champs back up at 3m around Leopardstown and looks tailor-made for an ease to the intermediate distance in March.

SOLID PERFORMER

Djelo has come a long way since finishing third to Grey Dawning at last year's festival.

He took his form to the next level when slamming last year's Ryanair winner Protektorat in the Peterborough Chase at Huntingdon in December. That rival gained revenge in the Fleur de Lys Chase next time but Djelo just didn't take to Windsor on that occasion.

He showed his true colours again when upped to 3m in the Denman Chase at Newbury in February. An RPR of 170 for that win puts him right in the mix.

DARK HORSE

French-trained **Il Est Francais** could go for the Champion Chase the previous day but would be a rival to fear if heading for the Ryanair instead.

His freewheeling style of running caught out all bar winner Banbridge in the King George VI Chase over 3m at Kempton on Boxing Day and his RPR of 173 there makes him one of the clear form picks.

Dropping him back to the intermediate distance would make a lot of sense.

VERDICT

If **Fact To File** heads for the Ryanair in preference to the Gold Cup, he'd be hard to look past. However, this year's edition is likely to be a deep one and **Djelo** and **Il Est Francais** would be formidable rivals. The Venetia Williams-trained Djelo rates the value pick. **DAVE ORTON**

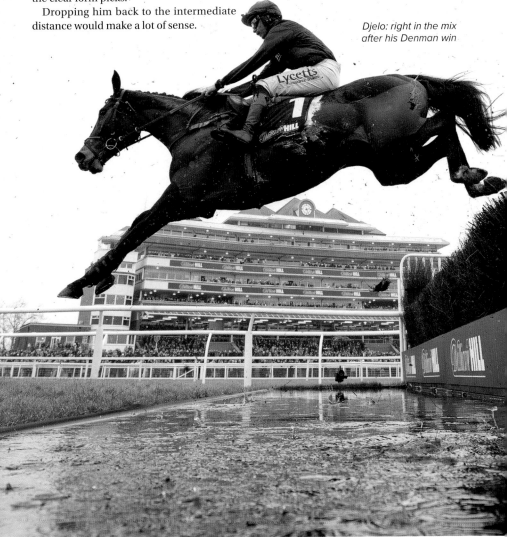

Djelo: right in the mix after his Denman win

Gidleigh Park: soft ground would put him in the reckoning

Majborough on another level

NOVICE CHASERS 2M
KEY FORM RACE

For the second year in a row the **Irish Arkle** at the Dublin Racing Festival provides the leading pointer to Cheltenham's Arkle and once again the Leopardstown prize went to Willie Mullins, courtesy of runaway winner Majborough.

Last season's Triumph Hurdle winner had impressed on his chasing debut at Fairyhouse in December but his nine-length romp at the DRF took his form to the next level. Despite pulling his way to the front and fiddling a few fences, he had plenty to spare over runner-up Touch Me Not, who ran to the same level as when second in the Henry VIII Novices' Chase on his previous outing.

SOLID PERFORMER

L'Eau Du Sud lines up unbeaten in four chase outings since starting out in handicap company at Stratford in October. His breakthrough win at the top level in Sandown's Henry VIII in December gives him a collateral line with biggest rival Majborough, through consistent runner-up Touch Me Not, and his slick fencing was advertised again in the Kingmaker Novices' Chase at Warwick in February.

DARK HORSE

Gidleigh Park was pulled up on his chasing debut but bounced back in style when running away with the Lightning Novices' Chase on Berkshire Winter Million weekend at Windsor in January.

Harry Fry's giant seven-year-old made those fences look small when making all and lowering the colours of Caldwell Potter and we know he likes Cheltenham, having won a Grade 2 novice hurdle there last season.

If it comes up genuinely soft on the opening day of the festival, he's well up to surprising a few.

VERDICT

With the Grade 1 novice chase over the intermediate trip having been discontinued in favour of a handicap, it seemed nailed on that we'd witness an ultra-competitive edition of the Arkle.

After the shock defection of ante-post favourite Sir Gino, however, the door was left wide open for **Majborough** to make it 3-3 over fences. **Gidleigh Park** can reward juicy each-way odds provided there's some rain about.

DAVE ORTON

NOVICE CHASERS 3M
KEY FORM RACE

Although Ballyburn might not have impressed everyone, it's safe to say he set the standard in the staying novice division with his RPR of 160 when landing the Grade 1 **Ladbrokes Novice Chase** at the Dublin Racing Festival in February.

Willie Mullins' seven-year-old got better the further he went over the 2m5½f trip, having been briefly headed at the final fence, and his mark took him closer to the form of his stunning novice hurdle success at last year's festival.

The DRF race was used as a final prep for last season's Brown Advisory winner Fact To File and has also been won by dual Gold Cup hero Galopin Des Champs.

SOLID PERFORMER

Ballyburn's stablemate **Dancing City**, a dual Grade 1 winner as a novice hurdler, has had an impressive transition to chasing this term and made it 2-2 in the Grade 3 Naas Novice Chase in January. That race over 3m1f proved a proper stamina test and there's a strong chance that the form of his three-and-a-half-length success over Bioluminescence – a leading hope for the Grade 2 Mares' Chase – will be well advertised at the festival.

DARK HORSE

Stellar Story comes into this year's festival somewhat under the radar, despite having won the Grade 1 Albert Bartlett for Gordon Elliott over hurdles last March.

He flopped behind stablemates Croke Park and Better Days Ahead on his second start as a chaser in a Grade 1 at Leopardstown's Christmas meeting. However, he got right back on track when looking somewhat unlucky not to successfully concede a penalty to Better Days Ahead with a fast-finishing second in a Grade 2 at Navan in February.

VERDICT

Ballyburn should take some stopping in the Brown Advisory in his quest for back-to-back festival wins. The likely odds won't make great appeal, however. If **Stellar Story** lines up in his own bid for a festival double, he certainly shouldn't be underestimated.

DAVE ORTON

Double shot for Stellar

*Stellar Story
(blue cap):
back on track
last time out*

Substance to Dock's form

*East India Dock:
solid form claims
in Triumph Hurdle*

NOVICE HURDLERS 2M-2M1F
KEY FORM RACE

One of the most dominant winners at the Dublin Racing Festival was Willie Mullins' Kopek Des Bordes, who blew away the opposition in the Grade 1 **Tattersalls Ireland Novice Hurdle**.

Admittedly five of his nine rivals were stablemates, but the way he eased clear between the last two flights was highly impressive. He jumped more fluently than on his debut over the course and distance on a foggy Boxing Day, and Mullins and Paul Townend were effusive in their praise of him afterwards.

Third-placed Good And Clever, trained by Warren Greatrex, was beaten 15 lengths further than he had been by Potters Charm in another Grade 1 at Aintree in December.

SOLID PERFORMER

It's a battle between substance and style in the Triumph Hurdle and **East India Dock** fits the bill in the former category.

A useful Flat handicapper for James Fanshawe, he's made a blistering start to his hurdles career with James Owen, backing up his debut success at Wincanton with a pair of Grade 2 victories at Cheltenham.

The half-brother to Burdett Road – arguably Britain's second-best chance in the Champion Hurdle – is an agile jumper and an uncomplicated ride who looks sure to run his race on the big day.

Conversely, his market rival Lulamba is a superb prospect but the form of his debut British win at Ascot is 11lb short of East India Dock's top RPR of 143.

DARK HORSE

Funiculi Funicula was making his first appearance for 15 months when disposing of his field in a Clonmel maiden hurdle in January, making all the running to win by a wide margin.

The form is hard to weigh up, with the opposition limited, but an RPR of 130+ is respectable and Mullins – yes, him again – has indicated he'll be on the boat to Cheltenham.

The five-year-old makes more appeal for the Supreme than the Turners, for which he's also entered.

VERDICT

It's hard to get away from **Kopek Des Bordes** in the Supreme, in which stablemate **Funiculi Funicula** can make the frame too. **East India Dock** can put one on the board for British stables in the Triumph.

RICHARD LOWTHER

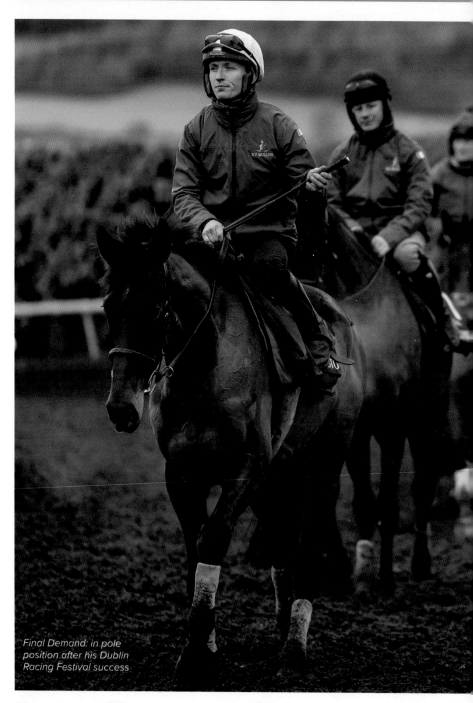

Final Demand: in pole position after his Dublin Racing Festival success

Final Demand has star quality

NOVICE HURDLERS 2M5F-3M

KEY FORM RACE

Final Demand announced himself as a genuine Grade 1 star in the **Nathaniel Lacy & Partners Solicitors Novice Hurdle** at the Dublin Racing Festival, storming clear to slam dependable yardstick Wingmen, who had been third in another top-level event at Naas the time before.

Final Demand had won in a "canter" at Limerick over Christmas, and that's not a description the Racing Post's comments-in-running team give out very often.

The DRF contest was over 2m6f, so Willie Mullins has a decision to make whether to go up in trip for the Albert Bartlett or drop back slightly in the Turners. The latter is looking more likely, but until the declarations are made you can't be sure.

SOLID PERFORMER

Defending a record of four from four over hurdles, **The Yellow Clay** will prove a tough opponent in the Turners or the Albert Bartlett. Following his win in a Grade 1 at Naas in January, his trainer Gordon Elliott ventured that the shorter Turners was the probable target, but he's ante-post favourite for the Albert Bartlett and plans aren't set in stone.

Owners Noel and Valerie Moran also have the Elliott-trained Wingmen, who was beaten a similar margin by The Yellow Clay at Naas as he was when behind Final Demand at the DRF.

DARK HORSE

John McConnell is based in County Meath but regularly has runners in Britain and his six-year-old **Intense Approach** has crossed the water for each of his last four races. Runner-up in a Grade 2 at Chepstow in October, he won at Cheltenham later that month to provide the trainer with his third victory in that race since 2020.

The previous two winners both went on to finish third in the Albert Bartlett and McConnell confirmed Intense Approach for that contest after he'd won at Musselburgh in February. His stamina is assured and he's still on an upward curve.

VERDICT

Willie Mullins sent out the first five in last season's Turners (then Gallagher) Novices' Hurdle, and with that feat still fresh in the memory it's impossible not to go with **Final Demand** this time. **The Yellow Clay** will give his all wherever he goes.

RICHARD LOWTHER

Ballyburn looks ready to double up again

LAST year Willie Mullins landed all eight Grade 1 races at the Dublin Racing Festival and proceeded to dominate Cheltenham the following month with nine winners. The correlation seemed strong, even if only four of his top-level scorers at the DRF repeated the trick in March.

This time Mullins won 'only' six Grade 1s at the DRF, perhaps offering a glimmer of hope to his rivals. Few will bank on any diminution of his powers at Cheltenham, however. Immediately after the DRF one bookmaker had eight or nine winners as the 6-4 favourite in betting on Mullins' tally at the festival.

Four of his six Grade 1 winners at the DRF were strong festival favourites immediately after Leopardstown. Galopin

Ballyburn: excellent chance to add Cheltenham success to Dublin Racing Festival win for the second year in a row

Des Champs (Gold Cup) and Kopek Des Bordes (Supreme Novices' Hurdle) looked to be bankers; less so the other two favourites, Ballyburn (Brown Advisory Novices' Chase) and Final Demand (Turners Novices' Hurdle).

Just over a week after the DRF, Irish Arkle winner Majborough joined the banker list when he took over as odds-on favourite for the Arkle at Cheltenham following the news that Nicky Henderson's Sir Gino had been ruled out.

That robbed the festival of one of the most hotly anticipated clashes of the week between the star five-year-olds but appeared to smooth the way for the richly talented Majborough to add the Arkle to last year's Triumph Hurdle success.

Mullins' other Grade 1 winner at this year's DRF, however, was still left facing a tough assignment at Cheltenham against a Henderson hotpot. State Man will have to defend his Champion Hurdle crown against the returning Constitution Hill, who was nine lengths superior when they met in the 2023 race.

Of Mullins' six top-level DRF winners, the one to back at odds-against is **Ballyburn**. Last year he started 1-2 in the Grade 1 2m5f novice hurdle and duly added a 13-length win to his seven-length success at the DRF. At the time most felt he was the proverbial 'could be anything' but his

comprehensive defeat by Sir Gino over 2m at Kempton's Christmas meeting was evidence enough that he could not be the dominant force in that chasing division.

Having gone back up to 2m5½f for his five-length win in the Grade 1 Ladbrokes Novice Chase at the DRF, Ballyburn looks well set to step up again in the Brown Advisory over 3m.

The main doubt seems to stem from the bubble bursting at Kempton, but that was against a top-class rival and there is nothing of the same calibre in the Brown Advisory. The rest of Ballyburn's form points to both a high-class performer and a dominant one even in good company.

Last year's DRF win over hurdles was decisive over Slade Steel, who took the Supreme Novices' Hurdle next time. This year Ballyburn won over fences at the DRF by five lengths from Croke Park and by just over ten lengths from stablemate Impaire Et Passe. Both the placed horses had been Grade 1 novice chase winners at the big Christmas meetings.

Seven of Mullins' nine Cheltenham winners last year had run at the DRF, emphasising that is the main place to look for his big chances. Three of those did not win at the DRF (form figures of U34) and chief among this year's beaten horses appears to be Fact To File, who realistically faced a losing battle when third behind Galopin Des Champs in the Irish Gold Cup.

Last year's Brown Advisory winner has a top RPR of 171 over fences and will have a

Majborough leads on his chase debut at Fairyhouse

first-rate chance dropping down to 2m5f in the Ryanair Chase. His RPR was 169 when he won the John Durkan over 2m3½f on his reappearance, which signalled his aptitude for the intermediate trip.

Spillane's Tower, the half-length runner-up in the John Durkan for Jimmy Mangan, looks set to be a chief rival again. Fact To File's greater experience and proven capability at Cheltenham could be telling advantages.

Absurde won the County Handicap Hurdle at 12-1 for Mullins last year, having finished fourth behind Ballyburn in the 2m Grade 1 novice hurdle at the DRF. This year's Absurde might be **Karniquet**, who took high rank in the County market after coming second to stablemate Kopek Des Bordes.

Another who would be interesting dropped into handicap company for Mullins is Willy De Houelle, who was fourth in the Grade 1 juvenile hurdle at the DRF and could be aimed at the Fred Winter on the opening day.

The two big Mullins hopes with most to prove after the DRF are fallers Lossiemouth and El Fabiolo. The mishaps are mounting up for El Fabiolo and he would have it all to do against Jonbon in the Champion Chase anyway. A move up in trip to the Ryanair is possible.

It is easier to see Lossiemouth coming back from her fall in the Irish Champion Hurdle, having looked set for a titanic battle with State Man. The Champion looks tough against Constitution Hill, who beat her by two and a half lengths in the Christmas Hurdle at Kempton, but so does the Mares' Hurdle against Brighterdaysahead. Remarkably, given her talent, Lossiemouth is likely to face an odds-on favourite wherever she goes.

The most likely types for Mullins to have been seen away from the DRF are his strong squad of mares and bumper runners. **Maughreen**, who won on her hurdling debut at Punchestown a few days before the DRF, has long been a leading fancy for the Mares' Novices' Hurdle.

Having been Champion Bumper favourite last year before suffering a setback, she is expected to get on the Cheltenham scoreboard this time.

Mullins had a winner (Bambino Fever) and runner-up (Sortudo) in the Grade 2 bumpers at the DRF. Perhaps Bambino Fever is the one for the Champion Bumper, but Mullins is likely to be mob-handed again and several won't have been anywhere near so highly tried.

Gordon Elliott was winless at the DRF, but in large part that was down to sending a smaller team that did not include several of his best hopes for Cheltenham. Brighterdaysahead (Mares' Hurdle) and Teahupoo (Stayers' Hurdle) are both odds-on for their festival targets and have been deliberately kept fresh.

It worked for Teahupoo last season to run only in the Hatton's Grace and then wait another three months until Cheltenham, and there was no reason for Elliott to change a winning formula.

Teahupoo will be the one to beat again in the Stayers', although the each-way pick is **Home By The Lee**. Joseph O'Brien's ten-year-old has been seventh, fifth and third in the last three runnings and is at least as good as ever judging by his Grade 1 win at Leopardstown's Christmas meeting.

Two leading novice hurdlers kept fresh by Elliott are Romeo Coolio and The Yellow Clay, who both look strong contenders for championship honours.

Romeo Coolio, who will go up against Kopek Des Bordes in the Supreme, is only

Uprating Horseboxes

As you may be aware, the DVSA is paying close attention to the horsebox industry and in particular, to lightweight horseboxes which they suspect may be operating overweight.

We have seen cases of horseboxes being stopped, checked and impounded on the roadside, owing to running overweight. The horses in transit have to be loaded into a different box and taken away, and the resultant fines are ever increasing in size. Yet, there is an alternative.

SvTech is keen to promote its uprating service for lightweight horseboxes (3500kg), whereby the horsebox can gain an extra 200-300kg in payload. This provides vital payload capability when carrying an extra horse and/or tack and offers peace of mind for the owner.

SvTech has carried out extensive work and testing on lightweight models and has covered uprates for most lightweight vehicles.

It is worth noting that some uprates require modifications or changes to the vehicle's braking, tyres and/or suspension, for which SvTech provides a simple purpose-built suspension assister kit. This will take between 1-2 hours for you to fit. Your horsebox will then go for a formal inspection to bring it into the 'Goods' category, and, depending on the vehicle's age, may also require fitment of a speed limiter, for which there are one or two options. Most importantly, vehicles registered after May 2002 must be fitted with manufacturer's ABS, if going above 3500kg.

If you're unsure, or don't believe that you need to uprate your lightweight horsebox, try taking it to a public weighbridge when you're fully loaded with your horse, tack, passenger, hay, etc. and weigh off each axle individually and the vehicle as a whole. There could be a distinct chance that you've overloaded one of the axles, even if you're within the GVW. If there is a problem, we can help. Call us to discuss your options.

Downplating Horseboxes

Do you own a 10 - 12.5 tonnes horsebox and do you want non-HGV licence holder to drive it? Your horsebox could be downplated to 7.5 tonnes so that any driver with a licence issued prior to 1st Jan 1997 could drive it.

- You are paying too much Vehicle Excise Duty.
- You want to escape the need for a tachograph.

The most important aspect when downplating is to leave yourself suitable payload to carry your goods. The Ministry requires that for horseboxes of 7500kg there is a minimum payload of 2000kg. Hence, when downplating to 7500kg, the unladen weight must not exceed 5500kg. For 3500kg horseboxes, you must ensure that you have a payload of at least 1000kg, thus, when empty it cannot weigh more than 2500kg.

Due to recent changes at DVSA, we are no longer required to make a mechanical change to the vehicle and, once downrated, we will be supplying you with a revised set of Ministry plating certificates, or if exempt, plating and testing, a converter's plate and certificate at the lower weight.

Depending upon vehicle usage, it is at the discretion of DVSA as to whether they will require a formal inspection of your vehicle.

TO DISCOVER YOUR OPTIONS, PLEASE DOWNLOAD, FILL IN AND RETURN OUR ENQUIRY FORM – WWW.SVTECH.CO.UK

SvTech

Special Vehicle Technology

T +44 (0)1772 621800
E webenquiries@svtech.co.uk

WHERE IRELAND HAS DONE BEST (AND WORST) IN THE PAST DECADE

	2015	2016	2017	2018	2019	2020	2021	2022	2023	2024
TUESDAY										
Supreme Novices' Hurdle	●		●		●		●		●	●
Arkle Novices' Chase	●	●		●	●	●			●	●
Ultima Handicap Chase										
Mares' Hurdle	●	●	●			●	●		●	
Champion Hurdle	●	●			●	●	●	●	●	●
Juvenile Handicap Hurdle				●	●	●	●	●	●	●
National Hunt Novices' Chase*	●		●			●	●	●	●	●
WEDNESDAY										
Turners Novices' Hurdle	●	●		●	●	●	●		●	●
Brown Advisory Novices' Chase	●			●			●			
Coral Cup Handicap Hurdle		●	●				●	●	●	●
Cross Country Chase**	●	●	●	●	●		●	●	●	
Queen Mother Champion Chase				●				●		●
Grand Annual Handicap Chase				●		●			●	
Champion Bumper				●	●	●	●	●	●	●
THURSDAY										
Mares' Novices' Hurdle *(nine runnings)*	●	●	●	●	●	●	●			
Jack Richards Novices' Handicap Chase ***										
Pertemps Handicap Hurdle	●	●	●				●	●		
Ryanair Chase	●	●	●				●	●		
Stayers' Hurdle	●	●	●				●	●		
Plate Handicap Chase	●		●				●	●		
Kim Muir Handicap Chase	●				●	●	●	●		
FRIDAY										
Triumph Hurdle	●				●		●	●	●	●
County Handicap Hurdle	●		●				●	●	●	●
Mares' Chase *(four runnings)*							●	●	●	●
Albert Bartlett Novices' Hurdle	●			●			●	●	●	●
Cheltenham Gold Cup		●	●		●		●	●	●	●
Hunters' Chase	●	●				●				
Martin Pipe Handicap Hurdle	●		●	●	●					

* becomes a handicap this year (previously a conditions race)
** reverts to a handicap this year (conditions race 2016-2023, not run in 2024)
*** new limited handicap for novices

4lb behind the favourite on RPRs. That does not look an insurmountable gap, even if both can be expected to improve from their last-time-out Grade 1 wins.

Elliott is leaning towards the Turners for **The Yellow Clay**, who made it four from four over hurdles with a good win in the Grade 1 Lawlor's of Naas over 2m4f in early January. It might depend on whether Mullins chooses the Turners or the Albert Bartlett

The Yellow Clay (red cap): strong Grade 1 novice hurdle contender for Gordon Elliott

for Final Demand, although The Yellow Clay would be a formidable rival for that DRF winner in any case.

Ireland's training titans also look set to go head to head again in the Champion Bumper, the pair having won seven of the last eight runnings between them. Elliott's main challenger appears to be Kalypso'chance, a Listed winner at Navan in December when interestingly he was ridden by Patrick Mullins. The winning RPR there was 130, compared with 124 for the Mullins-trained Bambino Fever at the DRF.

Elliott's handicap chances may well include Firefox (Grand Annual Chase), Wingmen (Coral Cup) and The Wallpark (Pertemps Final), if the latter goes there instead of the Stayers' Hurdle on the same day.

It will be interesting to see how Elliott fares in the Cross Country Chase now that it reverts to a handicap. He dominated the event in the last eight runnings as a conditions race but never won when it was a handicap before. Class acts Galvin and Delta Work will have to give plenty of weight now.

Henry de Bromhead was another big trainer who was winless at the DRF, which came at a time when his Knockeen stable was out of form.

Two winners in the first five weeks of 2025 was worrying, but these days Cheltenham without De Bromhead in the thick of the battle is hard to imagine.

A repeat win for Captain Guinness in the Champion Chase looks difficult but De Bromhead has plenty of promising younger horses, including the mares The Big Westerner and July Flower.

The Big Westerner is a leading fancy for the Albert Bartlett Novices' Hurdle after making it two out of two over hurdles in a Grade 2 over 2m7f at Limerick's Christmas meeting.

July Flower was trained early in her career by De Bromhead and then went back to France, where she was third in last year's French Champion Hurdle. On her first run back with De Bromhead in December, she was a Grade 3 winner at Leopardstown and took high rank in the Mares' Hurdle betting.

Another to note if the De Bromhead team is in better form by festival week is Workahead, who is set to go for the curtain-raising Supreme. The form has worked out well from his seven-length maiden hurdle victory at Leopardstown over Christmas.

Three winners at the DRF highlighted the growing power of Gavin Cromwell's stable and he came out of the weekend with the ante-post outright or joint-favourite in five Cheltenham races, more than any trainer bar Mullins.

Most of Cromwell's market leaders are in handicaps – DRF winner Backtonormal in the Plate/Kim Muir, Now Is The Hour in the revamped National Hunt Chase and Stumptown in the Cross Country.

Cromwell had his first handicap winner at last year's festival with Inothewayurthinkin in the Kim Muir and he looks set to have a strong hand in the staying chases this time. DRF winner Perceval Legallois is another possible, although the Grand National looks the main target.

Hello Neighbour was the other Cromwell winner at the DRF, landing the Grade 1 juvenile hurdle, and will be Ireland's main hope in the Triumph against British pair Lulamba and East India Dock.

Cromwell tends to be well stocked with mares and he has the favourite for the Mares' Chase in Bioluminescence, having

Lark In The Mornin: capable of more festival success

won last year's race with Limerick Lace. She needs soft ground. He also has a strong chance in the Mares' Novices' Hurdle with the highly rated Sixandahalf, whose clash with Maughreen could be a belter.

Like Cromwell, Joseph O'Brien had three DRF winners and will head to Cheltenham with high hopes of more success.

Stable star Banbridge has won Grade 1s at 2m, 2m4f and 3m in the past two years and O'Brien is keeping his options open for Cheltenham, while also being prepared to wait for Aintree. The King George VI Chase winner is around the same price for the Gold Cup and Ryanair Chase, although the latter looks much the easier assignment.

Solness, winner of the Grade 1 Dublin Chase at the DRF, looks to have an each-way chance in the Champion Chase and there is also Stayers' Hurdle each-way pick Home By The Lee.

Another good chance for O'Brien could be Lark In The Mornin, who won the juvenile handicap hurdle at last year's festival and could go for the County or the Martin Pipe Handicap Hurdle, another favourite race for his trainer.

Emmet Mullins is noted as a target trainer and he looks to have big threats with DRF winner McLaurey in the County and last year's close runner-up Its On The Line in the hunter chase. Vischio, his other DRF winner on her first run for the yard, is another to note if market moves develop in one of the handicaps.

■ PICK OF THE BUNCH

Ballyburn Class act in the Brown Advisory Novices' Chase

Home By The Lee Each-way shout in the Stayers' Hurdle

Karniquet One to note if dropped into handicap company

Maughreen Belated festival success awaits in the Mares' Novices' Hurdle

The Yellow Clay Battle-hardened top novice for Gordon Elliott

Joe Eccles picks a couple of handicappers to note from the Dublin Racing Festival

Sequestered
Trainer: Paul Gilligan
2nd, 2m5½f Grade 3 handicap chase

Gavin Cromwell's Backtonormal justified strong support with a comfortable success in the Grade 3 handicap chase.

An opening handicap mark of 130 underestimated Backtonormal and runner-up Sequestered can gain compensation next time if he doesn't face another such well-handicapped rival.

Paul Gilligan's seven-year-old bolted up in a 3m½f handicap chase at Leopardstown over Christmas and looked set to defy a 12lb rise when sauntering into the lead turning for home on his return visit.

Sequestered had to settle for second when Backtonormal hit top gear and was nudged up another 5lb for that showing, but he still looks capable of landing a big pot before the season is out. The Fulke Walwyn Kim Muir Handicap Chase could be the next target.

Storm Heart
Trainer: Willie Mullins
2nd, 2m Listed handicap hurdle

McLaurey justified favouritism for Emmet Mullins in the Listed handicap hurdle but Storm Heart was a big eyecatcher in second, beaten just a length.

The Gigginstown-owned five-year-old finished a 15-length fifth in last season's Triumph Hurdle behind stablemate Majborough after being sent off 7-2 favourite for Willie Mullins and Paul Townend.

He was then fourth in a Grade 1 at the Punchestown festival and returned to action only at the Dublin Racing Festival in a race his trainer and jockey won with Gaelic Warrior in 2023.

Storm Heart raced wide and had only a handful of his 17 rivals behind turning for home but came with a strong run in the home straight and may have troubled the winner but for a mistake at the final flight.

He's entitled to come on for that outing and, if the ground is testing, would have to be considered a big player in the County Handicap Hurdle, for which he was a best-priced 10-1 after the DRF.

Are results at the Dublin Racing Festival a good guide for Cheltenham? Andrew Dietz delves into the data

The Dublin Racing Festival (DRF) was introduced in 2018 as a key date on the jumps calendar, bringing together Ireland's best horses over two spectacular days at Leopardstown.

With signature races such as the Irish Champion Hurdle and Irish Gold Cup and more than €2 million in total prize-money, the DRF is a championship meeting in its own right. However, given it takes place the month before the Cheltenham Festival, it also serves as an ideally positioned stepping stone to jump racing's biggest meeting of all.

So how does the DRF fare overall as a prep for March?

Our data from the last seven years shows that 48 Cheltenham Festival winners ran at the DRF. That is an average of 6.86 winners per year, which initially seems a lot but might have been higher when you consider Ireland's dominance of the jumps in recent years.

Of those 48 winners, 22 won at the DRF, five came second, six third and four fourth. Surprisingly, a disappointing run at the DRF can be turned around at Cheltenham as eight of the winners were unplaced, two unseated their rider and one fell.

You won't be surprised to learn that Willie Mullins, by far and away the DRF's leading trainer, is responsible for exactly half of the tally of Cheltenham winners – 24 of the 48.

Focusing on Cheltenham's four championship races – the Champion Hurdle, Champion Chase, Stayers' Hurdle and Gold Cup – the DRF has produced a total of seven winners, including three in both the Champion Hurdle (Honeysuckle in 2021 and 2022 and State Man in 2024) and the Gold Cup (Minella Indo in 2021 and Galopin Des Champs in 2023 and 2024).

Captain Guinness is the sole Champion Chase winner (2024) to have run in the Dublin Chase (finished third), but Min improved on his second in the Dublin Chase when going on to win the Ryanair Chase in 2020.

No Stayers' Hurdle winner has prepped at the DRF, but there is not an equivalent race over the weekend at Leopardstown.

A main standout from the data is that the Grade 1 Tattersalls Ireland Novice Hurdle has been a notable breeding ground for Cheltenham winners, with no fewer than eight runners going on to claim glory at the festival.

Last year's race alone served up three festival winners with Ballyburn (first) in what is now the Turners Novices' Hurdle, Slade Steel (second) in the Supreme Novices' Hurdle and Absurde (fourth) in the County Handicap Hurdle.

The Grade 1 Ladbrokes Novice Chase is not far behind on six, including Brown Advisory winners Monkfish (2021) and Fact To File (2024) and last year's Arkle hero Gaelic Warrior.

Another notable trend shows the Grade 1 Juvenile Hurdle at the DRF has superseded Kempton's Adonis Juvenile Hurdle as the key trial for the Triumph Hurdle, with five of the last seven festival winners prepping in it.

Two won, two came second and one third, so do not discount the placed horses with a view to Cheltenham.

Four of the last seven winners of the Champion Bumper were victorious at the DRF, three in the Grade 2 bumper on day one and one in the Grade 2 mares' bumper on day two.

Also have a close check of the 2m2f mares' handicap hurdle as it has produced four festival winners since 2020. The 2021 edition was vintage as three Cheltenham winners came from it – Heaven Help Us (Coral Cup), Telmesomethinggirl (Mares' Novices' Hurdle) and Mrs Milner (Pertemps Final).

CHELTENHAM FESTIVAL WINNERS AT THE DUBLIN RACING FESTIVAL

◤ Wins ◤ Seconds ◤ Thirds ◤ Fourths ◤ Other

11*

WINNING STRIKE-RATE

46%

22/48 Cheltenham winners also won at the Dublin Racing Festival

4

22

6

5

CHELTENHAM WINNERS	DUBLIN FESTIVAL RACE
8	Tattersalls Ireland Novice Hurdle (Grade 1)
6	Ladbrokes Novice Chase (Grade 1)
5	Gannon's City Recovery & Recycling Services Juvenile Hurdle (Grade 1)
5	Irish Champion Hurdle (Grade 1)
4	Paddy Power Irish Gold Cup Chase (Grade 1)
4	Irish Stallion Farms EBF Paddy And Maureen Mullins Mares Handicap Hurdle (Listed)
3	Paddy Power Play Card (C & G) I.N.H. Flat Race (Grade 2)
2	Nathaniel Lacy & Partners Solicitors Novice Hurdle (Grade 1)
2	Goffs Irish Arkle Novice Chase (Grade 1)
2	Ladbrokes Dublin Chase (Grade 1)
2	Timeless Sash Windows Handicap Hurdle (Listed)
2	O'Driscolls Irish Whiskey Leopardstown Handicap Chase (Grade 3)
1	Coolmore N.H. Sires Luxembourg Irish EBF Mares I.N.H. Flat Race (Grade 2)
1	Ryanair Handicap Chase (Listed)
1	Race And Stay At Leopardstown Handicap Hurdle (Listed)

Eight unplaced, two unseated and one fell

Tipsters and bookmakers pick some eyecatchers from the Dublin Racing Festival . . .

'He could land a big one off his mark'

Richard Birch It has to be Final Demand. He simply took the breath away. A future leading Gold Cup contender, for sure.

David Jennings Wendrock. He was seventh of eight in the Grade 1 juvenile hurdle but led coming down to the last and looks an ideal type for the Fred Winter Juvenile Handicap Hurdle. With a more patient ride, he could be interesting at the festival.

Graeme Rodway Sea Of Sands was fifth behind Kopek Des Bordes and plenty of Cheltenham Festival handicap winners have finished down the field in that Grade 1. Sea Of Sands could well be the next.

Nick Watts Willy De Houelle is big on reputation but has come up short in three starts for Willie Mullins. However, he showed more behind Hello Neighbour in the Grade 1 juvenile hurdle and could be the type who runs well in the Fred Winter.

Bet365 Pat Cooney Willy De Houelle was disappointing in his first two runs over hurdles for Willie Mullins but jumped and settled better in the Grade 1 juvenile hurdle. The Fred Winter on the opening day could be just the right race for him.

Sea Of Sands: could be the latest to go from Grade 1 also-ran to handicap winner

Betfair Barry Orr Hello Neighbour is undefeated on the Flat and over hurdles. He seems to idle a bit but keeps getting the job done and is undoubtedly the best of the Irish in the Triumph Hurdle. With Lulamba and East India Dock dominating the market, he's being underrated and he's the one I'll be with.

Coral Andrew Lobo Backtonormal was impressive in winning the 2m5½f handicap chase. Gavin Cromwell has become a master of targeting races and I wonder if he'll go for the new novice handicap chase.

Ladbrokes John Priddey Last season's juvenile hurdlers were an excellent crop and Triumph fifth Storm Heart has to be interesting in the County after doing extremely well to get so close in the 2m handicap hurdle at Leopardstown.

Paddy Power Paul Binfield Grangeclare West returned to his Grade 1-winning novice form when just finding Galopin Des

Backtonormal and (inset) Jasmin De Vaux: two to note from Leopardstown

Champs too powerful in the Irish Gold Cup. Connections might keep him for Aintree but he'd have a solid each-way shout in the Gold Cup.

Tote Jamie Benson
Storm Heart was a never-nearer second in the hotly competitive 2m handicap hurdle despite making a momentum-killing mistake at the last.

Last season's juvenile form keeps being franked and a bit more of a staying test in the County could see him land a big one off a mark of 147.

William Hill Jamie McBride Jasmin De Vaux made a small step in the right direction when fourth behind Final Demand. While his jumping could do with sharpening up, he could run well in the Albert Bartlett.

How did this year's eight Grade 1 winners at the Dublin Racing Festival shape up? Racing Post analysts Tyrone Molloy and Justin O'Hanlon give their verdicts

Final Demand

Trainer: Willie Mullins
Won: Nathaniel Lacy & Partners
Solicitors Novice Hurdle, 2m6f
The least experienced in the field, Final Demand belied that lack of seasoning with an impressive performance, powering clear. On this evidence he should stay 3m but he also has a high cruising speed, so he should have no issue with dropping slightly in trip as well. His trainer suggested afterwards that he's adaptable enough to do either for his likely next assignment at Cheltenham. Betfair cut him to 9-4 (from 6) for the Turners Novices' Hurdle and 7-2 for the Albert Bartlett Novices' Hurdle. With improvement likely, he should be competitive in whichever race he runs. *(TM)*

Hello Neighbour

Gavin Cromwell
Gannon's City Recovery &
Recycling Services Juvenile Hurdle,
2m
Hello Neighbour had the hood on him for the first time, presumably to help him settle. That didn't really work as they went so steadily, but when the tempo increased he travelled into it like the best horse in the race. He didn't do a whole lot in front and it's hard to know how good he is as he seems to do only enough, but he's improving. He was trimmed to 9-2 by Paddy Power for the Triumph. *(JO'H)*

Majborough

Willie Mullins
Goffs Irish Arkle Novice Chase, 2m1f
Majborough justified his position at the head of the market with a destructive performance. He didn't always treat his fences with maximum respect, but such is his size and scope that any error he made didn't take anything out of him. But when he was good he was very good and none of his rivals could cope with his concussive galloping. This was just his second run over fences and he can only improve. *(JO'H)*

Galopin Des Champs

Willie Mullins
Paddy Power Irish Gold Cup, 3m½f
Galopin Des Champs proved again what a champion he is and that he can be ridden any way. He took them along and jumped superbly again. He briefly looked vulnerable but it's what he does from the last to the line that sets him apart and he pulled clear. Both here and at Cheltenham he just looks bombproof and things will have to go wrong for him to fail to win a third Cheltenham Gold Cup, for which he's now a top-priced 4-6 favourite. *(JO'H)*

Ballyburn

Willie Mullins
Ladbrokes Novice Chase, 2m5½f
Ballyburn bit off way more than he could chew over 2m at Kempton behind Sir Gino on his chase debut. He was far more at home over this longer trip and jumping at a somewhat more sedate pace. For all that, he did race a bit

keenly and to pull out what he did at the end was a fair performance in the circumstances. If he runs at Cheltenham he'll be stepping up to 3m. He's bred to stay it, but connections would certainly like to see him settle a bit better. He's now a top-priced 2-1 for the Brown Advisory. (JO'H)

Kopek Des Bordes
Willie Mullins
Tattersalls Ireland Novice Hurdle, 2m
Kopek Des Bordes posted a deeply impressive win on just his second hurdles start, having won a course-and-distance maiden five weeks earlier. Despite racing keenly, his jumping was much more fluent and he travelled with ease before powering clear without his rider needing to ask him a serious question. Still unbeaten, having won a bumper last season, he was cut into a best-priced 7-4 favourite for the Supreme Novices' Hurdle, which his trainer has won a record seven times. He'll take some stopping in that contest with further improvement likely. (TM)
Odds quoted as they stood after the DRF

Left from top: Final Demand, Hello Neighbour, Kopek Des Bordes and Solness

Solness
Joseph O'Brien
Ladbrokes Dublin Chase, 2m1f
Solness showed his breakthrough Grade 1 win over course and distance at Christmas was no fluke with a similar performance, making all at a strong pace and jumping accurately. However, he had to battle when the runner-up threatened to challenge and his will to win was evident. He has improved plenty this season and is a proper Grade 1 2m chaser but a sound surface seems important to him. The Queen Mother Champion Chase is next on his agenda (top price 12-1) and he can give a bold show there if the ground is suitable. (TM)

State Man
Willie Mullins
Irish Champion Hurdle, 2m
State Man earned an 11th Grade 1 but it turned into an easy success once the faller Lossiemouth had been negotiated. To his credit, he seemed to travel and gallop much better here than at Christmas up to the point when he was left clear. He could be forgiven for his concentration wavering in the circumstances. Although nothing whatsoever was learned, he was trimmed to a top-priced 8-1 for the Champion Hurdle. (JO'H)

Century up – and counting

WILLIE MULLINS crashed through the century barrier at the festival last year, winning both the Cheltenham Gold Cup and the Champion Hurdle in another dominant performance for his all-conquering Closutton stable.

The 18-time Irish champion trainer had nine winners last year – just shy of his record ten in 2022 – and his overall total has moved to 103. He has stretched his lead to 30 over Nicky Henderson in the all-time list, having gone past his British rival only in 2018, and has now been leading trainer at the festival for six years in a row (and 11 times in all).

Mullins has exceeded five winners at nine of the past ten festivals (he dipped slightly to four in 2019) and it was interesting that the bulk of last year's success came in races where he has been most dominant over the years, including the Champion Bumper, Mares' Hurdle, what is now the Turners Novices' Hurdle, County Hurdle, Arkle Chase and Brown Advisory Novices' Chase.

He went back to his cornerstone of landing the Champion Hurdle and Mares' Hurdle on the opening day, while continuing the more recent trend of doing well on the final day. Mullins took the Gold Cup for the fourth time in six years when Galopin Des

MOST SUCCESSFUL RACES

Champion Bumper ■■■■■■■■■■■■■	Mares' Novices' Hurdle ■■■■■
Mares' Hurdle ■■■■■■■■■■	Ryanair Chase ■■■■■
Supreme Novices' Hurdle ■■■■■■■	Triumph Hurdle ■■■■■
Turners Novices' Hurdle ■■■■■■■	Gold Cup ■■■■
County Hurdle ■■■■■■■	Martin Pipe Hcap Hurdle ■■■■
Arkle Chase ■■■■■■	National Hunt Chase ■■■■
Brown Advisory Novices' Chase ■■■■■■	Turners Novices' Chase* ■■■■
Champion Hurdle ■■■■■	*No longer held

Champs retained the crown last year and his Friday tallies since 2020 are four, two, five, two and three.

Hurdles (17 wins) just outweigh chases (16) on the Mullins roll of honour at the past five festivals, but the strike-rate is higher in chases (16 per cent against nine per cent).

The market is a strong pointer to Mullins' successes. Six of last year's nine winners went off favourite and only one of the nine was bigger than 6-1. At the five festivals since 2020, 22 of his 39 winners were favourite and eight were second favourite, cementing a trend established in 2014-2018 (the only break from the norm was in 2019).

The longer-priced winner last year was Absurde at 12-1 in the County Hurdle, which reinforced Mullins' strength in

handicap hurdles. He has had 12 handicap hurdle winners since 2010 (seven at double-figure odds) and excluding the Fred Winter Juvenile Handicap Hurdle, which he has never won, his strike-rate in that period is 12-139 (+18.75pts). The key targets have been the County (7-53, +48.25pts) and the Martin Pipe Conditional Jockeys' Handicap Hurdle (4-31, +4.5pts).

He remains the one to beat in races restricted to mares, having won ten out of 17 in the Mares' Hurdle, five of the nine runnings of the Mares' Novices' Hurdle and two of the four runnings of the Mares' Chase, and is strong in the Champion Bumper, where 12 of his 13 winners were five-year-olds (and seven of those had won their sole outing prior to arriving at Cheltenham).

FESTIVAL WINNERS BY RACE TYPE

- Hurdles **56**
- Chases **34**
- Bumpers **13**

1995

YEAR OF FIRST WINNER AT CHELTENHAM

37

CHELTENHAM FESTIVAL WINNERS IN THE LAST FIVE YEARS – 12% STRIKE-RATE

103

CHELTENHAM FESTIVAL WINNERS

MULLINS ON . . .

Ballyburn *Brown Advisory Novices' Chase*
I never lost faith in him. Kempton was disappointing, but I knew after two or three jumps that he needed to learn very quickly and he didn't. He's bred to get three miles. It was fascinating that he was able to do what he did over two miles. He's back on track now. All the schooling we did at home has paid off. He still has a lot to learn about settling in a race and once he does he could be a fair weapon over three miles.

Kopek Des Bordes *Supreme Novices' Hurdle*
Ted Walsh rang me the following morning [after the Dublin Racing Festival] and said he hadn't seen a performance like that since Golden Cygnet, which is something huge for someone like Ted to say. He went on two or three lengths ahead at the bend before the second-last, then Paul [Townend] got a grip on him and away he went again. It blew my mind against a field of top-class horses.

Big guns set to fire again

HENDERSON ON . . .

Jonbon *Champion Chase*
It was two heavyweights fighting for a title [against Energumene in the Clarence House] and it was a good, clean fight. Jonbon is still quite young and he's so professional now. He can dance at a fence and is very quick in and out when he's meeting one short, but what I loved was the way he quickened up going to the last. He'd fought off the enemy but still wanted to go and make a good show of it. What he did from the second-last to the line was the most impressive thing. He probably deserves a Champion Chase. That's the only race that's missing.

Lulamba *Triumph Hurdle*
It looked an impossible task [at Ascot] and I was prepared to get beat because of the hype, but we've got to eat humble pie a bit because the hype appeared to be correct. Nico [de Boinville] just said he was very classy, very good. He jumps, travels, he has pace, he's just a very straightforward, very good horse.

LAST year's festival was a disaster for Nicky Henderson, for so long accustomed to Grade 1 success and being the leading British trainer in the week that counts most in the jumps season.

For the first time since 2008, Henderson endured a winless four days last year. Stable stars Constitution Hill, Jonbon and Sir Gino all had to miss the meeting amid concerns over the health of his string and he sent out only 16 runners, half of whom were pulled up. The only bright spot was Luccia's game third in the Champion Hurdle at 33-1.

This year his Seven Barrows yard is expected to be back with a bang. Constitution Hill (Champion Hurdle) and Jonbon (Champion Chase) are set to line up as hot favourites, along with emerging star Lulamba (Triumph Hurdle), although Sir Gino will miss out again.

Henderson remains the most assured source of quality among the home team, having had at least two Grade 1 winners at seven festivals in a row up to 2022 and then another with Constitution Hill in the 2023 Champion Hurdle (his sole winner that year). Overall he has an excellent record of delivering with the hot ones in Grade 1 races. In the past decade he has sent out 18 favourites in that category and ten have won, returning a level-stakes profit of 4.83pts.

MOST SUCCESSFUL RACES

Champion Hurdle
■■■■■■■■■

Arkle Chase
■■■■■■■

Triumph Hurdle
■■■■■■■

Champion Chase
■■■■■■

Supreme Novices' Hurdle
■■■■■

Plate Handicap Chase
■■■■

Brown Advisory Novices' Chase
■■■■

Coral Cup
■■■■

Cathcart Chase*
■■■■

Kim Muir Handicap Chase
■■■

* No longer held

FESTIVAL WINNERS BY RACE TYPE

- ■ G1 hurdles **26**
- ■ G1 chases **22**
- ■ Non G1 chases **16**
- ■ Non G1 hurdles **9**

73
CHELTENHAM FESTIVAL WINNERS

1985
YEAR OF FIRST WINNER AT CHELTENHAM

9
CHELTENHAM FESTIVAL WINNERS IN THE LAST FIVE YEARS – 8% STRIKE-RATE

It has been a different story in handicaps. Only one of his seven favourites in the past decade has won (Dame De Compagnie at 5-1 in the 2020 Coral Cup), although three went close in second place.

Even so, Henderson's handicap runners are always worth a look, especially at longer odds. Eleven of his 14 handicap winners since 2005 were 12-1 or bigger, while the same number came over trips of at least 2m4f.

Amid last year's gloom there were still placed runs at big prices in handicaps from Lucky Place (fourth in the Coral Cup at 25-1) and Bold Endeavour (fourth in the Pertemps Final at 50-1).

Packed with staying power

GORDON ELLIOTT is a reliably powerful force at the Cheltenham Festival, even if he hasn't been able to get close to big Irish rival Willie Mullins in recent years.

Having been top trainer at the festival in 2017 (six winners) and 2018 (eight), Elliott last went close in 2020 when he tied with Mullins on winners (seven) but was ultimately beaten on third places. Last year he had three winners, finishing third behind

ELLIOTT ON . . .

Brighterdaysahead
Champion/Mares' Hurdle
We've been thrilled with her this season. Having a fourth run before Cheltenham might just have been one too many, so we decided to head straight there and hopefully have her in tip-top form for the festival. We're not going to decide [which race] until nearer the time.

Romeo Coolio
Supreme Novices' Hurdle
He won very nicely at Christmas. Looking at that, I'd say a fast gallop is what he needs. He looked good there and I just wanted to freshen him up for Cheltenham and get him into the best shape for the Supreme.

Mullins and Dan Skelton, but it was a sign of his stable strength that he had another five seconds and five thirds.

The three races he won last year were the Stayers' Hurdle with Teahupoo, the Albert Bartlett Novices' Hurdle with Stellar Story and the Martin Pipe Handicap Hurdle with Better Days Ahead. It was typical that those successes came in races where the accent is on stamina.

Fifteen of Elliott's 22 wins over hurdles have come at distances of 2m4f-plus, with three apiece in the Pertemps Final, Coral Cup and Martin Pipe. In the latter he has had three winners, three seconds and two thirds from 40 runners.

In similar vein, 12 of his 16 chase wins have come at distances in excess of 3m – albeit seven of them were provided by multiple festival scorers Cause Of Causes and Tiger Roll. His most successful festival race is the Cross Country Chase, although his five winners all came when it was a conditions race and it has now gone back to a handicap.

Elliott also has a notably good record with juvenile hurdlers, having won the division's handicap hurdle four times and the Triumph Hurdle twice, and they account for most of his hurdles wins over shorter trips. Six of his 37 runners in those races since 2013 have won (at odds of 25-1, 10-1, 33-1, 9-1, 15-2 and 18-1).

MOST SUCCESSFUL RACES

Cross Country Chase
■■■■■

Fred Winter Handicap Hurdle
■■■■

National Hunt Chase
■■■■

Coral Cup
■■■

Martin Pipe Handicap Hdle
■■■

Pertemps Network Final
■■■

Turners Novices' Hurdle
■■

Champion Bumper
■■

Kim Muir Handicap Chase
■■

Stayers' Hurdle
■■

Triumph Hurdle
■■

Turners Novices' Chase*
■■

No longer held

FESTIVAL WINNERS BY RACE TYPE

■ Grade 1 **14**
■ Non Grade 1 **26**

FESTIVAL WINNERS BY RACE DISTANCE

■ Below 2m4f **10**
■ 2m4f-3m **18**
■ Above 3m **12**

40
CHELTENHAM FESTIVAL WINNERS

2011
FIRST CHELTENHAM WINNER

15
CHELTENHAM FESTIVAL WINNERS IN THE LAST FIVE YEARS – 7% STRIKE-RATE

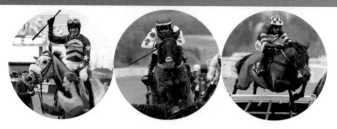

From left: big-race winners Kandoo Kid, Il Ridoto and festival hope Jubilee Alpha

Set for golden 50

PAUL NICHOLLS was successful last year with Pertemps Final winner Monmiral but the scoreboard does not tick over with the same regularity now as it did in his festival glory days when he was leading trainer six times, most recently with five winners in 2009.

The norm now is one or two winners, although a shutout remains a rarity. He failed to score in 2021 and 2022 but those were the first blanks since 2002.

The big difference nowadays is that Nicholls tends to have a small festival squad. Last year he had 13 runners and just five were priced at 10-1 or lower (Monmiral was 25-1).

Runners from Manor Farm Stables will always demand respect, however, given Nicholls' strong record across the rest of the season. His notable wins in the current campaign include the Paddy Power Gold Cup at Cheltenham with Il Ridoto as well as another big handicap chase with Kandoo Kid in the Coral Gold Cup at Newbury.

Handicap winners became the way on to the festival scoreboard for Nicholls from 2013 to 2018, and again with Monmiral last year, but there has been a Grade 1 resurgence in recent years. He won at the top level with Topofthegame (in what is now the Brown Advisory Novices' Chase in 2019), Frodon (Ryanair Chase, 2019), Politologue (Champion Chase, 2020), Stage Star (Turners Novices' Chase, 2023) and Stay Away Fay (Albert Bartlett Novices' Hurdle, 2023).

One key to finding a Nicholls handicap winner at the festival, especially over hurdles, is to identify a young, lightly raced type yet to be exposed to the handicapper. Eight of his 11 handicap hurdle winners were aged four or five, and ten of his 16 handicap winners overall have carried between 10st 10lb and 11st 11lb (two of the three above that weight were in the Martin Pipe).

It is worth noting that Nicholls has won the County Hurdle and the Grand Annual Chase four times apiece – both are over 2m, and that is another factor to take into account.

FESTIVAL WINNERS BY RACE TYPE

- G1 chases **19**
- G1 hurdles **10**
- Non G1 chases **9**
- Non G1 hurdles **11**

49
CHELTENHAM FESTIVAL WINNERS

1999
FIRST CHELTENHAM WINNER

4
CHELTENHAM FESTIVAL WINNERS IN THE LAST FIVE YEARS – 6% STRIKE-RATE

NICHOLLS ON . . .

Jubilee Alpha
Mares' Novices' Hurdle
She had a big weight [at Windsor last time] and the ground didn't really suit her, but she was very good. We've got a nice gap now to get her right. I know I can get her better than she showed there. We've got a few nice chances at Cheltenham and she's definitely one of them.

MOST SUCCESSFUL RACES

Champion Chase	Stayers' Hurdle
■■■■■■	■■■■
County Hurdle	Fred Winter
■■■■	Handicap Hurdle
Gold Cup	■■■
■■■■	Brown Advisory
Grand Annual	Novices' Chase
■■■■	■■■
Hunters' Chase	Ryanair Chase
■■■■	■■■

Great success in Grade 1s

TWO more Grade 1 wins last year cemented Henry de Bromhead's place among the big five trainers at the festival, a notable achievement given his smaller stable numbers compared with his rivals.

The Knockeen trainer was successful with Captain Guinness in the Queen Mother Champion Chase and Slade Steel in the Supreme Novices' Hurdle, giving him an eighth consecutive winning festival. The majority of his 23 festival winners have come in that period, establishing him as a powerful force.

Two winners put De Bromhead joint-fourth in last year's trainer standings. It is worth noting he was third for finishers in the first three (ten), which put him close behind Gordon Elliott (13) on

23
CHELTENHAM FESTIVAL WINNERS

2010
YEAR OF FIRST WINNER AT CHELTENHAM

16
CHELTENHAM FESTIVAL WINNERS IN THE LAST FIVE YEARS – 14% STRIKE-RATE

FESTIVAL WINNERS BY RACE TYPE

- ■ G1 chases **12**
- ■ G1 hurdles **7**
- ■ Non G1 chases **3**
- ■ Non G1 hurdles **1**

that measure and well ahead of the next best (Dan Skelton on five).

Only Willie Mullins remained out of reach (nine winners among 21 finishers in the first three).

De Bromhead is a clear leader in terms of strike-rate, however. In the past five years he has scored at 13.8 per cent, compared with 11.7 for Mullins and 7.1 for Elliott.

The quality of his string is evident in the fact that 18 of his 23 festival wins have been in Grade 1 contests and the good news with stronger fancies from Knockeen is that he usually does best with runners at 10-1 or lower. Fourteen of his last 15 winners were in that category, making it 19 out of 23 overall (and Special Tiara was only just outside at 11-1 in the 2017 Champion Chase).

Overall, at 10-1 or lower, De Bromhead has had 19 winners, 16 seconds and eight thirds from 77 runners since 2010 (25%, +29.53pts).

DE BROMHEAD ON . . .

Workahead *Supreme Novices' Hurdle*
He looked different gravy at Leopardstown and the form of the race has worked out well. It looks a very good Supreme but I think we're bang there.

The Big Westerner
Albert Bartlett Novices' Hurdle
She's a nice mare who's unbeaten and has done nothing wrong. She was impressive the way she picked up at Limerick and she's exciting.

MOST SUCCESSFUL RACES

Champion Chase	Gold Cup
■■■■	■■
Arkle Chase	Mares' Hurdle
■■	■■
Champion Hurdle	Ryanair Chase
■■	■■

Major hopes: Workahead (top) and The Big Westerner

DAN SKELTON took his festival tally into double figures last year with a memorable haul of four winners, which made him the top British trainer of the week and second only to Willie Mullins in the overall standings.

The Warwickshire trainer's best Cheltenham yet was mirrored by his stable's performance across the 2023-24 season. Skelton forced his way past Paul Nicholls and Nicky Henderson to finish best of British in the trainers' championship but could not resist the power of Mullins and had to settle for second place.

Having had just one Grade 1 festival winner before last year, Skelton added two more with Grey Dawning (Turners Novices' Chase) and Protektorat (Ryanair Chase). His other winners were Langer Dan (Coral Cup) and Unexpected Party (Grand Annual Handicap Chase).

That was a second consecutive Coral Cup for Langer Dan, cementing Skelton's reputation as a target trainer in the handicap hurdles. His favourite festival race is the County Handicap Hurdle, which he has won four times.

At 13-2 last year, Langer Dan became the fourth of Skelton's six handicap hurdle winners to go off 12-1 or lower. From a total of 31 handicap runners in that price bracket, he has also had runners-up at 7-2 and 13-2

Fancied runners worthy of note for target trainer

and three thirds at 6-1, 7-1 and 15-2.

Looking further into what the market reveals, Skelton has had only 28 festival runners priced under 10-1 and yet most have run well (winners at 5-2, 13-2, 8-1, 17-2 and 9-1, plus 12 others in the first four).

Skelton's strike-rate is

remarkable. Last year's four wins came from just 11 runners (a marked difference to Mullins' 75) and he is the leading trainer with fewer than 100 runners over the past five years (6-67, nine per cent). Perhaps most notably of all, he has a level-stake profit of +10.5pts in that period.

MOST SUCCESSFUL RACES

County Hurdle ■■■■   **Coral Cup** ■■

10
CHELTENHAM FESTIVAL WINNERS

2016
YEAR OF FIRST WINNER AT CHELTENHAM

6
CHELTENHAM FESTIVAL WINNERS IN THE LAST FIVE YEARS – 9% STRIKE-RATE

SKELTON ON . . .

The New Lion *Turners Novices' Hurdle*
We hoped he could develop into a very good hurdler and he's very exciting. What sets him apart is his mentality. Nothing stresses him out, he's very laid-back. It's heavy odds-on that we go in the Turners. We entered him in the Supreme just in case it was going to be heavy ground.

Protektorat *Ryanair Chase*
He was brilliant at Windsor and we were building up to that and Cheltenham. There'll be younger horses at Cheltenham and ones with a fancier depth of form, but we'll make them go, don't you worry about that.

DAN SKELTON IN THE COUNTY HURDLE

■ Wins **4**
■ Places **1**
■ Other **12**

WINNING STRIKE-RATE

24%
4-17

Profit/loss
+£73 to a £1 level stake

Year	Horse	SP
2016	*Superb Story*	8-1
2018	*Mohaayed*	33-1
2019	*Ch'Tibello*	12-1
2023	*Faivoir*	33-1

Small squads brimming with big challengers

TWO winners last year cemented Gavin Cromwell's place on the heels of the elite in the trainer standings over the past five festivals with five winners from just 31 runners (16%).

The County Meath trainer has the rare distinction of a level-stakes profit from all runners in that period, with his +8.63pts ranking second only to Dan Skelton among those in the upper echelon. Skelton and Cromwell are also closely matched with the top two winning tallies among trainers with fewer than 100 festival runners in the past five years (and overall behind only the big stables of Willie Mullins, Henry de Bromhead, Gordon Elliott and Nicky Henderson).

Cromwell's first four festival winners were in Grade 1 hurdles – starting with Espoir D'Allen in the 2019 Champion Hurdle – but he broke new ground last year over fences with Inothewayurthinkin in the Fulke Walwyn Kim Muir Handicap Chase and Limerick Lace in the Mares' Chase.

He remains a formidable opponent in Grade 1s. From 15 runners in that category at the festival, he has a 27 per cent strike-rate with a 35pts profit. He has also had two seconds, a third and two fourths in Grade 1s (giving him a 60 per cent rate of finishing in the first four) and it is clear Cromwell's top-level runners merit close consideration.

CROMWELL ON . . .

Sixandahalf *Mares' Novices' Hurdle*
She's had only one run over hurdles but is very good. We're looking forward to it and I think it'll take a nice one to beat her. She's a very good jumper.

JOSEPH O'BRIEN was back on the festival scoreboard last year and his success came on familiar territory with juvenile handicap hurdle winner Lark In The Mornin.

That made it four festival winners overall and his second in that race (following Band Of Outlaws in 2019) but it should be remembered that technically O'Brien had his first success in 2016 – also with a juvenile hurdler – when he oversaw Ivanovich Gorbatov's preparation for the Triumph Hurdle.

His other two wins came in the Martin Pipe Handicap Hurdle (Early Doors in 2019 and Banbridge in 2022), making O'Brien a trainer to note in that race too.

Outside the big five, O'Brien is the most likely trainer to have a finisher in the first three. Eighteen of his 69 runners at the six festivals starting with his official breakthrough year of 2019 have made the places at a strike-rate of 26 per cent, with four wins.

His biggest-priced festival winner was Banbridge at 12-1, which gives him a good strike-rate with the better fancies. From 37 runners at 12-1 or lower, he has had four wins, four seconds, four thirds and two fourths.

O'BRIEN ON . . .

Solness *Champion Chase*
We've ended up in Graded races and he just keeps going forward. I could see him running a big race. He'll jump and go and they'll have to come and get to him to beat him. That's the way he likes to run. He has a will to win.

SCULPTURE TO WEAR
by Rosemary Hetherington

Makers of the Finest Equestrian Jewellery

The Sculpture to Wear collection by Rosemary Hetherington was established in 1990 and is now celebrating 34 years of making the finest equestrian jewellery. We also offer a bespoke design service making unique pieces for discerning clients. The perfect gifts for family and friends.

Sculpture to Wear Limited
PO Box 24, Leyburn, North Yorkshire DL8 4YP
Telephone: 01969 624949   E: info@sculpturetowear.co.uk   www.sculpturetowear.co.uk

TUESDAY, MARCH 11 (OLD COURSE)

PAUL KEALY ON THE KEY PLAYERS

1.20 Sky Bet Supreme Novices' Hurdle   ITV/RTV
➤2m½f   ➤Grade 1   ➤£150,000

Ireland looks extremely likely to open the scoring in the traditional festival curtain-raiser and many will see Kopek Des Bordes as the first banker of the week for Willie Mullins. The five-year-old was so impressive in his Grade 1 win at the Dublin Racing Festival that Mullins said fellow trainer Ted Walsh had called the next day to compare him to Golden Cygnet, the fabled but ill-fated outstanding Supreme winner in 1978. The biggest danger is Gordon Elliott's Romeo Coolio, a Grade 1 winner at Christmas who has the advantages of more hurdling experience than the favourite and a previous run at Cheltenham, having been runner-up in last year's Champion Bumper. Henry de Bromhead, who won with Slade Steel last year, has the promising but inexperienced Workahead this time. Mullins has a host of other possibles and the highest-rated is Grade 2 winner Salvator Mundi. Britain would have a good chance only if The New Lion or Potters Charm were surprisingly rerouted from the Turners.

Kopek Des Bordes
5 b g; Trainer Willie Mullins
Hurdles form (left-handed) 11, best RPR 153

Runaway bumper winner on his racecourse debut a couple of weeks after last year's Cheltenham Festival, Kopek Des Bordes has needed just two runs over hurdles to become a very warm favourite for the meeting's curtain-raiser. He didn't impress everyone with his keenness and jumping on his hurdles debut in the fog at Leopardstown over Christmas and was installed at 20-1 in places for the Supreme after a two-and-three-quarter-length success from Kawaboomga (subsequent winner), but those odds had halved before he lined up at the Dublin Racing Festival in the Grade 1 Tattersalls Ireland Novice Hurdle and they were in freefall afterwards. The five-year-old, who is related to several winners in France (including one at Grade 1 level, who didn't do so well for Nicky Henderson) was still very keen, but his jumping was considerably better. Having joined the early leader three out, he shrugged off being hampered by a loose horse before the second-last and strolled to a 13-length victory. It looked a performance out of the top drawer for a novice and Racing Post Ratings back that up, a figure of 153 taking him to the top of the Supreme charts. That's bang on target for a Supreme winner, with only Altior, Shishkin and Appreciate It

having achieved a higher mark heading into the festival. That's pretty good for a horse who has run just twice over hurdles and is still clearly learning on the job, and it's hard to argue with his market position or the strength of it. To win a Grade 1 like that having been so free suggests a horse of unnatural ability. Trainer Willie Mullins' record with short-priced favourites is strong too, and getting stronger. He's 30-52 with horses under 2-1 at the festival in the last ten years and a seriously impressive 10-14 in the last two.

Going preference Has won on anything from yielding to soft

Star rating ✪✪✪✪✪

Romeo Coolio
6 b g; Trainer Gordon Elliott
Hurdles form 121, best RPR 149
Left-handed 1, best RPR 149
Right-handed 12, best RPR 135
Cheltenham form (bumper) 2, best RPR 135
At the festival 13 Mar 2024 Towards rear, headway on inner from 6f out, went second 2f out, led over 1f out, headed inside final furlong, kept on, finished second, beaten a length and three-quarters by Jasmin De Vaux in Champion Bumper

Had won only a five-runner point and a five-runner bumper before heading into last season's Champion Bumper, but had been talked up beforehand and had only a couple ahead of him in the betting overnight. That changed on the day, though, with concerns about the very soft ground causing a big drift. Romeo Coolio went off at 18-1, having touched 25s. He ran a blinder, though, travelling very strongly but ultimately having no answer to the finish of Jasmin De Vaux. A below-par effort at Punchestown after that was forgivable, and Romeo Coolio *(pictured)* has made a good fist of hurdling this season, winning two of his three starts. He didn't have much to beat first time at Down Royal and was then beaten by Tounsivator (no Cheltenham entries) in the Royal Bond at Fairyhouse, a race recently downgraded to Grade 2 status. There he travelled extremely well but didn't seem to have a change of gear when it mattered, so tactics were changed for the Grade 1 Future Champions Novice Hurdle at Leopardstown over Christmas, Sam Ewing utilising his mount's high cruising speed by making most and going for home a fair way out for a nine-length success. He's well up to Supreme standard on that evidence but is going to need to do better still to topple the favourite.

Going preference Deep ground when he finished second in the Champion Bumper, but has handled quicker going well over hurdles and is said to want it

Star rating ✪✪✪✪

Salvator Mundi
5 b g; Trainer Willie Mullins
Hurdles form 2611, best RPR 146
Left-handed 261, best RPR 146
Right-handed 1, best RPR 138
Cheltenham form 6, best RPR 130
At the festival 15 Mar 2024 Held up in rear, not fluent 3 out, headway after 2 out, no impression before last, weakened run-in, finished sixth, beaten 17 lengths by Majborough in Triumph Hurdle

Well touted having been second to Sir Gino on sole hurdles outing in France and bought by the same connections and sent to Willie Mullins. He wasn't considered as far forward as Sir Gino, though, with Mullins giving him his stable debut in last season's Triumph, primarily to give him some experience of travelling to Cheltenham with the Supreme in mind for the following season. Far from disgraced in finishing sixth to stablemate Majborough, Salvator Mundi got off the mark a couple of months later, beating moderate opposition by a yawning gap (62 lengths) at Tipperary, and he wasn't seen again until January when he lined up for the Grade 2 Moscow Flyer, a race his trainer has used as a Cheltenham prep for many of his better novice hurdlers, including Vautour, Douvan and Impaire Et Passe. An 8-15 chance, Salvator Mundi pulled hard and didn't jump particularly well off a slow gallop, but he won handily enough by three lengths from stablemate Kel Histoire, and that was enough to make him the new Supreme favourite until Kopek Des Bordes rocked up. It's hard to put a big figure on what he did at Punchestown as they went so slowly, but he gets extra credit for coming from last to first and doing it so well, and he's clearly one of the better 2m novices.

Going preference Three runs on soft and heavy, and he was a 1-12 shot when winning on quicker

Star rating ✪✪✪

Workahead
7 b g; Trainer Henry de Bromhead
Hurdles form (left-handed) 31, best RPR 141

Runaway point winner who is by Derby hero Workforce and a half-brother to Bronn, who finished third in the Brown Advisory two years ago and stays well. Workahead has only a Supreme entry, however, and both outings over hurdles have been at 2m. In the first he shaped with a fair degree of promise when just over nine lengths third to Champion Bumper winner Jasmin De Vaux in a maiden hurdle at Navan in December, and little more than two weeks later he got off the mark with a seven-length maiden success at Leopardstown from William Munny, who got a lot closer to the well-touted Kawaboomga next time. That's all we've seen of him, though, and it's fair to say he's going to find this much tougher on his first run outside maiden company unless he comes out soon.

Going preference Not enough evidence to go on

Star rating ✪✪

Kawaboomga
5 b g; Trainer Willie Mullins
Hurdles form 321, best RPR 136
Left-handed 32, best RPR 127
Right-handed 1, best RPR 136

AQPS bumper winner in France who finished third in his sole hurdle start there before joining Willie Mullins for this season. He was second favourite in the betting behind odds-on stablemate Kopek Des Bordes in a maiden hurdle at Leopardstown over Christmas and duly followed him home at a distance of two and three-quarter lengths without ever looking like troubling the winner. Since then, he has run in another maiden hurdle, beating William Munny a shade comfortably by one and a half lengths (runner-up had been a seven-length second to Workahead) with the pair 22 lengths ahead of the rest. It's promising, but it's only maiden form and he's shorter for the Turners despite having never run over further than 2m.

Going preference Has shown promise on anything from yielding to heavy

Star rating ✪✪

Funiculi Funicula
5 b g; Trainer Willie Mullins
Hurdles form 21, best RPR 130
Left-handed 2, best RPR 86
Right-handed 1, best RPR 130

Second in a hurdle at Auteuil in October 2023 but not seen again until this January when winning a Clonmel maiden hurdle by 17 lengths at odds of 4-7. Margin would not have been so big had second favourite, who

carries a rating of just 123, not fallen at the last, so no evidence that he's up to this level. Lightly raced, though, and Willie Mullins has no issues with running others against his big guns and often gets them among the places.

Going preference Has run only on soft or heavy

Star rating ✪

Karbau
5 b g; Trainer Willie Mullins
Hurdles form 41, best RPR 139
Left-handed 4, best RPR 123
Right-handed 1, best RPR 139

Yet another maiden hurdle winner in the hands of Willie Mullins who could come here or go in the Turners. Won the second of his two bumpers in France last April and, while he could manage only fourth on his stable debut at Naas in December when joint-favourite, he still showed plenty of promise. He then showed a lot more when jumping really well and cantering 16 lengths clear in a maiden at Punchestown in January, recording an RPR of 139, which is useful given the grade and style of success. His dam is a half-sister to the top-class Sir Des Champs, so he's going to stay further if needed, and this is one of the more interesting unexposed Mullins contenders.

Going preference Too early to say but heavy is no problem

Star rating ✪✪

Irancy
7 b g; Trainer Willie Mullins
Hurdles form (right-handed) 31, best RPR 123

A half-brother to the useful Darasso but who has evidently had his problems. Didn't make his hurdling debut until December 2023, finishing third of 24 to Firefox at Fairyhouse some 762 days after his French bumper win, and it was almost a year before we saw him again. This time he won, by nine lengths at Punchestown in November, but he hasn't been seen since. Is still among the entries but form is some way off the best of these so far.

Going preference French bumpers on bad ground, hurdles win on good

Star rating ✪

Kel Histoire
5 ch g; Trainer Willie Mullins
Hurdles form (right-handed) 12, best RPR 132

Bumper winner in France who made a pleasing debut for Mullins when scoring at Cork in December and was sent off second favourite for the Moscow Flyer after that. Ran well enough there, battling back to take a three-length second after being hampered just before the last, but had no answer to Salvator Mundi's change of gear, and that would seemingly put him some way down the pecking order.

Going preference Yielding ground for maiden win but arguably better form in defeat on soft at Punchestown

Star rating ✪

Kiss Will
5 bz g; Trainer Willie Mullins
Hurdles form (right-handed) 1, best RPR 126

Yet another wide-margin maiden winner from the Mullins camp, which houses the hot favourite and all but a handful of those in the top dozen in the betting. This one finished second in a 1m5f French bumper in September 2023 and made his hurdling debut in January, scoring by 13 lengths at Fairyhouse from a rival making his racecourse debut. It's not easy to rate that form highly but he clearly has promise.

Going preference Not enough to go on

Star rating ✪

James's Gate
8 b g; Trainer Martin Brassil
Hurdles form 4311, best RPR 136
Left-handed 41, best RPR 136
Right-handed 31, best RPR 130
Cheltenham form (bumper) 3, best RPR 133
At the festival 16 Mar 2022 Took keen hold, chased leader, pushed along over 2f out, ridden and kept on from over 1f out, finished third, beaten six and a quarter lengths by Facile Vega in Champion Bumper

Fragile sort who was third in the 2022 Champion Bumper but was beaten at long odds-on at Punchestown the following month and then went missing for 20 months. When he came back he didn't fare so well as, after a fourth of 23 on his maiden hurdle

debut, he was a 24-length third of four to Mystical Power in the Moscow Flyer in January last year. Another 11-month absence followed but he has got his act together now, winning his maiden at Punchestown and following up in a novice at Navan. Clearly still has plenty of ability but would have run

Kopek Des Bordes: Racing Post Rating of 153 is bang on target for a Supreme winner

in a handicap at the Dublin Racing Festival if he hadn't had a cough, and perhaps that will be the best route for him, although he now needs to squeeze in another run to be eligible.

Going preference Seems to act on anything

Star rating ○

OTHERS TO CONSIDER

Despite having red-hot favorite Kopek Des Bordes in the race, Willie Mullins still had another 12 to choose from after the scratching stage. Some of those have already been mentioned, but **Karniquet** was left out because he has already been readily dealt with by the stable's number one. None of the others left in (Inn At The Park, Kappa Jy Pyke, Sea Of Sands, You Oughta Know) have had the required runs to qualify for a handicap this year, but that doesn't mean they will take up the Grade 1 option, and all of them need to improve in a big way anyway. **The New Lion** and **Potters Charm** were surprisingly left in, but they're not two-milers and neither is **Sixmilebridge**. Grade 1 Formby runner-up **Miami Magic** is, but he needs to leave that form well behind. Fergal O'Brien's **Tripoli Flyer** has looked very promising in winning his last two hurdles by wide margins, but they came at lowly level at Market Rasen and Musselburgh and it's hard to get that excited about his chance in this.

VERDICT

KOPEK DES BORDES has done plenty wrong in his two races, notably with his refusal to settle, but that only makes it more frightening that he already has the best form. He's clearly learning on the job and has a huge engine, and he'll surely be hard to beat. On RPRs he isn't a country mile clear of nine-length Future Champions Novice Hurdle winner **Romeo Coolio**, who has the advantage of Cheltenham experience having run a fine second in the Champion Bumper last year, but the favourite has run only twice and there will likely be even more to come when he decides to settle. Gordon Elliott's contender looks the most likely danger, while at a bigger price **Karbau**, who jumped so well and won in a canter at Punchestown, could prove a useful second or third string for Willie Mullins.

SUPREME NOVICES' HURDLE RESULTS AND TRENDS

FORM		WINNER	AGE & WGT	Adj RPR	SP	TRAINER	BEST RPR LAST 12 MONTHS (RUNS SINCE)
24	3-112	Slade Steel D	6 11-7	154ᵀ	7-2	H de Bromhead (IRE)	2nd Leopardstown Gd1 novice hurdle (2m) (0)
23	1111	Marine Nationale D	6 11-7	158·⁷	9-2	B Connell (IRE)	won Fairyhouse Gd1 novice hurdle (2m) (0)
22	11	Constitution Hill D	5 11-7	159·¹	9-4j	N Henderson	won Gd1 Tolworth Hurdle (2m) (0)
21	2-111	Appreciate It D	7 11-7	162ᵀ	8-11f	W Mullins (IRE)	won Leopardstown Gd1 novice hurdle (2m) (1)
20	1-F11	Shishkin D	6 11-7	161·²	6-1	N Henderson	won Huntingdon Listed nov hurdle (2m3½f) (0)
19	4P-11	Klassical Dream D	5 11-7	154·⁸	6-1	W Mullins (IRE)	won Leopardstown Gd1 novice hurdle (2m) (0)
18	12231	Summerville Boy D	6 11-7	157·³	9-1	T George	won Gd1 Tolworth Hurdle (2m) (0)
17	11RR6	Labaik D	6 11-7	150·⁸	25-1	G Elliott (IRE)	won Navan Gd3 novice hurdle (2m) (3)
16	61111	Altior CD	6 11-7	163ᵀ	4-1	N Henderson	won Kempton Class 2 novice hurdle (2m) (0)
15	2111	Douvan D	5 11-7	160·³	2-1f	W Mullins (IRE)	won Punchestown Gd2 novice hurdle (2m) (0)

WINS-RUNS: 4yo 0-2, 5yo 3-55, 6yo 6-64, 7yo 1-8, 8yo 0-3 **FAVOURITES:** -£3.65

TRAINERS IN THIS RACE (w-pl-r): Willie Mullins 3-7-32, Nicky Henderson 3-4-14, Gordon Elliott 1-3-9, Barry Connell 1-0-1, Henry de Bromhead 1-2-9, Alan King 0-0-4, Paul Nicholls 0-0-3, Nigel Twiston-Davies 0-0-2, Dan Skelton 0-0-2, Ben Pauling 0-0-2, Warren Greatrex 0-0-2, Paul Hennessy 0-0-1, Fergal O'Brien 0-0-1

FATE OF FAVOURITES: 1220441120 **POSITION OF WINNER IN MARKET:** 1203331133

Key trends

➤ Rated within 8lb of RPR top-rated, ten winners in last ten runnings

➤ Adjusted RPR of at least 154, 9/10

➤ Previously contested a Graded race, 9/10

➤ Won last time out, 8/10

➤ Ran within the last 66 days, 8/10

➤ Won at least 50 per cent of hurdle starts, 7/10

Other factors

➤ Only one winner had come via the Flat. Six of the other nine started their careers in bumpers, earning an RPR of at least 110. Two started over hurdles in France, while another went hurdling straight from a point-to-point

➤ Only one winner had run in the Champion Bumper (Appreciate It second in 2020)

2.00 My Pension Expert Arkle Novices' Chase ITV/RTV
➤2m ➤Grade 1 ➤£200,000

This was shaping up as potentially one of the best Britain v Ireland showdowns of the festival until the news came that Nicky Henderson's Sir Gino – hugely impressive on his chasing debut at Christmas – had been ruled out due to a serious infection in the ligaments of his near hind leg. He had been odds-on favourite but that mantle passed to Willie Mullins' Majborough, like Sir Gino an outstanding juvenile hurdler last season and now a high-performing chaser at an early age. Last year's Triumph Hurdle winner has outstanding claims, having recorded a Racing Post Rating of 164 in winning the Grade 1 Irish Arkle at the Dublin Racing Festival. This is a race in which favourites do well, with eight of the last ten winning, including all seven priced at 2-1 or shorter. Britain still appears to have the main danger in Dan Skelton's L'Eau Du Sud, also a Grade 1 winner in the Henry VIII Novices' Chase and with more experience than the favourite after going on to make it four out of four over fences in the Grade 2 Kingmaker at Warwick. Other possibles include the Gordon Elliott-trained pair Firefox and Touch Me Not – runner-up to both Majborough and L'Eau Du Sud in their Grade 1s – along with Jango Baie, who may give Henderson a runner at least.

Majborough
5 b g; Trainer Willie Mullins
Chase form 11, best RPR 164
Left-handed 1, best RPR 164
Right-handed 1, best RPR 151
Cheltenham form (hurdles) 1, best RPR 147
At the festival 15 Mar 2024 Jumped left on occasions, in touch with leaders, headway 3 out, went second home turn, soon hung left and ridden, jumped left and challenging last, soon led, kept on well, won Triumph Hurdle by a length and a half from Kargese

Took advantage of Sir Gino's absence from last season's Triumph, beating stablemate Kargese by a length and a half. At the time it was considered a weak renewal, not least because Sir Gino wasn't there, but it hasn't turned out that way. The runner-up, as well as finishing second to Sir Gino at Aintree, went on to win at Punchestown, while fourth-placed Nurburgring won the Galway Hurdle, fifth-placed Storm Heart returned from an absence to be second in a big handicap hurdle at the Dublin Racing Festival and the sixth, Salvator Mundi, is now one of the main fancies for the Supreme. It turns out it was a vintage running after all, which makes it all the more impressive that Majborough could win it on only his third

racecourse start. He has made a reasonably smooth transition to fences as well, winning on both outings, starting with a six-and-a-half-length success from the useful Tullyhill, when he jumped to his left at times but only needed nudging out to win. Next time it was the Grade 1 Irish Arkle, in which Majborough turned in a performance almost as good as that of the now-absent Sir Gino at Kempton, returning an RPR of 164 for an eased-down nine-length win from Touch Me Not, who had been a lot closer when second to L'Eau Du Sud in the Henry VIII at Sandown. There were mild negatives as his jumping was a bit novicey at times and he edged to his left on a few occasions as well, but there's no denying the engine as the time was very good. As far as the jumping is concerned, Majborough seemed far more proficient when asked for a leap by rider Mark Walsh rather than when left to pop them on his own, so it'll be interesting to see if he's ridden with that in mind next time. The market did have Sir Gino as a very strong favourite, but that mantle has been passed on to Majborough and there's little doubt he deserves it.

Going preference Acts on any ground
Star rating ✪✪✪✪✪

L'Eau Du Sud *(right)*
7 gr g; Trainer Dan Skelton
Chase form 1111, best RPR 155
Left-handed 111, best RPR 153
Right-handed 1, best RPR 155
Cheltenham form (all) P21, best RPR 153
At the festival 15 Mar 2024 Held up in rear, midfield 3rd, went third 2 out, led narrowly but not fluent last, kept on run-in, headed towards finish, finished second, beaten a length by Absurde in County Handicap Hurdle

Useful and improving handicap hurdler last season, who finished second in the Betfair (now William Hill) Hurdle at Newbury and then in the County Hurdle. Has taken his form to a new level over fences, though, largely jumping well (though sometimes a bit big) on his way to winning all four of his chase outings. Started off in handicap company, making a mockery of his mark of 138 with a ten-length win at Stratford, and followed that with an 11-length success in the Grade 2 Arkle Trial at Cheltenham in November, jumping really on that occasion and cruising to victory. It was the Grade 1 Henry VIII at Sandown next and he got the job done with a near four-length success from subsequent Majborough victim Touch Me Not, although this time his jumping wasn't altogether foot perfect as he gave some of his fences plenty of air and was a bit awkward at the last two. The jumping was much better on his final prep in the Kingmaker at Warwick, although his length success from a rallying Rubaud wasn't quite as impressive as everyone was expecting, L'Eau Du Sud hanging on in the end by a length. In fairness, Rubaud is a four-time Grade 2 winner over hurdles who started the season rated 9lb superior to L'Eau Du Sud and was getting 5lb, so time may tell it was an excellent effort, especially as they went fast enough and Harry Skelton probably pushed the button a shade too early, going for home three out. There's no pretending any of his form is up to the level of Majborough at the moment, so he's going to need more. On the upside, he has more experience than him, has already jumped really well at Cheltenham and will be far happier taking a lead in the early stages.

Going preference Acts on any ground
Star rating ✪✪✪✪

Firefox
7 b g; Trainer Gordon Elliott
Chase form 1323, best RPR 149
Left-handed 23, best RPR 149
Right-handed 13, best RPR 148
Cheltenham form (hurdles) 3, best RPR 143
At the festival 12 Mar 2024 Midfield, steady headway when not fluent 3 out, pushed along when hampered and outpaced before last, soon stumbled, rallied and went third inside final 110yds, did well in the circumstances, finished third, beaten five lengths by Slade Steel in Supreme Novices' Hurdle

Talented performer who has never finished out of the first four in any code, but hasn't done much winning since taking three of his four bumpers. His sole hurdles success came in a maiden in December 2023 when he beat none other than Ballyburn, and after that he went 4322 in Grade 1s, including at Cheltenham, Aintree and Punchestown. It has been a similar story over fences this term, with a beginners' chase success at Down Royal followed by form figures of 323 in Graded events, and he was put well in his place when third to Majborough at a distance of 13 lengths at the DRF. Has run to an RPR of between 147 and 150 on his last five outings in Graded company, whether over hurdles or fences, and that seems to be what he is. That ought to mean not good enough to win an

Arkle, given Majborough's peak effort is 164, but Sir Gino's absence hasn't exactly inspired others to have a crack – there were only 15 left after the scratchings in February – and the pick of his 2m form entitles him to be fighting it out for the places. He has run four times over fences, and his half-length Grade 1 third over 2m4f suggests he does stay that trip, so he could go handicapping, although he'd have to defy a mark in the 150s.

Going preference Seems perfectly versatile

Star rating✪✪

Gidleigh Park
7 b g; Trainer Harry Fry
Chase form P1, best RPR 154
Left-handed 1, best RPR 154
Right-handed P
Cheltenham form (hurdles) 16, best RPR 136
At the festival 15 Mar 2024 Took keen hold, towards rear, some headway and held up in midfield after 8th, weakened approaching last, finished sixth, beaten 16 lengths by Stellar Story in Albert Bartlett Novices' Hurdle

Slammed the very useful The Jukebox Man by six lengths on his bumper debut in March 2023 and won his first three novice hurdles last season from 2m to 2m4½f, including a Grade 2 at Cheltenham on Trials day. After that he was sent off at just 9-2 for the Albert Bartlett at the festival and, while finishing a creditable sixth of the 13 runners, it was quite apparent he didn't stay. His first effort over fences in November couldn't have gone much worse as he was none too fluent in the jumping department and was pulled up before the sixth. However, he was reported to have had an irregular heartbeat, and he put that run behind him when scoring quite impressively dropped to 2m around Windsor's tight circuit in January. There he led all the way, going clear at the fifth, and found plenty once challenged to beat the well-touted but disappointing (in relation to price tag anyway) Caldwell Potter by four lengths. He's got the speed for 2m on that evidence, but he'll be trying to lead a much better horse at Cheltenham if he attempts to take on the positively ridden Majborough.

Going preference Acts well on soft, once a non-runner due to good

Star rating ✪✪

Touch Me Not
6 br g; Trainer Gordon Elliott
Chase form 2122, best RPR 151
Left-handed 2, best RPR 151
Right-handed 212, best RPR 151

Needed four attempts to get off the mark over hurdles last season, scoring in a lowly Tramore maiden in April, but has quickly left that form behind since being sent over fences despite the fact he fell in his only point (was clear at the last). He jumped really well on his debut at Punchestown in October, making most before being reeled in at the line, and he went back there for the Grade 2 Craddockstown Novice Chase the following month, running out a comfortable winner from short-priced stablemate Farren Glory. After that he gave L'Eau Du Sud a bit of a fright in the Henry VIII at Sandown, eventually going down by just under four lengths, and then followed Majborough home at a respectable distance of nine lengths in the Irish Arkle. On that evidence, he's not going to be winning at Cheltenham, at least not in Grade 1 company, but he has had four starts over fences now, which means handicaps such as the Grand Annual, or the returning novice handicap over 2m4f (has a winning half-brother at the trip), are a possibility. An Irish chase mark of 151 is the problem but he's only six.

Going preference Seems okay on most surfaces

Star rating ✪

Jango Baie
6 b g; Trainer Nicky Henderson
Chase form 12, best RPR 158
Left-handed 1, best RPR 157
Right-handed 2, best RPR 158
Cheltenham form 1, best RPR 157

Grade 1 novice hurdle winner over 2m at Aintree last season thanks to the heavy fall of Farren Glory, but showed better form afterwards upped in trip, notably when a slightly unlucky second back at Aintree in a Grade 3 2m4f handicap hurdle at the Grand National meeting, staying on strongly after being hampered. He took that form to a new level again on his chase debut and it came at Cheltenham, which is rare enough for a Nicky Henderson-trained horse over fences.

There he was receiving 8lb from the more experienced Springwell Bay, but he won with seemingly tons in hand from a horse who would run away with a Cheltenham handicap (by nine lengths) off a mark of 145 next time. Jango Baie just failed to double his Grade 1 haul in the Scilly Isles Novices' Chase a Sandown next time, going down by a short head to the promising Handstands after a sustained duel from two out. With the pair having pulled 17 lengths clear of the third, the race confirmed both as very useful performers. He's another who would no doubt have been heading straight for the old Turners if it still existed, but the choices are now to send him here, go for the mile-longer Brown Advisory or wait for Aintree, where he clearly operates so well. All options are possible, but with this race looking sure to cut up further and the same connections' Jingko Blue in the three-miler, he could well find himself in the line-up on day one. His form over further arguably gives him the edge on some of the shorter-priced runners, so if he can repeat it at 2m he'd be a frame contender.

Going preference No obvious preference
Star rating ✪✪

Only By Night

7 b m; Trainer Gavin Cromwell
Chase form 111, best RPR 139
Left-handed 1, best RPR 134
Right-handed 11, best RPR 139

Achieved a peak RPR of just 121 over hurdles last season, so would be some way from a typical Arkle winner should she take part. She has at least looked considerably better in three outings over fences, winning at Tipperary in November and then taking a Cork Grade 2 in comfortable enough style the following month. Her final run came in February when she went to Exeter for a Listed mares' chase and, despite a slow jump at the last, had enough in reserve to win by a length. A top RPR of 139 tells you she has improved for fences, but even with the 7lb mares' allowance she has tons to find.

Going preference Acts on good to soft and slower
Star rating ✪

Kalif Du Berlais

5 b g; Trainer Paul Nicholls
Chase form F114, best RPR 152
Left-handed 11, best RPR 152
Right-handed F4, best RPR 135
Cheltenham form 1, best RPR 152

Talked up by Paul Nicholls as one of the most exciting young horses he'd had for a while after beating Givemefive in the Dovecote at Kempton last season but was put firmly in his place at Aintree when only a distant third to Sir Gino and Kargese in the 4-Y-O Juvenile Hurdle. However, it was over fences that Nicholls expected him to make his mark, and after a faltering start when he fell on his debut at Carlisle (had jumped beautifully until then), he started to show what he was made of. A battling success at Newbury's Coral Gold Cup meeting was far from eye-popping, but it was essentially his first full race of the season and he improved dramatically on that when scoring very easily by nearly ten lengths over the New course at Cheltenham off a mark of 141. That was only a three-runner affair, but the runner-up gave substance to the form by winning pretty handily at Sandown next time and went up 5lb for it. Kalif Du Berlais also went to Sandown next time, but was a clear non-stayer in finishing last of four to Handstands in the Grade 1 Scilly Isles over 2m4f on heavy ground. Afterwards it was suggested he would go straight for the 2m Maghull at Aintree but, with Sir Gino coming out and the field falling apart, connections (whose other entry Caldwell Potter is earmarked for the novice handicap chase on the Thursday) may change their minds. That said, some of the owners are also involved in L'Eau Du Sud.

Going preference Seems versatile enough
Star rating ✪✪

OTHERS TO CONSIDER

Ballyburn remained among the entries after the scratchings but has been deliberately left out here as I couldn't see why Willie Mullins would want to run him against his own odds-on favourite when he will be favourite for the Brown Advisory the following day. He would arguably still be the form choice if something happens to Majborough, but

ARKLE CHASE RESULTS AND TRENDS

	FORM WINNER	AGE & WGT	Adj RPR	SP	TRAINER	BEST RPR LAST 12 MONTHS (RUNS SINCE)
24	1-11U **Gaelic Warrior** D, BF	6 11-7	164ᵀ	2-1f	W Mullins (IRE)	won Limerick Gd1 novice chase (2m3½f) **(1)**
23	2-111 **El Fabiolo** D	6 11-7	174ᵀ	11-10f	W Mullins (IRE)	won Leopardstown Gd1 novice chase (2m1f) **(0)**
22	B1111 **Edwardstone** D	8 11-4	174ᵀ	5-2f	A King	won Sandown Gd1 novice chase (1m7½f) **(2)**
21	1-111 **Shishkin** C, D	7 11-4	180ᵀ	4-9f	N Henderson	won Doncaster Gd2 novice chase (2m½f) **(0)**
20	11121 **Put The Kettle On** CD	6 10-11	165⁻⁹	16-1	H de Bromhead (IRE)	won Cheltenham Gd2 novice chase (2m) **(0)**
19	6-231 **Duc Des Genievres**	6 11-4	165⁻⁵	5-1	W Mullins (IRE)	won Gowran Park novice chase (2m4f) **(0)**
18	3-111 **Footpad** D	6 11-4	178ᵀ	5-6f	W Mullins (IRE)	won Leopardstown Gd1 novice chase(2m1f) **(0)**
17	-1111 **Altior** C, D	7 11-4	185ᵀ	1-4f	N Henderson	won Newbury Gd2 ch (2m½f) **(0)**
16	-1111 **Douvan** C, D	6 11-4	180ᵀ	1-4f	W Mullins (IRE)	won Leopardstown Gd1 novice chase (2m1f) **(1)**
15	1-F11 **Un De Sceaux** D	7 11-4	181ᵀ	4-6f	W Mullins (IRE)	won Leopardstown Gd1 novice chase (2m1f) **(0)**

WINS-RUNS: 5yo 0-7, 6yo 6-24, 7yo 3-41, 8yo 1-12, 9yo 0-5, 10yo 0-1 **FAVOURITES:** £6.04

TRAINERS IN THIS RACE (w-pl-r): Willie Mullins 6-3-17, Nicky Henderson 2-3-6, Henry de Bromhead 1-2-14, Gavin Cromwell 0-1-2, Gordon Elliott 0-1-6, Joseph O'Brien 0-2-2, Ben Pauling 0-0-2, Dan Skelton 0-0-2, Paul Nicholls 0-0-2

FATE OF FAVOURITES: 1111061111 **POSITION OF WINNER IN MARKET:** 1111371111

will surely stay at longer distances from now on. **Springwell Bay** is another who has form better than some who are likely to line up, but it's over a different trip and he's one of the horses most inconvenienced by the lack of the old Turners as he looks a pure 2m4f horse. He did once run a close second over 3m in a Pertemps qualifier, but hasn't run over 2m since his novice hurdle season. **Jeannot Lapin** won a beginners' chase at 150-1 on his debut and arguably improved when beaten 18 lengths by Majborough, but he's a rank outsider here, as are **Jordans**, **San Salvador** and **Fascile Mode**, while we have already established that **Caldwell Potter** is going for a handicap.

VERDICT

I really want to make a case for L'Eau Du Sud, but that's only because I backed him a while ago and it will be a case of hoping rather than expecting. As a horse used to being held up in big-field handicap hurdles, he'll be much better suited taking a lead as opposed to forcing it as he did at Warwick last month, but whether he has the required class to deal with MAJBOROUGH is another matter. Last year's Triumph winner may not quite be the force of nature that Sir Gino looked like at Kempton, but he's certainly not far off it, and if his jumping stands up to the test he'll surely be hard to beat. There are some straws to clutch at given the way he ran down a few fences at Leopardstown

Key trends

➤ Adjusted RPR of at least 164, 10/10

➤ Rated within 9lb of RPR top-rated, 10/10

➤ Aged six or seven, 9/10

➤ SP no bigger than 5-1, 9/10 (exception 16-1)

➤ Finished in the first two on all completed chase starts, 9/10

➤ RPR hurdles rating of at least 152, 8/10

➤ Three to five chase runs, 8/10

Other factors

➤ Nine winners had previously won a 2m-2m1f Graded chase

➤ Eight winners started favourite and all were RPR top-rated

➤ Seven winners had previously run at the festival, showing mixed form in a variety of hurdle races

last time when allowed to do his own thing but Mark Walsh will surely be alive to that this time. Of the ones at much bigger prices Jango Baie could run a big race if he can handle the drop to 2m, and so could Kalif Du Berlais if allowed to take his chance, but it's hard to see this race attracting anything but a small field and it ought to be Majborough's for the taking.

2.40 Ultima Handicap Chase
3m1f ▸ Premier Handicap ▸ £150,000 — ITV/RTV

This prestigious 3m1f handicap chase is one of the most important of its type in the jumps season and, as well as being a major prize in its own right, often draws runners who will head on to other big races in the spring, including the Grand National.

LAST YEAR'S WINNER Chianti Classico became the second winner of this race for trainer Kim Bailey, 25 years after his first success with Betty's Boy. The 6-1 shot continued the trend of most winners coming from high in the betting market and was the eighth novice to land the race in the last 21 runnings.

FORM The only winner in the last 19 runnings without any previous course experience was the Irish-trained Dun Doire in 2006, although Chianti Classico's previous visit hadn't been positive (pulled up in the Albert Bartlett Novices' Hurdle – then again, so was Monty's Star and he returned to finished second in last year's Brown Advisory Novices' Chase). With his first victory in 2016, Un Temps Pour Tout became the first horse since Dixton House in 1989 to land the prize having not won a race over fences before, although he was part of the recent trend towards inexperienced chasers. In the last ten years only The Druids Nephew (2015) and Vintage Clouds (2021) had run more than ten times over fences before landing the prize.

WEIGHT AND RATINGS The low to mid 140s is a fruitful place to look (Chianti Classico last year became the 11th winner in the last 17 runnings rated 140-146). It has been more possible for higher-rated runners to win in recent years: Un Temps Pour Tout (off 155 in 2017) carried 11st 12lb, the highest winning weight since Different Class with 11st 13lb in 1967, and Beware The Bear scored off 151 in 2019.

AGE Eight-year-olds have won the race ten times since the turn of the millennium, along with six seven year-olds. Together they account for two-thirds of winners (16-24) in that period.

TRAINERS Jonjo O'Neill (now training jointly with son AJ) and David Pipe are the two most successful current trainers with three wins each. Three of the last four runnings have gone to the north, with Sue Smith's Vintage Clouds in 2021 followed by Corach Rambler's double for Lucinda Russell in 2022-23. While Irish-bred horses account for 15 of the last 17 winners, those trained across the Irish Sea have not done so well, having been successful only twice since 1966 with Youlneverwalkalone (2003) and Dun Doire (2006).

BETTING Only four favourites have been successful since 1977, but most winners have been well fancied with 19 of the last 25 returned at 10-1 or lower. Chianti Classico was joint-third favourite last year at 6-1. The successful favourites since 1977 were Antonin (4-1 in 1994), Wichita Lineman (5-1 in 2009), Coo Star Sivola (5-1 in 2018) and Corach Rambler (6-1jf in 2023).

ONES TO WATCH Masaccio (Alan King) and **Johnnywho** (Jonjo and AJ O'Neill) are a couple of interesting novices. Both have competed without success in Graded races, including when second and third respectively behind the highly regarded The Jukebox Man at Newbury. Another whose form ties in is **Lowry's Bar** from the stable of Philip Hobbs and Johnson White.

Masaccio: solid novice chase form

ULTIMA HANDICAP CHASE RESULTS AND TRENDS

	FORM WINNER	AGE & WGT	OR	SP	TRAINER	BEST RPR LAST 12 MONTHS (RUNS SINCE)
24	P-112 **Chianti Classico** BF	7 11-4	143-3	6-1	K Bailey	2nd Kempton Class 2 hcap chase (3m) (0)
23	U1-54 **Corach Rambler** CD	9 11-5	146-4	6-1j	L Russell	won Ultima Handicap Chase (3m1f) (2)
22	3114U **Corach Rambler** C, D, BF	8 10-2	140-2	10-1	L Russell	won Chelt Class 3 nov hcap chase (3m1½f) (2)
21	8-753 **Vintage Clouds** D	11 10-11	143-7	28-1	S Smith	5th Warwick Class 2 hcap chase (3m) (1)
20	-3124 **The Conditional** CD, BF	8 10-6	139-3	15-2	D Bridgwater	2nd Newbury Gd3 hcap chase (3m2f) (1)
19	4P-41 **Beware The Bear** C	9 11-8	151T	10-1	N Henderson	won Cheltenham Class 2 hcap chase (3m3½f) (0)
18	53421 **Coo Star Sivola** C, D	6 10-10	142-2	5-1f	N Williams	won Exeter Class 3 nov hcap chase (3m) (0)
17	-1036 **Un Temps Pour Tout** CD	8 11-12	155-10	9-1	D Pipe	won Ultima Handicap Chase (3m1f) (5)
16	-1224 **Un Temps Pour Tout** D, BF	7 11-7	148-15	11-1	D Pipe	2nd Newbury Gd2 novice chase (2m7½f) (1)
15	-1275 **The Druids Nephew**	8 11-3	146T	8-1	N Mulholland	2nd Cheltenham Gd3 hcap chase (3m3½f) (1)

WINS-RUNS: 5yo 0-2, 6yo 1-12, 7yo 2-48, 8yo 4-74, 9yo 2-44, 10yo 0-28, 11yo 1-9, 12yo 0-2 **FAVOURITES:** -£0.50

FATE OF FAVOURITES: 0021P32015 **POSITION OF WINNER IN MARKET:** 2531530513

OR 130-140 2-7-65, **141-150** 6-16-111, **151-164** 2-7-42

Key trends

➤ Ran no more than five times that season, 10/10

➤ Won over at least 3m, 9/10

➤ Officially rated 139-151, 9/10

➤ Aged seven to nine, 8/10

➤ Ran at a previous festival, 8/10

➤ No more than ten runs over fences, 8/10

➤ Top-three finish on either or both of last two starts, 7/10

➤ Carried no more than 11st 5lb, 7/10 (dual winner accounts for two exceptions)

Other factors

➤ Six had recorded a top-four finish at a previous festival

➤ Seven winners had run well in a handicap at Cheltenham earlier in the season (three won, two placed and two fourth). The 2017 winner Un Temps Pour Tout had run well in a Grade 2 hurdle at the course

➤ This was once seemingly an impossible task for novices but five of the last ten winners have been first-season chasers

3.20 Close Brothers Mares' Hurdle ITV/RTV
> 2m4f > Grade 1 > £120,000

Coming on the same afternoon as the Champion Hurdle, this Grade 1 continues to offer an alternative route to top festival honours for the best mares – arguably to the detriment of the showpiece feature – and the old arguments have resurfaced over where Brighterdaysahead and Lossiemouth should run.

The Gordon Elliott-trained Brighterdaysahead rates as the best mare around after her stunning display in the Grade 1 Neville Hotels Hurdle at the Leopardstown Christmas meeting, where she left last year's Champion winner State Man trailing and came home 30 lengths clear.

Lossiemouth won this race last year by three lengths from Telmesomethinggirl, taking Willie Mullins' score to ten in the 17 runnings. She has raced against the boys this season, most recently taking a heavy fall four out in the Irish Champion Hurdle when going head to head with State Man.

If at least one of the big two went to the Champion, the chances would improve for July Flower (Henry de Bromhead) and the Mullins pair Kargese and Jade De Grugy.

MARES' HURDLE RESULTS AND TRENDS

	FORM WINNER	AGE & WGT	Adj RPR	SP	TRAINER	BEST RPR LAST 12 MONTHS (RUNS SINCE)
24	211-1 **Lossiemouth** C	5 11-5	164^T	8-13f	W Mullins (IRE)	won Cheltenham Gd2 hurdle (2m1f) (0)
23	1-132 **Honeysuckle** CD	9 11-5	169^T	9-4j	H de Bromhead (IRE)	won Gd1 Champion Hurdle (2m½f) (3)
22	371P1 **Marie's Rock**	7 11-5	151^{-10}	18-1	N Henderson	won Kempton Class 3 hcap hurdle (2m5f) (2)
21	2-331 **Black Tears** D	7 11-5	156^{-9}	11-1	D Foster (IRE)	won Punchestown Gd3 hurdle (2m4f) (0)
20	1-111 **Honeysuckle** D	6 11-5	169^{-2}	9-4	H de Bromhead (IRE)	won Gd1 Hatton's Grace Hurdle (2m4f) (1)
19	112-3 **Roksana** D	7 11-5	153^{-8}	10-1	D Skelton	2nd Aintree Gd2 novice hurdle (3m½f) (1)
18	/1-11 **Benie Des Dieux** D	7 11-5	156^{-13}	9-2	W Mullins (IRE)	Seasonal debutante (0)
17	12212 **Apple's Jade** D, BF	5 11-5	171^T	7-2	G Elliott (IRE)	won Aintree Gd1 juvenile hurdle (2m1f) (5)
16	1-111 **Vroum Vroum Mag** D	7 11-5	160^T	4-6f	W Mullins (IRE)	won Ascot Gd2 hurdle (2m7½f) (0)
15	7521 **Glens Melody** D	7 11-5	162^{-11}	6-1	W Mullins (IRE)	won Warwick Listed hurdle (2m5f) (0)

WINS-RUNS: 5yo 2-8, 6yo 1-26, 7yo 6-43, 8yo 0-30, 9yo 1-16, 10yo 0-1, 11yo 0-1 **FAVOURITES:** -£5.09

TRAINERS IN THIS RACE (w-pl-r): Willie Mullins 4-7-29, Henry de Bromhead 2-2-8, Gordon Elliott 1-3-5, Dan Skelton 1-1-6, Fergal O'Brien 0-0-2, Jamie Snowden 0-0-1, Jessica Harrington 0-1-4, Paul Nolan 0-1-1

FATE OF FAVOURITES: F133F22411 **POSITION OF WINNER IN MARKET:** 2132423811

Key trends

> Top-four finish in a Grade 1 or 2 hurdle, 9/10

> At least eight career starts, 8/10

> Adjusted RPR of at least 156, 8/10

> Rated within 10lb of RPR top-rated, 8/10

> Won last time out, 7/10

Other factors

> A runner priced 16-1 or bigger has finished in the first three in eight of the last ten runnings

> Willie Mullins has trained four of the last ten winners

> Quevega used to come here fresh when defending her crown but eight of the last nine winners had between two and five outings that season

4.00 Unibet Champion Hurdle — ITV/RTV
➤2m½f ➤Grade 1 ➤£450,000

Essentially this boils down to Constitution Hill and State Man, the last two Champion winners, versus each other and possibly against one or both of Brighterdaysahead and Lossiemouth unless they go for the Mares' Hurdle 40 minutes earlier. If they all line up, it could be a race for the ages. Even if they don't, which seems the more likely scenario, there is still the potential for an outstanding performance from at least one of the combatants. Nicky Henderson's Constitution Hill was magnificent in the 2023 Champion, beating State Man by nine lengths, but health issues forced him to miss last year's race and he hasn't yet scaled his former heights even though he remains unbeaten after ten races over hurdles. The Willie Mullins-trained State Man took the crown in his old rival's absence 12 months ago and has a deserved reputation as 'Mr Reliable', although there was an off-day at Christmas before he bounced back to land a third Irish Champion Hurdle at the Dublin Racing Festival. Gordon Elliott's Brighterdaysahead has beaten State Man twice this season, most eyecatchingly in that Christmas contest at Leopardstown, and rates as the best mare in training after her spectacular 30-length success. Close behind her is Mullins' Lossiemouth, who won last year's Mares' Hurdle and might take the step up to the Champion this time. She has met both of her big male rivals this season, finishing well against Constitution Hill in the Christmas Hurdle at Kempton but then taking a crashing fall when upsides State Man in the Irish Champion. Provided there are no lasting effects, she is capable of a big run wherever she lines up.

Constitution Hill
8 b g; Trainer Nicky Henderson
Hurdles form 1111111111, best RPR 177
Left-handed 11111, best RPR 177
Right-handed 11111, best RPR 175
Cheltenham form 111, best RPR 177
At the festival 15 Mar 2022 Travelled strongly, tracked leaders, left in second 3 out, led going easily 2 out, nudged along and went clear on turn before last, shaken up and went further clear final 110yds, eased towards finish, impressive, won Supreme Novices' Hurdle by 22 lengths from Jonbon
14 Mar 2023 Travelled strongly, prominent, pressed leader from 3rd, led going easily 3 out, shaken up and went clear before last, impressive, won Champion Hurdle by nine lengths from State Man

The outstanding hurdler of his and almost any other generation and still a perfect 10-10 over hurdles despite enduring a troubled season and a half with various health issues. His 22-length Supreme Novices' Hurdle win in 2022 remains the most jaw-dropping performance from a novice hurdler most of us have ever seen, and he was at least as good when toying with State Man in the Champion a year later, cruising to success by nine lengths and recording an RPR of 177, which is way out of reach for mere mortals. That was two years ago, though, and Constitution Hill, who was not so impressive upped to 2m4f at Aintree next time, has had his share of problems since. Not quite ready to defend his Fighting Fifth crown last season, he did return in the Christmas Hurdle, where he looked as good as ever in strolling to a near ten-length success from Rubaud, although with the runner-up rated only 149, it was hard to put a big figure on the performance (RPR 158). Things went pear-shaped afterwards, though, as he missed the International at Cheltenham in January due to a poor scope, while a dreadful gallop at Kempton followed by an unsatisfactory blood test meant he was ruled out of a defence of his crown at Cheltenham. Things went from bad to worse after that as at the end of March Constitution Hill was in a veterinary hospital being monitored for suspected colic and was reportedly "very ill". Constitution Hill went for a wind operation in May and connections started to make bullish noises about him again in the summer, but he then appeared to have another poor

Jaydon Lee and Nicky Henderson after Constitution Hill's win in the International at Cheltenham in January

gallop with rising star Sir Gino at Newbury in the autumn. While trainer Nicky Henderson said at the time he was satisfied, it was the latter who lined up in Constitution Hill's place in the Fighting Fifth in November. When he finally made his reappearance in the Christmas Hurdle, exactly a year had passed since he'd last been seen on a racecourse and nobody, perhaps with the exception of those in the stable, really knew what to expect. What we got was a strong indication that Constitution Hill retains at least a large share of his ability as he had no trouble laying up with a hot gallop set by Burdett Road and breezed into the lead at the second-last before having to be shaken up to fend off Lossiemouth by two and a half lengths. With the latter having struggled to go the early gallop and the 142-rated four-year-old Burdett Road beaten only nine lengths, it was again hard to put a big figure on the performance (RPR 162), but we shouldn't underestimate how much this great horse had been through just to get there, and it was certainly a huge step in the right direction. Unfortunately we were always unlikely to find out if he's right back to his best before the festival as there's nothing good enough in Britain to give him a race, and that was borne out by his three-length success from Brentford Hope in the International on Trials day in January (RPR just 150). He was never out of a canter in a very slowly run race (ten seconds slower than the Triumph Trial) and the only real talking point was the chance he took at the last, which caused a few gasps from the crowd. By the time he lines up it will be very nearly two years since he ran within 10lb of his career-best Champion Hurdle win and the question remains just how close can he get to it, for while we can be hopeful he is just as good as he was, we certainly can't be confident. And if the two crack mares turn up, he might need to be – although that, unfortunately, is a big if.

Going preference Acts on anything
Star rating ✪✪✪✪✪

Lossiemouth: targeted at the 2025 Champion ever since winning the Triumph Hurdle two years ago

Lossiemouth
6 gr m; Trainer Willie Mullins
Hurdles form 11121111112F, best RPR 156
Left-handed 112111F, best RPR 156
Right-handed 11112, best RPR 152
Cheltenham form 111, best RPR 156
At the festival 17 Mar 2023 In touch with leaders, carried right 3rd, headway and prominent 3 out, led after 2 out, hung left approaching last, ridden and kept on well run-in, won Triumph Hurdle by two and a quarter lengths from Gala Marceau
12 Mar 2024 Travelled strongly, in rear, headway before 3 out, prominent 2 out, smooth headway and led approaching last, ridden final 110yds, readily, won Mares' Hurdle by three lengths from Telmesomethinggirl

Dual Cheltenham Festival winner who has been targeted at the 2025 Champion Hurdle ever since landing the 2023 Triumph Hurdle, and despite things not going according to plan so far this season, it's still the preferred option according to Willie Mullins. Connections decided to wait a year after her Triumph success given what is usually a tricky season for former juvenile hurdlers, so instead Lossiemouth had a very light campaign and went down the Mares' Hurdle route. She didn't make her return that season until the International on Trials day at Cheltenham, taking advantage of Constitution Hill's absence to cruise home by nine and a half lengths from Love Envoi in a weak renewal, while next time she duly took the Mares' Hurdle, scoring by three lengths from Telmesomethinggirl. Another mares' Grade 1 over 2m4f completed that season, but it was into open company on her return in December, when she made the usually best-fresh Teahupoo look pedestrian in the 2m4f Hatton's Grade, coming from last to first to win going away on the bridle. That was an incredibly slowly run affair, however, and a much sterner test awaited in the shape of Constitution Hill in the Christmas Hurdle at Kempton. There she gave the impression she was struggling to keep up in the early stages with the lightning pace set by Burdett Road, but in the end she stayed on strongly for a two-and-a-half-length second to the Champion Hurdle favourite, who arguably had to work harder for that win than any other.

It's quite likely that Lossiemouth suffered a bit of a culture shock at Kempton as it was nearly a year since she'd run over less than 2m4f and was probably the fastest she'd ever been asked to go in the early stages of a race, and she at least showed she had no problem with a searching gallop in the Irish Champion at the DRF next time as she set it ahead of State Man before taking a crashing fall four out. That was hardly an ideal prep and the question of where she stands in relation to stablemate and reigning title-holder State Man remains – while she was odds-on favourite, both Willie Mullins and Paul Townend were adamant that he was still their number one and so far the form book backs that up given her career-best RPR is just 156.

Going preference Acts on all ground but could probably do with a test at this trip
Star rating ❍❍❍

Brighterdaysahead
6 b m; Trainer Gordon Elliott
Hurdles form 11121111, best RPR 165
Left-handed 1211, best RPR 165
Right-handed 1111, best RPR 159
Cheltenham form 2, best RPR 142
At the festival 14 Mar 2024 Took keen hold, in touch with leaders, mistake 4 out, slightly hampered when prominent 2 out, challenging approaching last, briefly disputed lead last, no extra inside final 110yds, finished second, beaten a length and three-quarters by Golden Ace in Mares' Novices' Hurdle

Brighterdaysahead: big decision to be made between the Champion Hurdle and the Mares' Hurdle

Gordon Elliott was happy to tell punters going into last year's festival that Brighterdaysahead could be the best mare he's ever trained, so it came as a shock when she went down by just under two lengths to Golden Ace in the Mares' Novices' Hurdle, with many blaming rider Jack Kennedy for not making it enough of a test. Brighterdaysahead duly bolted up back at 2m4f at Aintree after that, and it's fair to say that what she's done this season makes it all the more baffling that she surrendered her unbeaten record when it mattered. A cosy Grade 3 win at Elliott's favourite early-season hunting ground Down Royal kickstarted her season and she made the most of her fitness after that to edge out State Man in the Grade 1 Morgiana, returning an RPR of 159, which elevated her to the top mare in training. State Man was a 4-9 chance that day and went off at the same price to gain his revenge in the Neville Hotels Hurdle at Leopardstown over Christmas, but it was Brighterdaysahead who came out on top again – and how. Elliott's mare chased stablemate King Of Kingsfield off a solid gallop, with the rest of the field largely ignoring them, and she didn't come back, strolling home by 30 lengths. However, State Man was reported to have never travelled, and it's clear that he couldn't have run to form as he was passed on the run-in by the ten-year-old Winter Fog. Whatever happened to him, the time was very good and Brighterdaysahead earned an RPR of 165, a figure for a mare over hurdles that has been bettered only by Annie Power (170) and Elliott's Apple's Jade (168) in the last 15 years. If she's not his best-ever mare, she's very close to it at the age of just six. She would be clear second favourite for the Champion if confirmed a runner, but connections are eyeing what would appear a gimme for the Mares' Hurdle 40 minutes earlier on the same day. It's hard to blame connections for running a top mare in a mares' championship (Annie Power, Apple's Jade and Honeysuckle all ran in it before having a go at the Champion) and this sort of thing is always likely to happen when a good mare comes along while the two races occupy the same spot in the calendar. In fairness to connections a decision hasn't been made yet,

and she may well line up in the big one, but she's hardly an ante-post proposition.

Going preference All ground comes alike

Star rating ✪✪✪

State Man
8 ch g; Trainer Willie Mullins
Hurdles form 2F1111112111111231, best RPR 168
Left-handed 2F111211131, best RPR 168
Right-handed 111112, best RPR 168
Cheltenham form 121, best RPR 166
At the festival 18 Mar 2022 Towards rear of midfield and on outer, smooth headway from 2 out, led approaching last, ridden final 110yds, ran on well, won County Handicap Hurdle by a length and a quarter from First Street 14 Mar 2023 Towards rear, headway on outer when good jump 5 out, soon in touch with leaders, went second after 2 out, pushed along before last, kept on but no match for winner, finished second, beaten nine lengths by Constitution Hill in Champion Hurdle 12 Mar 2024 Prominent on inner, not fluent 3 out, switched right and pressed leaders going easily home turn, led approaching last, ridden and kept on run-in, won Champion Hurdle by a length and a quarter from Irish Point

Duly took advantage of Constitution Hill's absence to land last year's Champion Hurdle, but made a meal of it to beat Irish Point by only a length and a quarter and his RPR of 160 was one of the lowest ever recorded by a winner of the race, pouring fuel on the notion that he's not quite as happy at Cheltenham as he is elsewhere despite boasting festival form figures of 121. He beat Irish Point a good deal more comfortably at Punchestown a few weeks later (despite winning by only two lengths), and while he was beaten at odds-on by the race-fit Brighterdaysahead in the Morgiana on his return, he wasn't far off his best form. Expected to reverse the form in the Neville Hotels Hurdle at Leopardstown over Christmas, he then turned in his worst performance for more than two years, trailing in third at a distance of 31 lengths with his rider Paul Townend reporting that he never travelled at any point. That was clearly a blip from one of the most consistent horses in training and State Man looked in much better fettle when landing his third Irish Champion

Hurdle at the DRF, although it was way too early to say what would have happened had Lossiemouth not taken a crashing fall four out. The Willie Mullins-trained eight-year-old arguably doesn't get the credit he deserves, largely because he's been in the presence of Constitution Hill, but he has won 11 Grade 1s himself and is clearly top class when on song, which is most of the time. It's hard to see Townend deserting him at Cheltenham and he remains one of only four horses who can realistically win this year – and one of those might not even run.

Going preference No issues to report

Star rating ✪✪✪

Burdett Road
5 b g; Trainer James Owen
Hurdles form 112132, best RPR 155
Left-handed 121, best RPR 143

Right-handed 132, best RPR 155
Cheltenham form 121, best RPR 143

One-time Triumph Hurdle favourite who was put well in his place by Sir Gino on Trials day last year, going down by ten lengths, and went back to the Flat, where it was finally discovered with a runaway Newmarket success that he was far happier being a front-runner. Given that knowledge he returned to hurdles with a potentially tasty hurdles mark of just 133 and duly took advantage of it to make all in the Greatwood Handicap Hurdle. An attempt to pick up some place money in Grade 1 company followed, but that arguably just ruined his handicap mark, as while he did finish a nine-length third to Constitution Hill and Lossiemouth, he went up a further 8lb following his Greatwood rise and is now on 150. That's arguably put him in no-man's

CHAMPION HURDLE RESULTS AND TRENDS

	FORM WINNER	AGE & WGT	Adj RPR	SP	TRAINER	BEST RPR LAST 12 MONTHS (RUNS SINCE)
24	1-111 **State Man** C, D	7 11-10	174^T	2-5f	W Mullins (IRE)	won Gd1 Irish Champion Hurdle (2m) (0)
23	11-11 **Constitution Hill** CD	6 11-10	180^T	4-11f	N Henderson	won Gd1 Christmas Hurdle (2m) (0)
22	1-111 **Honeysuckle** CD	8 11-3	177^T	8-11f	H de Bromhead (IRE)	won Punchestown Gd1 Hurdle (2m) (2)
21	11-11 **Honeysuckle** C, D	7 11-3	174^T	11-10f	H de Bromhead (IRE)	won Gd1 Irish Champion Hurdle (2m) (0)
20	19-11 **Epatante** D	6 11-3	168^T	2-1f	N Henderson	won Gd1 Christmas Hurdle (2m) (0)
19	4-111 **Espoir D'Allen** D	5 11-10	162^{-17}	16-1	G Cromwell (IRE)	won Limerick Gd3 hurdle (2m) (1)
18	1-111 **Buveur D'Air** CD	7 11-10	175^T	4-6f	N Henderson	won Gd1 Aintree Hurdle (2m4f) (3)
17	1-111 **Buveur D'Air** D	6 11-10	163^{-7}	5-1	N Henderson	won Gd1 Aintree novice hurdle (2m½f) (1)
16	1F-11 **Annie Power** C, D	8 11-3	173^T	5-2f	W Mullins (IRE)	won Gd1 Punchestown Mares Hurdle (2m2f) (1)
15	1-111 **Faugheen** C, D	7 11-10	173^{-4}	4-5f	W Mullins (IRE)	won Gd1 Christmas Hurdle (2m) (0)

WINS-RUNS: 5yo 1-21, 6yo 3-24, 7yo 4-26, 8yo 2-18, 9yo 0-8, 10yo 0-4, 11yo 0-2, 12yo 0-1 **FAVOURITES:** £6.56

TRAINERS IN THIS RACE (w-pl-r): Nicky Henderson 4-5-23, Willie Mullins 3-9-26, Gordon Elliott 0-2-7, Kerry Lee 0-1-1

FATE OF FAVOURITES: 1101611111 **POSITION OF WINNER IN MARKET:** 1121411111

Key trends
➤Won last time out, 10/10

➤Won a Grade 1 hurdle, 9/10

➤Rated within 7lb of RPR top-rated, 9/10 (seven top-rated)

➤Aged between six and eight, 9/10

➤No more than 12 hurdle runs, 8/10

➤Adjusted RPR of at least 168, 8/10

Other factors
➤Katchit (2008) broke a longstanding trend when he became the first five-year-old to win since See You Then in 1985 but in 2019 Espoir D'Allen became the second in just over a decade (28 from that age group had failed in the interim)

➤Three winners had not run since the turn of the year (two trained by Nicky Henderson)

land as he couldn't get near the front two at Kempton despite neither being at their best. Couldn't hold Golden Ace in the Kingwell and will need some flops to make the frame.

Going preference Fast-ground winner on the Flat and no problem with soft

Star rating ✪

OTHERS TO CONSIDER

Only ten horses remained after the scratchings. Of the five not yet mentioned, **King Of Kingsfield** might well be in the field to do the donkey work should Brighterdaysahead be declared and probably won't run if she doesn't. **Brentford Hope** and **Winter Fog** might try to pick up a little share of the money, while **Golden Ace** has a festival win over Brighterdaysahead from last season and did land the Kingwell, but it was hardly strong form. **Senecia** would be a social runner but might nick a bit of cash given the prize-money goes down to eighth.

VERDICT

I can't remember being less sure about a race that has only four potential winners and I can't see myself having a bet. The hope is that **CONSTITUTION HILL** *bounces back to put up the sort of performance that wowed everyone in the 2022 Supreme and 2023 Champion, but while the signs are good that he's retained all his ability after his many problems, he hasn't yet proved it on the figures. Indeed, in terms of RPRs over the last 12 months, he's only fourth on the list and some 10lb behind* **Brighterdaysahead**

State Man (right) and Irish Point fight out last year's finish

when the mares' allowance is taken into account. The gap is hugely unlikely to be anywhere near that much, if anything at all once Constitution Hill is asked to extend fully, but we won't know that for sure until he is. On the upside, he retains all the swagger in the early stages that has been a feature of the way he races since he first set out on a racecourse. It's quite possible too, perhaps even likely, that Brighterdaysahead will go for the Mares' Hurdle 40 minutes earlier, just like Annie Power, Honeysuckle and Gigginstown's Apple's Jade, who flopped when favourite for this in 2019. All three mares had a Cheltenham Festival win under their belts before taking on the big boys and Brighterdaysahead doesn't have that, having inexplicably been beaten by **Golden Ace** *as a novice last year.* **Lossiemouth** *is a more likely runner, but she's already been beaten by Constitution Hill at Kempton and then took a heavy fall at Leopardstown when deserted by Paul Townend, who rode State Man to success instead. She still has it to prove at 2m, but* **State Man** *doesn't come without worries either, as he made a meal of winning a very weak Champion Hurdle last year and hasn't been in the same all-conquering form as 12 months ago. It's a less than confident vote for the jolly.*

4.40 **Fred Winter Juvenile Handicap Hurdle** ITV/RTV
➤2m½f ➤Premier Handicap ➤£80,000

First run in 2005, this is a fiercely competitive and often wide-open handicap hurdle for four-year-olds only. While the championship event in this division is Friday's Triumph Hurdle, there is often plenty of quality lurking in this race – among last year's placed horses were subsequent winners at Listed level and at the Punchestown festival, as well as the Galway Hurdle runner-up.

LAST YEAR'S WINNER Lark In The Mornin scored at 9-1, becoming the second winner for Joseph O'Brien (after Band Of Outlaws in 2019) and the seventh in a row for Ireland (eighth place was the best Britain could manage last year). He was the second German-bred winner in recent years (after Aramax in 2020). It is also notable that seven French-breds have won in 20 runnings.

FORM Thirteen of the 20 winners had won on one of their last two starts.

WEIGHT AND RATINGS Lark In The Mornin last year became the third winner in four years off a low mark in the 120s (he was rated 122, plus runner-up Eagles Reign was 123 and fourth-placed Harsh, also trained by O'Brien, was 121).

TRAINERS Gordon Elliott and Paul Nicholls have had three winners, as well as several placed horses. O'Brien is a big player with his strong juvenile hurdling team.

BETTING Eight of the last 13 winners were at least 18-1, although that has shifted in recent years (four of the last six were no bigger than 10-1).

ONES TO WATCH Stencil, ten-length runner-up to East India Dock in Cheltenham's Triumph Trial, could well come here for Noel George and Amanda Zetterholm. **Total Look** (Gavin Cromwell), **Willy De Houelle** (Willie Mullins) and O'Brien's **Galileo Dame** and **Naturally Nimble** (a German-bred) are strong Irish possibles.

FRED WINTER JUVENILE HANDICAP HURDLE RESULTS AND TRENDS

	FORM	WINNER	AGE & WGT	OR	SP	TRAINER	BEST RPR LAST 12 MONTHS (RUNS SINCE)
24	263	**Lark In The Mornin**	4 11-0	122-8	9-1	J O'Brien (IRE)	3rd Punchestown maiden hurdle (2m½f) (0)
23	52154	**Jazzy Matty** D, BF	4 10-6	125-2	18-1	G Elliott (IRE)	won Fairyhouse maiden hurdle (2m) (2)
22	6541	**Brazil** D	4 11-9	137-6	10-1	P Roche (IRE)	won Naas novice hurdle (2m) (0)
21	2217	**Jeff Kidder** D	4 10-8	125-4	80-1	N Meade (IRE)	7th Leopardstown Gd 2 novice hurdle (2m) (0)
20	31F31	**Aramax** D	4 11-8	138-6	15-2	G Elliott (IRE)	won Naas novice hurdle (2m) (0)
19	311	**Band Of Outlaws** D	4 11-8	139-5	7-2f	J O'Brien (IRE)	won Naas novice hurdle (2m) (0)
18	127	**Veneer Of Charm** D	4 11-0	129-14	33-1	G Elliott (IRE)	2nd Fairyhouse hurdle (2m) (1)
17	2P614	**Flying Tiger** D	4 11-5	134-2	33-1	N Williams	won Newbury Class 4 hurdle (2m½f) (1)
16	322	**Diego Du Charmil** BF	4 11-1	133-17	13-2	P Nicholls	2nd Enghien hurdle (2m½f) (0)
15	3-421	**Qualando**	4 11-0	131-9	25-1	P Nicholls	4th Auteuil Listed hurdle (2m1½f) (2)

FAVOURITES: -£5.50 **FATE OF FAVOURITES:** 00231P2206 **POSITION OF WINNER IN MARKET:** 0200130473

Key trends
➤Top-three finish in at least one of last two starts, 9/10
➤Three to five hurdle runs, 9/10
➤Had lost maiden tag over hurdles, 8/10
➤Won within last three starts, 8/10
➤Officially rated 125 to 137, 7/10

Other factors
➤Two of the four winners who had run on the Flat had earned an RPR of at least 87; the other six were unraced on the Flat
➤Three winners were French-bred
➤Seven winners were beaten on their first two starts over hurdles

5.20 National Hunt Novices' Handicap Chase RTV
> 3m6f   > £100,000

This is the longest and oldest race at the festival, although five years ago the race distance was reduced to 3m6f and with two fewer fences to jump. There are more big changes this year with the removal of the race's Grade 2 status and its downgrading to a 0-145 novice handicap, plus the traditional stipulation that only amateur jockeys can ride in the race has been removed.

LAST YEAR'S WINNER Following the trend of recent years, there were only seven runners and Corbetts Cross (15-8 second favourite) won from 7-4 favourite Embassy Gardens. It was the growing uncompetitiveness of the race that prompted this year's changes and a bigger field (up to a maximum of 18) will be expected now.

WEIGHT AND RATINGS A recent rise in quality was reflected in the ratings, with most recent winners in the 150s. This will change now that the ratings band has been set at an upper limit of 145.

ONES TO WATCH Gavin Cromwell's **Now Is The Hour** has been the clear ante-post favourite, although the Kim Muir is also a possibility. **Haiti Couleurs** (Rebecca Curtis) and **Transmission** (Neil Mulholland) have good credentials after finishing first and second in a 3m1½f novice handicap chase at Cheltenham in December.

NATIONAL HUNT CHASE RESULTS AND TRENDS

FORMWINNER	AGE & WGT	Adj RPR	SP	TRAINER	BEST RPR LAST 12 MONTHS (RUNS SINCE)
24 -312F **Corbetts Cross** BF	7 11-7	157⁻⁴	15-8	E Mullins (IRE)	won Fairyhouse chase (2m5½f) (2)
23 3-213 **Gaillard Du Mesnil**	7 11-7	167ᵀ	10-11f	W Mullins (IRE)	3rd Gd1 Brown Advisory Nov Chase (3m½f) (4)
22 4-311 **Stattler**	7 11-6	166ᵀ	2-1	W Mullins (IRE)	won Naas Gd3 novice chase (3m1f)(0)
21 -1111 **Galvin** C	7 11-6	167ᵀ	7-2	I Ferguson (IRE)	won Cheltenham Class 2 nov chase (3m½f) (0)
20 2152F **Ravenhill**	10 11-6	156⁻⁸	12-1	G Elliott (IRE)	2nd Listowel hcap chase (3m) (1)
19 12324 **Le Breuil**	7 11-6	155⁻⁹	14-1	B Pauling	3rd Newbury Gd2 novice chase (2m7½f) (2)
18 112BU **Rathvinden**	10 11-6	167ᵀ	9-2	W Mullins (IRE)	2nd Fairyhouse Gd1 novice chase (2m4f) (2)
17 22133 **Tiger Roll** C	7 11-6	159⁻⁶	16-1	G Elliott (IRE)	won Limerick hcap chase (3m) (2)
16 -3P62 **Minella Rocco**	6 11-6	159⁻⁷	8-1	J O'Neill	2nd Ascot Gd2 novice chase (3m) (0)
15 20-75 **Cause Of Causes**	7 11-6	159⁻²	8-1	G Elliott (IRE)	2nd Kim Muir hcap chase (3m1½f) (3)

WINS-RUNS: 5yo 0-1, 6yo 1-15, 7yo 7-66, 8yo 0-40, 9yo 0-9, 10yo 2-6, 12yo 0-1 **FAVOURITES:** -£8.09

TRAINERS IN THIS RACE (w-pl-r): Gordon Elliott 3-2-13, Willie Mullins 3-3-15, Ben Pauling 1-0-5, Emmet Mullins 1-0-1, Paul Nicholls 0-1-4, Gavin Cromwell 0-0-1, Dan Skelton 0-0-1, Nicky Henderson 0-1-5, Rebecca Curtis 0-0-6, Neil Mulholland 0-0-3, Nigel Twiston-Davies 0-0-5

FATE OF FAVOURITES: 045UFU3212 **POSITION OF WINNER IN MARKET:** 3592543212

Key trends
> Hurdles RPR of at least 134, 10/10

> Adjusted RPR of at least 156, 9/10

> Top-two finish in a chase over 3m+, 9/10

> Ran at least four times over fences, 9/10

> Rated within 7lb of RPR top-rated, 8/10

> Top-three finish on last completed start, 8/10

> Aged seven, 7/10

> Had won over at least 3m (hurdles or chases), 7/10

Other factors
> The last two winners to have had less than four chase runs were both trained by Willie Mullins (Back In Focus in 2013 and Stattler in 2022)

PAUL KEALY ON
THE KEY PLAYERS

1.20 Turners Novices' Hurdle

ITV/RTV

➤2m5f ➤Grade 1 ➤£150,000

Willie Mullins is the leading trainer in this race with seven wins and he has another strong candidate in Final Demand, who took over favouritism after his impressive Grade 1 victory at the Dublin Racing Festival. His Racing Post Rating jumped 20lb to a division-leading 154 with that 12-length success, giving Mullins an excellent chance of a fourth Turners in a row. Britain has a serious challenger in the Dan Skelton-trained The New Lion, also an impressive Grade 1 winner in the Challow at Newbury. The Mullins squad also looks set to include Kawaboomga, who is talented but lacks Graded experience, while another to note from the home team is Nigel Twiston-Davies's course-and-distance winner Potters Charm. Some of the others with good Graded form, such as Gordon Elliott's The Yellow Clay, may go elsewhere.

Final Demand

6 b g; Trainer Willie Mullins
Hurdles form 11, best RPR 154
Left-handed 1, best RPR 154
Right-handed 1, best RPR 134

Point winner in March last year who didn't make his debut for Willie Mullins until the end of December at Limerick, where he ran out a deeply impressive 15-length winner from the front. It's always hard to put a level on a maiden hurdle success, but subsequent wins for the second and third suggested it was an above-average race and Final Demand surged to the head of the Turners betting when adding another wide-margin victory to his name in the Grade 1 Nathaniel Lacy & Partners Solicitors Novice Hurdle at the Dublin Racing Festival. That was a bit of a strange race as nothing really managed to get into it from behind, the prominently ridden Final Demand picking off leading pair Wingmen and Mozzies Star (rated just 127) off the home turn and powering away. The runner-up had been beaten almost as far by The Yellow Clay the time before and is clearly not a top dog at Gordon Elliott's, but there was no denying the winner's supremacy and an RPR of 154 puts him at the top of the charts of the likely runners. Since that Leopardstown Grade 1 was upped to 2m6f the winner has never gone on to score in a Cheltenham novice hurdle (last one to do so was Nicanor in 2006 when the race was run over 2m4½f), but that will certainly change at some point and this

might be the year. He's in the Albert Bartlett as well, and is clearly going to stay strongly, but this is the preference.

Going preference Has raced only on yielding to soft or soft

Star rating ✪✪✪✪

The New Lion

6 b g; Trainer Dan Skelton
Hurdles form (left-handed) 111, best RPR 152

Began his career in a bumper at Market Rasen last April, winning handily enough after missing three previous engagements due to unsuitably soft ground, and since then he has quickly developed into the leading British contender for this. After a smooth success on his hurdles debut at Chepstow in October, he had to work a little harder at Newbury the following month (next three home all won since), and that probably didn't prepare us for what he was going to do in the Grade 1 Challow back there in December. Sent off second favourite to the well-touted Regent's Stroll, The New Lion travelled very strongly throughout, led after the last and cruised to a near five-length victory. It was undeniably impressive, although there are warning signs about the form as runner-up Wendigo had been beaten in a maiden at Hexham and had only a Ludlow success to his name, while the third, Bill Joyce, was beaten further next time and Regent's Stroll, back in fourth, was also turned over at a short price next time and is beginning to look like a busted flush. Still, you can only beat what is put in front of you and The New Lion clearly did it with plenty in hand. If the Leopardstown Grade 1 has been a bad guide to Cheltenham novice winners then the same is true of the Challow, though, and no winner has gone on to take this race, although Wichita Lineman did win the Albert Bartlett in 2007.

Going preference Three times a non-runner due to soft or heavy ground, but handles soft as well as quicker

Star rating ✪✪✪✪

The Yellow Clay *(right)*
6 b g; Trainer Gordon Elliott
Hurdles form 1111, best RPR 148
Left-handed 111, best RPR 148
Right-handed 1, best RPR 116
Cheltenham form (bumper) 6, best RPR 125
At the festival 13 Mar 2024 Prominent, weakened from over 1f out, finished sixth, beaten 12 lengths by Jasmin De Vaux in Champion Bumper

Very useful bumper horse who won two of five starts in that sphere and finished sixth in the Champion Bumper at Cheltenham, but has done an awful lot better since being stepped up in trip over hurdles. He has won all four starts, including an eight-length romp in the Lawlor's of Naas with Final Demand's victim Wingmen three lengths further back in third. Trainer Gordon Elliott nominated this race after that January success, but the market has been shouting very loudly for the Albert Bartlett since, so he's dealt with in more detail in Friday's section.

Going preference Best form on soft but acts on anything

Star rating ✪✪✪

Kawaboomga
5 b g; Trainer Willie Mullins
Hurdles form 321, best RPR 136
Left-handed 32, best RPR 127
Right-handed 1, best RPR 136

Bumper winner in France who finished third on his hurdles debut there in March and then second to stablemate Kopek Des Bordes on his Irish debut for Willie Mullins at Leopardstown just after Christmas. Although beaten just under three lengths, he was no

match for the winner, who did plenty wrong (pulled hard, jumped poorly), but he did get off the mark in useful style at Fairyhouse a month later. That's still only maiden form, though, and it leaves him with a lot to find with the principals.

Going preference Not much to go on, but okay on yielding and soft

Star rating ✪✪

James's Gate
8 b g; Trainer Martin Brassil
Hurdles form 4311, best RPR 136
Left-handed 41, best RPR 136
Right-handed 31, best RPR 130
Cheltenham form (bumper) 3, best RPR 133
At the festival 16 Mar 2022 Took keen hold, chased leader, pushed along over 2f out, ridden and kept on from over 1f out, finished third, beaten six and a quarter lengths by Facile Vega in Champion Bumper

Third to Facile Vega in the 2022 Champion Bumper, but then missed more than a year and hardly suggested he would be a Grade 1 hurdles performer in just two outings in the 2023-24 season, finishing fourth in a maiden at Leopardstown and then a 24-length third of four to Mystical Power in the Moscow Flyer. However, he has got his act together this season, winning a maiden at Punchestown in December and following up in a novice by three-quarters of a length, albeit in receipt of 3lb from a rival rated just 134. He was going to run in a handicap off his mark of 136 at the DRF but came out due to a cough and it remains to be seen where he goes next. Not quite sure why he's single figures in places for this as he has huge amounts to find.

Going preference Seems to act on anything

Star rating ✪

Potters Charm
6 b g; Trainer Nigel Twiston-Davies
Hurdles form (left-handed) 11112, best RPR 146
Cheltenham form 112, best RPR 146

Wide-margin winner of a heavy-ground bumper last spring for Nigel Twiston-Davies, having been nearest at the finish when second in a point the previous November, and has quickly developed into a high-class novice.

He made steady progress initially, scoring at Worcester on his debut in September and then Cheltenham the following month, where he beat Gordon Elliott's Minella Sixo (twice placed in Graded company since) by two and a quarter lengths. Potters Charm then announced himself as a big-league player by slamming the well-backed odds-on shot Valgrand by an easy 11 lengths back at Cheltenham in a Grade 2 Albert Bartlett Trial (though over the Turners distance) in November. The runner-up has admittedly gone backwards since, but Potters Charm didn't as he dropped back to 2m1f for the Grade 1 Formby at Aintree and ran out a two-and-a-quarter-length winner, albeit giving the impression that 2m1f around there was way too short. The original plan was to head straight back to Cheltenham for this, but connections eyed what they thought was an easy pot back there on Trials day instead, and paid for it with an eight-and-a-half-length defeat at the hands of 9-1 chance Sixmilebridge. That was undoubtedly a backward step even if he was conceding 5lb to the winner, but it's hard to believe he was the same horse who won there in November as he looked beaten a long way out, and was apparently very quiet for a day or two afterwards. It was almost certainly the wrong move to go again after having a harder race than it looked at Aintree, but at least there is the best part of seven weeks to freshen him up. The yard's The New One was beaten on Trials day before going on to win this in 2013, and Potters Charm, rated easily their best novice since, deserves more respect than he's getting from the layers on his best form.

Going preference Has won on anything from good to heavy

Star rating ✪✪✪

Sixmilebridge
6 b g; Trainer Fergal O'Brien
Hurdles form 2111, best RPR 145
Left-handed 21, best RPR 145
Right-handed 11, best RPR 130
Cheltenham form (all) 01, best RPR 145
At the festival 13 Mar 2024 In touch with leaders, lost position over 3f out, soon weakened, finished 17th, beaten 44 lengths by Jasmin De Vaux in Champion Bumper

Bumper winner for Ben Pauling but finished tailed off in the big one at Cheltenham, after which he was sent for a wind operation and moved by his owners to Fergal O'Brien. Beaten at odds of 11-10 on his hurdles debut at Stratford in October, he then won a couple of hurdles at Leicester and Huntingdon, being sent off at odds-on each time and winning well without really setting the world alight. It was a different story on Trials day at Cheltenham, though, as he powered away from Potters Charm for an eight-and-a-half-length win, which puts him firmly in the picture, even if there's the suspicion that the runner-up wasn't quite at his best. He's also in the Supreme, but O'Brien rates him a three-miler over fences for the future, so there's surely next to no chance he goes there, and while he's qualified for the EBF Final at Sandown, he'll have ruined his mark for that.

Going preference Has won on good to soft and heavy

Star rating ✪✪

OTHERS TO CONSIDER
A surprisingly healthy 52 entries remained after the final scratching stage in February, although they included the likes of **Kopek Des Bordes** and **Jet Blue**, who are surely heading to the Supreme and Albert Bartlett respectively. Henry de Bromhead's **The Big Westerner** was an impressive enough winner from Mozzies Sister in a Grade 2 at Limerick but over 2m7f and she's more likely to head

down the Albert Bartlett route as well. Warren Greatrex's **Good And Clever** has finished third in a couple of Grade 1s but doesn't seem to have the pace for 2m, so could well step up in trip here, although he'll also need to improve in a big way as well. **Fingle Bridge** was left in by Olly Murphy after his February defeat of Regent's Stroll, but it was strongly hinted that Aintree would be the plan. **Bill Joyce** needs to improve markedly on his Challow and Cheltenham runs, while there's the usual stack of Willie Mullins contenders to consider outside of his big guns, the pick of whom might well be **Kappa Jy Pyke** (also in Supreme), who ought to have no problem with a step up in trip and who impressed Paul Townend when scoring at Punchestown on his second maiden hurdle outing.

VERDICT

*There's no doubt **Final Demand** and **The New Lion** are the ones to beat, but they both won races last time that have routinely seen the winners fail at Cheltenham. That is surely no more than a long-term statistical blip, but there are reasons to question what they beat, especially The New Lion, with the form having taken some knocks. Of course, they may simply be exceptional winners of average races, as that does happen, but I'm happy to give **POTTERS CHARM** another chance at an each-way price. He looked the real deal when scoring at Cheltenham in November and may have had a harder race than it looked when winning the Formby at Aintree on a drop in trip that didn't seem to suit. He's worth a chance to prove his Trials day defeat wasn't him at his best.*

TURNERS NOVICES' HURDLE RESULTS AND TRENDS

	FORM WINNER	AGE & WGT	Adj RPR	SP	TRAINER	BEST RPR LAST 12 MONTHS (RUNS SINCE)
24	1-211 Ballyburn	6 11-7	164ᵀ	1-2f	W Mullins (IRE)	won Leopardstown Gd1 novice hurdle (2m) (0)
23	1-11 Impaire Et Passe	5 11-7	158-4	5-2	W Mullins (IRE)	won Punchestown Gd2 novice hurdle (2m) (0)
22	1-311 Sir Gerhard C	7 11-7	159ᵀ	8-11f	W Mullins (IRE)	won Leopardstown Gd1 novice hurdle (2m) (0)
21	1-211 Bob Olinger	6 11-7	159-5	6-4f	H de Bromhead (IRE)	won Naas Gd1 novice hurdle (2m4f) (0)
20	1-111 Envoi Allen C	6 11-7	161ᵀ	4-7f	G Elliott (IRE)	won Fairyhouse Gd1 novice hurdle (2m) (1)
19	-11d11 City Island	6 11-7	152-5	8-1	M Brassil (IRE)	won Naas novice hurdle (2m3f) (0)
18	1-111 Samcro	6 11-7	161ᵀ	8-11f	G Elliott (IRE)	won Navan Gd3 novice hurdle (2m4f) (1)
17	5-211 Willoughby Court D	6 11-7	154-5	14-1	B Pauling	won Warwick Gd2 novice hurdle (2m5f) (0)
16	1-111 Yorkhill	6 11-7	159-8	3-1	W Mullins (IRE)	won Sandown Gd1 novice hurdle (2m) (0)
15	-1142 Windsor Park	6 11-7	154-3	9-2	D Weld (IRE)	2nd Leopardstown Gd1 novice hurdle (2m2f) (0)

WINS-RUNS: 5yo 1-35, 6yo 8-63, 7yo 1-13 **FAVOURITES:** -£0.98

TRAINERS IN THIS RACE (w-pl-r): Willie Mullins 4-8-30, Gordon Elliott 2-2-9, Ben Pauling 1-1-6, Henry de Bromhead 1-0-4, Martin Brassil 1-0-2, Nigel Twiston-Davies 0-0-2, Alan King 0-2-3, Dan Skelton 0-1-5, Paul Nicholls 0-0-3, Fergal O'Brien 0-0-6, Nicky Henderson 0-1-9, Warren Greatrex 0-0-2, Rebecca Curtis 0-0-1, Olly Murphy 0-0-1

FATE OF FAVOURITES: 3221P11161 **POSITION OF WINNER IN MARKET:** 3251411121

Key trends

▶Started career in Irish points or bumpers, ten winners in last ten runnings

▶Two or three hurdle runs, 10/10

▶Rated within 5lb of RPR top-rated, 9/10

▶Adjusted RPR of at least 154, 9/10

▶Won at least 50 per cent of hurdle runs, 9/10

▶First or second in all hurdle runs, 9/10

▶Won a Graded hurdle, 9/10

▶Scored over at least 2m4f, 8/10

▶Aged six, 8/10

Other factors

▶Five of the last ten favourites have obliged and in that period only Willoughby Court's SP (14-1 in 2017) was bigger than 8-1

2.00 Brown Advisory Novices' Chase ITV/RTV
➤ 3m½f ➤ Grade 1 ➤ £200,000

Three of last year's festival winners are in the reckoning for this Grade 1 staying novice chase, which in terms of competitiveness may be the race that benefits most from the removal of the 2m4f Grade 1. Ante-post favourite Ballyburn is one of those who may have gone for the old Turners, given that he won the Grade 1 novice hurdle over the intermediate distance last year, but he will have to move up in trip now. The Willie Mullins-trained seven-year-old has strong form credentials after his Grade 1 win over 2m5½f at the Dublin Racing Festival, even if questions remain about his jumping. The other festival winners from last year are Better Days Ahead (Martin Pipe Handicap Hurdle) and Stellar Story (Albert Bartlett Novices' Hurdle), who are both trained by Gordon Elliott and are closely matched on their February meeting in a Grade 2 at Navan, which Better Days Ahead won by a neck. Dancing City and Lecky Watson, third and fifth behind Stellar Story in the Albert Bartlett, are also in the mix for Mullins, while Elliott's challenge could be bolstered by Croke Park, runner-up to Ballyburn at the DRF. Nicky Henderson has the chief home hopes in Jango Baie and Jingko Blue.

Ballyburn
7 b g; Trainer Willie Mullins
Chase form 121, best RPR 160
Left-handed 1, best RPR 160
Right-handed 12, best RPR 158
Cheltenham form (hurdles) 1, best RPR 166
At the festival 13 Mar 2024 Took keen hold, raced in second, led after 2 out, shaken up and 6 lengths ahead last, easily, won Gallagher Novices' Hurdle by 13 lengths from Jimmy Du Seuil

Superstar novice hurdler who put up officially the best-ever performance by a winner of what last year was the Gallagher Novices' Hurdle, scoring by 13 lengths from stablemate Jimmy Du Seuil. He was expected during the off-season to be prepared for the Turners' Novices' Chase this term, but those plans were thrown up in the air by the powers that be at Cheltenham deciding to bin that race and bring back the novice handicap chase instead. That left connections in a quandary, as the only choices were the Arkle and Brown Advisory, and while he'd won easily in Grade 1 company over 2m as a hurdler, his pedigree was telling everyone he's a 3m chaser. It didn't help that the bookmakers made him favourite for both, but Ballyburn started out being prepared for the Arkle until his run against Sir Gino at Kempton over Christmas

– a month after a straightforward success at 2-13 at Punchestown – forced a rethink. There he was continually outjumped by the Nicky Henderson-trained five-year-old, who won in a 'canter' by seven and a half lengths. It was still far from a bad run from a horse who was conceding 6lb to a dual Grade 1 winner over hurdles, but Ballyburn didn't jump like a speed chaser, so going up in distance was the only option. He did that on his next start in the 2m5½f Ladbrokes Novice Chase at the DRF, where despite racing keenly he stayed on for a five-length victory over Croke Park. That gives him the best form and he should learn to settle now he's being trained for longer distances, while travelling at a more sedate pace certainly helped him in the jumping department. That said, he doesn't look an absolute natural (reportedly had several intensive schooling sessions in the run-up to Leopardstown) and, while he definitely goes there as the one to beat, he doesn't look quite as invincible as he did as a novice hurdler. Sir Gino's absence from the Arkle has probably increased his prospects of going back in trip, but not by a lot.

Going preference Acts on any ground
Star rating ✪✪✪✪✪

Dancing City

8 ch g; Trainer Willie Mullins
Chase form 11, best RPR 149
Left-handed 1, best RPR 149
Right-handed 1, best RPR 139
Cheltenham form (hurdles) 3, best RPR 144
At the festival 15 Mar 2024 Prominent, ridden and went third approaching last, hit last, soon no extra, finished third, beaten seven and a quarter lengths by Stellar Story in Albert Bartlett Novices' Hurdle

Had a superb novice season over hurdles last term, causing a 16-1 shock in his first Grade 1 at the DRF but then proving it to be no fluke by finishing third in the Albert Bartlett and winning at both Aintree and Punchestown. He has done everything that has been asked of him over fences too, first winning his beginners' chase at Punchestown in December and then taking a Grade 3 at Naas at the end of January. He won that comfortably enough by three and a half lengths from the lightly raced Bioluminescence, but with only five runners it wasn't the deepest of races. That said, he jumped really well in the main (got a bit high at a couple, but nothing to worry about) and that will stand him in good stead for the tougher challenges ahead. It looks like he'll be at least as good over fences as he was over hurdles and that puts him firmly in the picture, albeit his odds are on the short side in relation to what he has achieved.

Going preference Comparable form on good/yielding and heavy
Star rating ✪✪✪

Better Days Ahead

7 b g; Trainer Gordon Elliott
Chase form (left-handed) 121, best RPR 152
Cheltenham form 01, best RPR 147
At the festival 15 Mar 2023 Always towards rear, finished 16th, beaten 24 lengths by A Dream To Share in Champion Bumper
15 Mar 2024 Midfield, headway 7th, prominent 3 out, ridden after 2 out, went third approaching last, led run-in, kept on well, won Martin Pipe Handicap Hurdle by a length and a half from Waterford Whispers

Went down the handicapping route over hurdles at last season's Cheltenham Festival, winning the biggest plot race of the meeting, the Martin Pipe, by a length and a half from

Dancing City: Grade 3 winner at Naas on his second chase start

Waterford Whispers, with the first six home from a field of 21 being the first six in the betting. The Martin Pipe has a rich history of producing top-class staying chasers (think Galopin Des Champs, Banbridge, Don Poli, Sir Des Champs), so much was expected of Better Days Ahead over fences and he's getting there slowly. A four-length scorer from Supreme Novices' Hurdle winner Slade Steel on his chase debut at Navan in November, he then failed to quite get to grips with stablemate Croke Park in the Grade 1 Racing Post Long Distance Novice Chase at Leopardstown in December, failing by a head to get up. After that it was his turn to hold on, this time by a neck from another stablemate, Stellar Story, in a Grade 2 at Navan in early February. That doesn't quite tell the story, though, as the runner-up, who was conceding 5lb, wasn't vigorously ridden until after the last. Still, he's going the right way, and that will have put him spot on.

Going preference Acts on any but goes very well on soft/heavy
Star rating ✪✪✪

Croke Park

7 b g; Trainer Gordon Elliott
Chase form 1112, best RPR 152
Left-handed 12, best RPR 152
Right-handed 11, best RPR 148

Won his first two novice hurdles for Gordon Elliott last season, but then made no show in Grade 1 company in January at Navan and at Aintree in April. After a break he had to work hard enough to get off the mark in a four-runner beginners' chase at Fairyhouse in November, but finished with blood in both nostrils. That hardly prepared anyone for what he was going to do next and he was sent off as the 22-1 outsider of five for the Grade 1 Bar One Drinmore Novice Chase at Fairyhouse in December, but won it by a neck from Heart Wood, with even-money favourite Firefox just a short head away in third. Croke Park went on to prove that was no fluke, though, by taking the Grade 1 Racing Post Long Distance Novice Chase by a head from Better Days Ahead at Leopardstown, and he was far from disgraced when seen off

by Ballyburn over a shorter trip at the DRF. He's compiling a pretty good CV and, while he needs more to trouble Ballyburn, there's no reason why he won't continue to progress.

Going preference Has won on heavy, best form on better ground
Star rating ✪✪

Lecky Watson

7 ch g; Trainer Willie Mullins
Chase form 11, best RPR 154
Left-handed 1, best RPR 137
Right-handed 1, best RPR 154
Cheltenham form (hurdles) 45, best RPR 142
At the festival 15 Mar 2023 In touch with leaders on outer, shaken up 2f out, ridden over 1f out, disputed lead when hampered inside final furlong, soon lost ground, no impression final 110yds, finished fourth, beaten five and a half lengths by A Dream To Share in Champion Bumper
15 Mar 2024 Midfield, hit 8th, ridden after 2 out, no impression approaching last, finished fifth, beaten six and a half lengths by Stellar Story in Albert Bartlett Novices' Hurdle

Good efforts to be placed in a couple of 2m-2m4f Graded novice hurdles at Navan and Naas last winter, but appeared to have his limitations exposed in the spring, finishing fifth in the Albert Bartlett and occupying the same spot at Punchestown. However, he has made fair progress in two outings over fences this term, beating Slade Steel (was second to him over hurdles at Navan) by a length and a quarter on his debut and enjoying a cosy eight-length win from Down Memory Lane in a Grade 3 at Punchestown next time. He earned an RPR of 154 there, which puts him in the picture for sure, but that can only be a tentative figure as there were four runners, he set a steady pace and still didn't jump particularly well. This will provide a much sterner test of his jumping and he needs to satisfy the stamina question too.

Going preference Best form on soft, can go on quicker
Star rating ✪✪

Jango Baie

6 b g; Trainer Nicky Henderson
Chase form 12, best RPR 158
Left-handed 1, best RPR 157

Right-handed 1, best RPR 158
Cheltenham form 1, best RPR 157

Fortunate winner of last season's Grade 1 Formby Novices' Hurdle at Aintree thanks to the heavy fall of Farren Glory, but showed better form afterwards upped in trip, notably when a slightly unlucky second back at Aintree in a Grade 3 2m4f handicap at the Grand National meeting, staying on strongly after being hampered. He took that form to a new level again on his chase debut, making it at Cheltenham, which is rare enough for a Nicky Henderson-trained horse over fences. There he was receiving 8lb from the more experienced Springwell Bay, but he won with seemingly tons in hand from a horse who would run away with a Cheltenham handicap (by nine lengths) off a mark of 145 next time. Jango Baie just failed to double his Grade 1 haul in the Scilly Isles Novices' Chase at Sandown next time, going down by a short head to the promising Handstands after a sustained duel from two out. With the pair pulling 17 lengths clear of the third, the run confirmed both as very useful performers. He's another who would no doubt have been heading straight for the old Turners if it still existed, but it's this race, the Arkle or Aintree now. While there's every chance he'll stay 3m, connections have another one in the same colours who already does. Given this one runs so well at Aintree, don't be surprised if that's where he goes.

Going preference No obvious preference
Star rating ✪✪

Stellar Story
8 b g; Trainer Gordon Elliott
Chase form (left-handed) 142, best RPR 153
Left-handed 42, best RPR 153
Right-handed 1, best RPR 136
Cheltenham form (hurdles) 1, best RPR 151
At the festival 15 Mar 2024 Raced in second, challenging 2 out, ridden and outpaced approaching last, 4 lengths down when overjumped last, kept on well and led final strides, won Albert Bartlett Novices' Hurdle by a head from The Jukebox Man

Looked to have limitations exposed from an early stage over hurdles, but not the first horse to cause a shock when it mattered in the Albert Bartlett at the festival and roared home at odds of 33-1, turning a four-length deficit into a head victory at the line over The Jukebox Man. His fourth to Dancing City at Punchestown after that was a reasonable enough effort and he was always going to go chasing this season. There are way too many Graded chases in Ireland, evidenced by the fact Stellar Story has run in three, faced only nine rivals in total and come up against just three horses who are not in the same stable (one of them a 300-1 shot), but he did well in two of them. His sole success came by a short head over stablemate Search For Glory on his debut at Punchestown in the three-runner Grade 2 Florida Pearl, but next time some sloppy jumps in the fog contributed to a tailed-off last of four in the Racing Post Long Distance Novice Chase. However, he fared much better next time at Navan in February, just failing to get up against Better Days Ahead, to whom he was conceding 5lb. Indeed, there were many who thought a more vigorous ride from Danny Gilligan from the second-last may have made the difference, so he's arguably a shade bigger in the betting than he should be in relation to his fellow festival winner. His record strongly suggests he's going to need soft ground, though.

Going preference Looks a case of the softer the better
Star rating ✪✪✪

Gorgeous Tom
7 b g; Trainer Henry de Bromhead
Chase form 1F14, best RPR 147
Left-handed 1F, best RPR 125
Right-handed 14, best RPR 147

Slow-burner over hurdles who needed four attempts in maiden company before getting off the mark at Naas in April, but then beat the useful Mistergif at Punchestown the following month. Having made no show when only 7-1 for the Galway Hurdle in August, he was switched to chasing later that month, winning a small race at Wexford. After that he went to Tipperary and was made 5-4 favourite for a Grade 3 only to fall at the ninth, but he made amends for that by winning another one at Cork in November albeit only by beating the horse he'd already taken care of on his debut (Monbeg Park, rated 133). Although only fourth of five in the Grade 1 Drinmore next time, Gorgeous Tom looked like being dropped completely at the second-last but ended up rattling home to be beaten only a length and was well in front by the time the jockeys had pulled them all up. That suggested he's going to be well worth a try at 3m, especially given his dam is a half-sister to Foxhunter winner and Grand National runner-up Cappa Bleu. Has had the required four runs over fences (only three are needed for the novice handicaps), so it'll be interesting to see if he receives a handicap entry in one of the longer races.

Going preference Has won on heavy, improvement has come on quicker ground
Star rating ✪✪

Jingko Blue
6 b g; Trainer Nicky Henderson
Chase form 11F, best RPR 150
Left-handed 11, best RPR 150
Right-handed F
Cheltenham form (hurdles) P
At the festival 13 Mar 2024 Prominent and disputing third, hit fluent 4th, mistake and jockey lost iron briefly 5th, dropped to rear 3 out, soon weakened, pulled up last in Gallagher Novices' Hurdle won by Ballyburn

In the same ownership as Jango Baie and one of the few Henderson horses who got a run at last season's festival. However, he was one of the ones who performed so poorly (pulled up in Ballyburn's Gallagher) that it led to others being pulled out. That experience hasn't appeared to have done him any harm, though, as he has added to his point win and two hurdles successes by going 2-3 over fences. On the first occasion he made light of a handicap mark of 140 by cruising to a nine-and-a-half-length success over 2m4f at Uttoxeter, while at Windsor's Winter Million meeting he proved two and a quarter lengths too good for Lowry's Bar over 3m. That was only a three-runner race, but the runner-up had been seriously progressive in handicaps before that and Jingko Blue dealt with him quite comfortably in the end, although a late mistake didn't help the runner-up. An early unseat in the Reynoldstown (seemed to lose

footing on landing rather than belting fence) was hardly an ideal prep, but at least he won't have had a hard race and he could still be the Henderson runner to end up here.

Going preference Has run only on good to soft or soft
Star rating ✪✪

OTHERS TO CONSIDER
While only ten stood their ground for the Arkle once the scratchings were made, there's a chance of a more competitive heat here, with 23 sill in the field. The Willie Mullins-trained **Quai De Bourbon** is worth a mention given he's been to Cheltenham and was an excellent third in the Martin Pipe, although he's started slowly over fences, winning his beginners' chase at the second time of asking, and needs to prove his stamina. **Search For Glory** has been second and third in Graded races following his debut chase win, although he was beaten a long way when fancied for a handicap at the DRF and he may go down that route again. As in the Arkle, **Springwell Bay** has form considerably better than most in the field after his runaway handicap win at Cheltenham, but it was at 2m4f and he didn't look so convincing when behind Hyland at the longer trip earlier in the season. **Champ Kiely** was beaten a long way by Ballyburn at the DRF, but that was his second run after 20 months off the track and he may well have bounced. His other form suggests he's better than that, albeit he needs to find some more at the age of nine. The Changing Man finally got his head in front in a chase when romping home in a seriously depleted Reynoldstown at Ascot, but the favourite unseated early, the original second favourite didn't run and the third favourite was beaten by halfway, so it's hard to know what he achieved in beating the 127-rated Leave Of Absence, even if he won by 24 lengths.

VERDICT
*There's no doubt last year's Gallagher winner **Ballyburn** is the one to beat, but he doesn't boast the aura of invincibility he had 12 months ago, and on RPRs over fences he's only just ahead of **Jango Baie***

BROWN ADVISORY NOVICES' CHASE RESULTS AND TRENDS

FORM WINNER	AGE & WGT	Adj RPR	SP	TRAINER	BEST RPR LAST 12 MONTHS (RUNS SINCE)
24 2-211 **Fact To File**	7 11-7	171ᵀ	8-13f	W Mullins (IRE)	won Leopardstown Gd 1 nov chase (2m5½f) (0)
23 2-011 **The Real Whacker** CD	7 11-7	167⁻³	8-1	P Neville	won Cheltenham Gd 2 novice chase (2m4½f) (0)
22 -1111 **L'Homme Presse** C	7 11-4	173⁻⁴	9-4f	V Williams	won Sandown Gd1 novice chase (2m4f) (0)
21 1-111 **Monkfish** C, D	7 11-4	180ᵀ	1-4f	W Mullins (IRE)	won Leopardstown Gd1 nov chase (2m5½f) (0)
20 1-11F **Champ** D, BF	8 11-4	169⁻⁵	4-1	N Henderson	Fell Cheltenham Gd 2 novice chase (2m4½f) (0)
19 12-22 **Topofthegame** D	7 11-4	170ᵀ	4-1	P Nicholls	2nd Kempton Gd 1 novice chase (3m) (0)
18 13112 **Presenting Percy** C, D, BF	7 11-4	171⁻¹	5-2f	P Kelly (IRE)	won Fairyhouse hcap chase (3m5f) (1)
17 -21F1 **Might Bite** C, D	8 11-4	175ᵀ	7-2f	N Henderson	Fell Kempton Gd 1 novice chase (3m) (1)
16 4F121 **Blaklion** C, D	7 11-4	172⁻¹	8-1	N Twiston-Davies	won Wetherby Gd 2 novice chase (3m) (0)
15 1-211 **Don Poli** C, D	6 11-4	165⁻²	13-8f	W Mullins (IRE)	won Leopardstown Gd1 novice chase (3m) (0)

WINS-RUNS: 5yo 0-1, 6yo 1-17, 7yo 7-53, 8yo 2-18, 9yo 0-2 **FAVOURITES:** £6.74

TRAINERS IN THIS RACE (w-pl-r): Willie Mullins 3-5-19, Nicky Henderson 2-2-10, Nigel Twiston-Davies 1-0-3, Gordon Elliott 0-2-7, Olly Murphy 0-0-1, Rebecca Curtis 0-0-1, Henry de Bromhead 0-3-6, P Hobbs & J White 0-0-1

FATE OF FAVOURITES: 1311331121 **POSITION OF WINNER IN MARKET:** 1311331141

and **Springwell Bay**. It's quite possible that neither of those two will run given doubts over their stamina and, while Ballyburn has yet to try 3m and was keen when upped to 2m5½f at Leopardstown, he's bred to get it and will surely settle down once he's trained for long distances. I have this feeling he's not going to be quite so good over fences for some reason, though, largely because I think he finds jumping them a bit of an effort. While he has a huge engine, this race may be a little more open than the market suggests. The Mullins second-string **Dancing City** is likeable, of course, but he's desperately short given a peak RPR of 149 in two chase outings and a top effort of 151 over hurdles. That chase figure puts him behind a few here, including **Lecky Watson**, **Better Days Ahead**, **Croke Park** and **Jingko Blue**. **STELLAR STORY** is another one too, as he was quite an eyecatcher when second to Better Days Ahead given he wasn't asked for his full effort until after the last and was conceding 5lb to the neck winner. His record suggests he's going to need very soft ground, but if he gets it I can see last year's Albert Bartlett winner roaring up the hill again to grab at least a slice of the action. I half-expect the stoutly bred **Gorgeous Tom** to go for a handicap, possibly the National Hunt Chase, but if he comes here I'd be tempted with an each-way bet on him too, as he'll leave his other form well behind when he gets a test of stamina.

Key trends
- Rated within 5lb of RPR top-rated, 10/10
- Contested a Graded chase, 10/10 (six won)
- Top-two finish last time out, 9/10 (exception fell)
- Six to 12 hurdle and chase runs, 9/10
- Aged seven or eight, 9/10
- Adjusted RPR of at least 167, 9/10
- Ran three to five times over fences, 8/10

Other factors
- Of the combined 40 chase starts of winners, only 2016 scorer Blaklion had finished outside the first three when completing (five had fallen)
- Six winners had previously run at the festival – two in the Albert Bartlett (P1), one in the Turners (2), one in the Martin Pipe (1), one in the Pertemps Final (1) one in the Coral Cup (2) and one in the Champion Bumper (2)

2.40 Coral Cup Handicap Hurdle ITV/RTV
➤2m5f ➤Premier Handicap ➤£110,000

This highly competitive handicap hurdle was introduced in 1993 and regularly attracts a maximum field (currently set at 26).

LAST YEAR'S WINNER Langer Dan became the first dual winner of the race when scoring at 13-2 for Dan Skelton. He was 9-1 the previous year, but even with his back-to-back successes there have been just five winners at single-figure odds since 2004.

FORM Eleven of the last 15 winners had won or finished second last time out.

WEIGHT AND RATINGS Langer Dan carried 11st 8lb to victory last year off a mark of 141 (in 2023 he won off the same mark carrying 11st 4lb). He made it six winners in the past decade rated in the narrow 138-143 band.

AGE This race tends to suit younger, less exposed types, and the number of hurdles runs is a key factor. Only four of the last 17 winners were into double figures.

TRAINERS Nicky Henderson is the most successful trainer with four wins.

BETTING Only three favourites (outright or joint) have won in 31 runnings.

ONES TO WATCH Skelton has another likely type in **Be Aware**, rated 137 after finishing second in the Greatwood and third in the Ladbrokes Handicap Hurdle at Ascot. Ben Pauling's **Fiercely Proud**, who went up to 137 after winning the Ascot race, is also in the picture. Gordon Elliott's **The Enabler** could get in on a low mark.

CORAL CUP RESULTS AND TRENDS

FORM WINNER	AGE & WGT	OR	SP	TRAINER	BEST RPR LAST 12 MONTHS (RUNS SINCE)
24 -6P90 **Langer Dan** CD	8 11-8	141⁻¹	13-2	D Skelton	won Coral Cup hcap hurdle (2m5f) **(4)**
23 1-378 **Langer Dan**	7 11-4	141ᵀ	9-1	D Skelton	won Aintree Gd3 hcap hurdle (2m4f) **(3)**
22 F1P83 **Commander Of Fleet** D	8 11-5	152⁻⁴	50-1	G Elliott (IRE)	won Navan hcap hurdle (3m½f) **(3)**
21 75441 **Heaven Help Us** C	7 10-2	138⁻⁴	33-1	P Hennessy (IRE)	won Leopardstown hcap hurdle (2m2f) **(0)**
20 21/51 **Dame De Compagnie** C, D	7 10-12	140ᵀ	5-1f	N Henderson	won Cheltenham Class 2 hcap hdl (2m4½f) **(0)**
19 144-P **William Henry** C, D	9 11-10	151⁻⁶	28-1	N Henderson	4th Ayr Class 2 hcap hurdle (2m5½f) **(1)**
18 115-0 **Bleu Berry**	7 11-2	143⁻⁵	20-1	W Mullins (IRE)	won Fairyhouse Gd2 novice hurdle (2m) **(2)**
17 48124 **Supasundae**	7 11-4	148⁻²	16-1	J Harrington (IRE)	won Punchestown hurdle (2m4f) **(2)**
16 P-421 **Diamond King**	8 11-3	149⁻⁵	12-1	G Elliott (IRE)	won Punchestown hurdle (2m4f) **(0)**
15 1-31 **Aux Ptits Soins**	5 10-7	139⁻⁴	9-1	P Nicholls	won Auteuil hurdle (2m1½f) **(0)**

WINS-RUNS: 5yo 1-37, 6yo 0-66, 7yo 5-68, 8yo 3-44, 9yo 1-19, 10yo 0-14 **FAVOURITES:** -£4.00

FATE OF FAVOURITES: 3004710PP0 **POSITION OF WINNER IN MARKET:** 2660010053

Key trends

➤Aged seven or eight, 9/10

➤Not run for at least 32 days, 8/10

➤Won between 2m2f and 2m6f over hurdles, 8/10

➤Carried at least 10st 12lb, 8/10

➤Officially rated 138 to 149, 8/10

➤No more than four runs that season, 7/10

➤No more than nine hurdle runs, 7/10

➤Won a race earlier in the season, 6/10 (four won last time out)

Other factors

➤The three winners to have had more than nine hurdle runs came in the last three runnings – Commander Of Fleet in 2022 (13 hurdle runs) and Langer Dan in the last two years (16 and 21)

3.20 Glenfarclas Cross Country Handicap Chase ITV/RTV
▶3m5½f   ▶Limited handicap   ▶£75,000

This unusual event, introduced when the festival expanded to four days in 2005, began as a handicap but was changed to a conditions race in 2016. Now it reverts back to a handicap, although with a 19lb weight range in an effort to attract high-quality chasers. Last year's race was abandoned after heavy rain made parts of the cross-country course unraceable.

IRELAND v BRITAIN Ireland has won 16 of the 19 runnings. Enda Bolger dominated in the early years when it was a handicap but he was joined on five winners by Gordon Elliott, who took charge after the change to a conditions race. Philip Hobbs is the only trainer to have won for Britain, with Balthazar King in 2012 and 2014 (both when it was a handicap), and Easysland scored for France in 2020.

ONES TO WATCH The cross-country handicaps at Cheltenham's pre-Christmas meetings may become more of a pointer now. Nicky Henderson's **Mister Coffey** finished runner-up in both, on the second occasion to the Gavin Cromwell-trained **Stumptown**, who has long been ante-post favourite for this. Cromwell also has **Vanillier**, while Elliott's classy pair **Galvin** and **Delta Work** will enter calculations.

CROSS COUNTRY RESULTS AND TRENDS

FORM	WINNER		AGE & WGT	OR	SP	TRAINER	BEST RPR LAST 12 MONTHS (RUNS SINCE)
24	Abandoned						
23	3-136 Delta Work	CD	10 11-7	173-2	11-10f	G Elliott (IRE)	won Cheltenham cross-country chase (3m6f) **(3)**
22	3-466 Delta Work	C	9 11-4	175-1	5-2f	G Elliott (IRE)	4th Down Royal Gd1 chase (3m) (2)
21	52-P6 Tiger Roll	CD	11 11-4	178-3	9-2	D Foster (IRE)	2nd Cheltenham cross-country chase (3m6f) (1)
20	-1111 Easysland	CD	6 11-4	166-18	3-1	D Cottin (FR)	won Cheltenham cross-country chase (3m6f) **(1)**
19	11-41 Tiger Roll	CD	9 11-4	159T	5-4f	G Elliott (IRE)	won Grand National hcap chase (4m2½f) (2)
18	P-2P5 Tiger Roll	C	8 11-4	150-8	7-1	G Elliott (IRE)	won Cheltenham Gd2 NH Chase (4m) (4)
17	-5P05 Cause Of Causes	C	9 11-4	142-3	4-1	G Elliott (IRE)	won Kim Muir Hcap Chase (3m2f) (5)
16	18119 Josies Orders	CD	8 11-4	148-7	15-8f	E Bolger (IRE)	won Cheltenham cross-country chase (3m6f) (1)
15	4172F Rivage D'Or		10 10-10	134-4	16-1	T Martin (IRE)	2nd Kilbeggan hcp chase (3m1f) (2)

WINS-RUNS: 6yo 1-6, 7yo 0-8, 8yo 2-17, 9yo 3-28, 10yo 2-31, 11yo 1-19, 12yo 0-22, 13yo 0-3, 14yo 0-3, 15yo 0-1

FAVOURITES: £1.73 **FATE OF FAVOURITES:** 013312211 **POSITION OF WINNER IN MARKET:** 712312211

Key trends

▶Won over at least 3m, 9/9

▶At least 14 chase runs, 8/9

▶Trained in Ireland, 8/9 (exception trained in France)

▶Top-three finish within last two completed starts, 7/9

▶Won or placed in a cross country race at Cheltenham or Punchestown, 5/9

Other factors

▶The last eight winners were owned by Gigginstown (five) or JP McManus (three)

▶Two winners since 2008 had landed the PP Hogan at Punchestown in February, while 2013 winner Big Shu was runner-up in that event

▶Since 2015, only six British-trained runners have made the first four

4.00 BetMGM Queen Mother Champion Chase ITV/RTV
➤ 2m   ➤ Grade 1   ➤ £400,000

Jonbon was one of the Nicky Henderson stars forced to miss last year's festival owing to concerns over the health of the Seven Barrows string but he is set to line up with a big chance this time. He has won five out of five since that disappointment, advancing his career-best Racing Post Rating three times during that impressive run. This season he has scored by wide margins in the Tingle Creek at Sandown and the Clarence House at Ascot, latterly defeating dual Champion Chase winner Energumene to take his RPR to 177. The big question is whether he can reproduce his best at Cheltenham, where he has won on only two of his five visits (in contrast to his 100 per cent record elsewhere). Willie Mullins has three of the main threats in Gaelic Warrior, Energumene and El Fabiolo but there are question marks with them as well, concerning form, age and jumping. King George VI Chase runner-up Il Est Francais would be an intriguing contender if dropped back to this trip by Noel George and Amanda Zetterholm, while Dublin Chase one-two Solness (Joseph O'Brien) and Marine Nationale (Barry Connell) add further Grade 1 quality to the mix.

Jonbon
8 b g; Trainer Nicky Henderson
Chase form 11121111211111, best RPR 177
Left-handed 11211211, best RPR 172
Right-handed 111111, best RPR 177
Cheltenham form (all) 22121, best RPR 169
At the festival 15 Mar 2022 Tracked leader, joined leader after 5th, disputing lead when left in lead 3 out, headed and pushed along 2 out, ridden and outpaced on turn before last, soon no chance with winner, finished second, beaten 22 lengths by Constitution Hill in Supreme Novices' Hurdle
14 Mar 2023 Jumped slightly left throughout, raced in second, pushed along after 3 out, drifted left when challenging 2 out, soon ridden, 3 lengths down last, hung left and no extra run-in, beaten five and a half lengths by El Fabiolo in Arkle Novices' Chase

Teak-tough performer who has won 17 of 20 starts in all and 12 of 14 chases, and seems better than ever at the age of nine. He's always had a huge reputation, not least because he's a half-brother to Douvan and cost JP McManus £570,000, but he's now almost doubled that in prize-money and looks quite a bargain. Denied a chance to run in last season's Champion Chase due to the form of Nicky Henderson's yard, Jonbon went to Aintree instead and took the step up to 2m4f in his stride by winning the Melling Chase from Conflated, and he then went to one of his favourite stomping grounds, Sandown, to dish out a four-length defeat to El Fabiolo, who had been a 2-9 chance when pulled up in the Champion Chase due to a bad early error and again didn't jump too well. Jonbon has since gone 3-3 this season, making a little bit of a meal of beating Boothill in the Shloer at Cheltenham on his reappearance but then taking his form to a new level with runaway wins in the Tingle Creek at Sandown (by eight lengths from Quilixios, his fifth Grade 1 win in five starts at that track) and in the Clarence House at Ascot by six and a half lengths from dual Champion Chase winner Energumene. While he has gone from strength to strength this season, many of those expected to provide the stiffest competition have not, so it's no wonder he has become quite a warm favourite, although the fact that nine of the last 12 odds-on favourites have been beaten makes his shortening odds look like a poisoned chalice. More worrying than SP stats, of course, is whether Jonbon is truly at home at Cheltenham. He has run there five times, yet all three of his career defeats have been there and his best RPR of 169 is 8lb below his peak effort elsewhere. That said, you'd hardly forgive him for being blown away by Constitution Hill in the 2022 Supreme, nor by El Fabiolo in the 2023 Arkle. On the plus

Jonbon: best Cheltenham RPR of 169 is 8lb below his peak effort elsewhere

side, he's a perfect 8-8 when ridden by Nico de Boinville, for whom he usually jumps really well. There's no denying he deserves his place at the head of the market, and if ever a horse deserved to seal his legacy with a win at the festival it's him as he always gives his best.

Going preference Has top-class form on all surfaces

Star rating ✪✪✪✪✪

Il Est Francais

7 b g; Trainer Noel George & Amanda Zetterholm
Chase form 11151P2, best RPR 173
Left-handed 1151P, best RPR 156
Right-handed 12, best RPR 173

Has come from nowhere to be challenging for second favouritism for Champion Chase glory despite not having run over anywhere near as short as 2m since scoring over 2m1½f on his chase debut in France in 2023. Indeed, at this time last year he was being touted as a future challenge for Gold Cup honours, having looked a potential superstar when running away with the Kauto Star Novices' Chase at Kempton in a time much faster than the King George later on the card. However, things haven't gone to plan since then as he suffered two heavy defeats in his next three French outings and then found himself pegged back by Banbridge in the King George, having held a clear lead turning into the home straight. However, it's really difficult to suggest he didn't stay given he thumped the rest of the field by ten lengths, and it remains to be seen if he's a proper two-miler, especially given there's no shortage of potential pacesetters among this year's entries. Still, this could be where he ends up as connections say they're likely to head here if Fact To File is directed towards the Ryanair, which also seems likely after his apparent non-staying efforts behind Galopin Des Champs at Leopardstown. Still, that's very strange reasoning considering that Jonbon, as things stand, has considerably better form in the book over 2m than Fact To File has over 2m5f.

Going preference Two standout British efforts came on good ground but has won on heavy in France

Star rating ✪✪

Gaelic Warrior: last year's Arkle winner needs soft ground to be effective at two miles

Gaelic Warrior

7 b g; Trainer Willie Mullins
Chase form 11U1223, best RPR 172
Left-handed U123, best RPR 172
Right-handed 112, best RPR 158
Cheltenham form (all) 221, best RPR 172
At the festival 15 Mar 2022 Jumped right throughout, led, pushed along home turn, 2 lengths ahead last, soon ridden and faced strong challenge, headed inside final 110yds, kept on well, finished second, beaten a short head by Brazil in Fred Winter Juvenile Handicap Hurdle 15 Mar 2023 Took keen hold, midfield, headway and prominent after 2 out, pushed along and went second 4 lengths down last, soon edged right, kept on final 110yds, no match for winner, finished second, beaten six and a half lengths by Impaire Et Passe in Ballymore Novices' Hurdle 12 Mar 2024 Travelled strongly, prominent, switched right and pressed leaders going easily 2 out, led approaching last, pushed along and went clear run-in, impressive, won Arkle Chase

by eight and a half lengths from Found A Fifty

Arkle winners have a very good record of at least hitting the frame in the Champion Chase the following season, but it's fair to say Gaelic Warrior has not exactly enhanced his claims despite not having moved out dramatically in the market. He looked a superstar in a first-time hood in last season's Arkle, which came after he'd unseated by diving right at the last when already well held by Fact To File at Leopardstown. Despite worries about him going left-handed, Gaelic Warrior jumped as straight as he ever has and was always cruising off the solid gallop, and he pulled right away to win by eight and a half lengths from Found A Fifty, with a further four and three-quarters back to Il Etait Temps, both of whom went on to Grade 1 success at Aintree the following month. Unfortunately it hasn't been plain

sailing for Gaelic Warrior since, as Il Etait Temps then reversed the form at Punchestown in early May, while in two starts this season the Willie Mullins-trained seven-year-old has still been a long way off that Cheltenham form. He was expected to need his first run in the Grade 1 Paddy's Rewards Club Chase at Leopardstown over Christmas, when he found surprise winner Solness three and three-quarter lengths too good for him, but instead of building on that he took a backward step when only a 14-length third to the same horse in the Dublin Chase at the DRF. That was an unsatisfactory race as the field, having not learned their lesson from Christmas, let the winner get away from them again, but Gaelic Warrior looked very laboured throughout and couldn't even go with runner-up Marine Nationale. In his defence, connections keep running him at Leopardstown, where he has never seemed that happy, but there's also a chance that a horse who won a 3m Grade 1 novice hurdle by ten lengths almost two years ago is no longer quick enough for 2m. The ground was as heavy as it has been for years on day one at Cheltenham last year (despite the clerk of the course refusing to call it heavy until afterwards), so perhaps he just needs a real test at the trip to slow the others down. Connections seem to have taken that on board now as well, and if conditions aren't testing they'll consider going back up in trip for the Ryanair on the Thursday.

Going preference Probably prefers soft and definitely needs it to be effective at 2m

Star rating ✪

Energumene
11 br g; Trainer Willie Mullins
Chase form 11111211131112, best RPR 179
Left-handed 11131, best RPR 179
Right-handed 111211112, best RPR 178
Cheltenham form 131, best RPR 179
At the festival 16 Mar 2022 Held up in rear, not fluent 2nd, mistake 7th, headway on outer going easily before 4 out, soon tracked leaders, disputed lead 3 out, led clearly 2 out, good jump last, shaken up and went clear run-in, readily, won Champion Chase by eight and a half lengths from Funambule Sivola
15 Mar 2023 Travelled strongly, jumped right on occasions, prominent, disputed lead 6th, good jump 4 out, mistake 3 out, soon led clearly going easily, edged left home turn, clear when another good jump last, kept on well run-in, impressive, won Champion Chase by ten lengths from Captain Guinness

A match for any of these at his best, but the dual Champion Chase winner, who thrashed last year's winner Captain Guinness by ten lengths when landing his second crown, suffered an injury and was off for 593 days after beating Chacun Pour Soi at Punchestown in April 2023 and hasn't quite returned to his best in two outings this term. He was a ten-length winner on his return in the Grade 2 Hilly Way at Cork on his belated return in December, but hadn't quite dealt with Banbridge (who was giving him 10lb) when that one unseated at the last. It was still a really encouraging return to action and Energumene showed

all his customary enthusiasm both there and at Ascot when taking on Jonbon in the Clarence House at Ascot in January, although he proved no match for him from two out and went down by six and a half lengths. He's still clearly capable of high-class form, but whether he can take it that little bit higher to win another Champion Chase at the age of 11 remains to be seen. He's arguably the best jumper in the field, though, so don't rule it out. Connections may favour a tilt at the Ryanair if the ground isn't soft enough to make it a test at 2m.

Going preference Goes well on soft but versatile

Star rating ✪✪✪✪

El Fabiolo
8 b g; Trainer Willie Mullins
Chase form 111111P2F, best RPR 178
Left-handed 111PF, best RPR 178
Right-handed 1112, best RPR 174
Cheltenham form 1P, best RPR 172
At the festival 14 Mar 2023 Prominent, not fluent 1st, led just after 2 out, 3 lengths ahead when not fluent last, soon ridden, kept on strongly and went further clear final 110yds, ridden out, won Arkle Novices' Chase by five and a half lengths from Jonbon
13 Mar 2024 Prominent, lost position when not fluent 1st, dropped to last when bad mistake and almost fell 5th, soon pulled up in Champion Chase won by Captain Guinness

Three-time Grade 1 winner in his novice chase season, looking for all the world as though he would dominate the division for a while with comfortable wide-margin wins in the Irish and British Arkles and at Punchestown as well. All went swimmingly in the early part of last season, when he racked up two more successes, his eight-and-a-half-length Dublin Chase win taking his form to a new level, and he went to Cheltenham looking almost bombproof for a first Champion Chase, going off at odds of 2-9 in the absence of both Jonbon and Energumene. Then disaster struck – as it seems to do so many times with odds-on shots in this race – when a dreadful mistake at the fifth fence dropped him back to last and left Paul Townend with no choice but to pull him up. After that he jumped stickily when beaten four lengths by Jonbon in the Celebration Chase at Sandown, and after being difficult to train this season he got only as far as the second fence in the Dublin Chase. He had been backed from 8-1 after the declaration stage to just 3-1, so someone was clearly hoping he'd come back to form straight away, but at the very least he could ideally have done with a full race. He quite clearly comes with risks attached, but has better form than quite a few around him in the betting if he gets it right and returns to his best.

Going preference Jumping much more of an issue than ground

Star rating ✪✪

Solness
7 b g; Trainer Joseph O'Brien
Chase form 21122513040132411, best RPR 166
Left-handed 112301211, best RPR 166
Right-handed 22514034, best RPR 149
Cheltenham form 0, best RPR 119
At the festival 13 Mar 2024 Raced wide, towards rear throughout, finished 11th, beaten 42 lengths by Unexpected Party in Grand Annual Handicap Chase

Looked thoroughly exposed as a chaser after 11 outings before the autumn of this season, but has won four times since then (once over hurdles) and gone from a useful 148-rated performer to a dual Grade 1 winner in the space of the last five months. His two big runs came at Leopardstown, the first over Christmas when he was a 28-1 winner of the Paddy's Rewards Club Chase, seemingly taking advantage of the easy lead he'd been given and the lack of race fitness of favourite Gaelic Warrior, who was beaten just under four lengths into second. There were enough reasons to think that was a bit of a fluke, but Solness wasn't having any of it and he repeated the feat in the Dublin Chase in February, once again going clear early and staying there to the very end. While he was closed down by Marine Nationale, with the winning distance two lengths, he still found enough after the last and the rest, including Gaelic Warrior, were 14 lengths adrift. It's hard to know where the improvement has come from, and there's a chance he was simply ignored both times and is flattered, but we'll

find out at Cheltenham as that won't happen given the number of potential pacesetters among the entries.

Going preference Has won on soft, but the quicker the better

Star rating ✪✪✪

Marine Nationale
8 b g; Trainer Barry Connell
Chase form (left-handed) 15232, best RPR 163
Cheltenham form (hurdles) 1, best RPR 158
At the festival 14 Mar 2023 Travelled strongly, towards rear of midfield, headway on outer 3 out, shaken up and went second before last, edged left and led when bumped run-in, ridden inside final 110yds, won going away, readily, won Supreme Novices' Hurdle by three and a quarter lengths from Facile Vega

Looked a potential star for Barry Connell when sprinting away after the last to win the Supreme Novices' Hurdle in 2023, and it took just one run over fences the next season for him to assume the mantle of an odds-on shot for the Arkle, his eight-and-a-half-length beginners' chase success marked by a superb round of jumping. However, things went pear-shaped at the Dublin Racing Festival as he could manage only fifth of six to Il Etait Temps and that was it for the season, a suspensory ligament injury ruling him out of Cheltenham and everything else. Progress this season has been slow but steady, as after being beaten at odds of 8-11 by Quilixios at Naas in November he improved on that effort to be third to Solness at Leopardstown over Christmas and then got closer to him in the Dublin Chase in February. If you're of the opinion that Solness was allowed to steal that race, you have to be impressed with the way Marine Nationale separated himself from the rest of the field as he was 12 lengths clear of Gaelic Warrior at the line. He's one of several contenders on the comeback trail but is certainly going the right way and is still young enough to have his best days ahead of him.

Going preference Acts on good and soft

Star rating ✪✪✪

OTHERS TO CONSIDER
Banbridge remained in all the major Grade 1 chases when the scratchings were made,

CHAMPION CHASE RESULTS AND TRENDS

	FORM WINNER	AGE & WGT	Adj RPR	SP	TRAINER	BEST RPR LAST 12 MONTHS (RUNS SINCE)
24	2-1P3 **Captain Guinness** D	9 11-10	169-14	17-2	H de Bromhead (IRE)	2nd Gd 1 Celebration Chase (1m7½f) (3)
23	1-113 **Energumene** CD, BF	9 11-10	181T	6-5f	W Mullins (IRE)	won Punchestown Gd1 chase (2m) (2)
22	1-112 **Energumene** D	8 11-10	183-2	5-2	W Mullins (IRE)	2nd Gd1 Clarence House Chase (2m1f) (0)
21	11-13 **Put The Kettle On** CD	7 11-3	170-10	17-2	H de Bromhead (IRE)	3rd Leopardstown Gd 1 Chase (2m1f) (0)
20	22-25 **Politologue** D	9 11-10	175-9	6-1	P Nicholls	2nd Gd 1 Champion Chase (2m) (3)
19	1-111 **Altior** CD	9 11-10	187T	4-11f	N Henderson	won Gd 1 Champion Chase (2m) (4)
18	111-1 **Altior** CD	8 11-10	181T	Evensf	N Henderson	won Gd 1 Celebration Chase (1m7½f) (1)
17	-6315 **Special Tiara** D	10 11-10	174-8	11-1	H de Bromhead (IRE)	3rd Gd 1 Champion Chase (2m) (4)
16	P2-11 **Sprinter Sacre** CD	10 11-10	177-1	5-1	N Henderson	won Kempton Gd2 chase (2m) (0)
15	5-311 **Dodging Bullets** CD	7 11-10	178-6	9-2	P Nicholls	won Gd1 Clarence House Chase (2m1f) (0)

WINS-RUNS: 6yo 0-1, 7yo 2-17, 8yo 2-25, 9yo 4-23, 10yo 2-9, 11yo 0-4, 12yo 0-1, 13yo 0-1 **FAVOURITES:** -£4.44

TRAINERS IN THIS RACE (w-pl-r): Nicky Henderson 3-0-5, Henry de Bromhead 3-3-13, Paul Nicholls 2-2-10, Willie Mullins 2-4-13, Alan King 0-1-5, Venetia Williams 0-1-3, Joe Tizzard 0-0-1, Harry Fry 0-0-1

FATE OF FAVOURITES: P201143P1P **POSITION OF WINNER IN MARKET:** 3241122213

but there's talk of him going for the Gold Cup and, while he beat Energumene in the Hilly Way, this is surely the least likely option. It seems harsh to relegate defending champion **Captain Guinness** to the 'others' section, but on this season's form he deserves it. While he'll probably bounce back in some way, he's ten now and this will be much more hotly contested than a year ago. The likes of Game Spirit 1-2-3 **Master Chewy**, **Libberty Hunter** and **Matata** are all worthy of a place, but a place is all they can realistically hope for.

VERDICT

*At the start of the season I was convinced **Jonbon** would find himself getting displaced as a Champion Chase contender by some up-and-comers, but I couldn't have been more wrong as he has gone from strength to strength while many of his expected main rivals have faltered. I'd quite like to see him get a Champion Chase on his impressive CV but I'm not sure I could back him at shorter than evens given not only the poor record of favourites in this but his record at Cheltenham. His best RPR there is just 169, and if he genuinely can't better it he brings plenty of rivals into the equation. The likes of El Fabiolo, **Energumene** and **Gaelic Warrior** all have better RPRs to their names at Cheltenham, although they clearly all come with risks attached. I can see the latter returning to form should the ground*

Key trends

➤ Won over at least 2m1f, 9/10

➤ No more than 10lb off RPR top-rated, 9/10 (three were top-rated)

➤ Adjusted RPR of at least 174, 8/10

➤ Grade 1 chase winner, 8/10

➤ Won Graded chase within last two starts, 8/10

➤ No older than nine, 8/10

➤ Between seven and 16 runs over fences, 7/10

Other factors

➤ Five winners had previously won at the festival

➤ In the past ten years 36 French-breds have run, yielding four wins, eight seconds and six thirds

*get very soft, but that's far from a given, so I've slowly come round to the idea that **MARINE NATIONALE** might be the one to give Jonbon the most to do. He does have to improve to do so, but Barry Connell has him going back in the right direction, and if we accept that everyone let Solness get away with an easy and long lead at Leopardstown last time, we can upgrade his two-length second given he was the only one to get within 14 lengths of the winner.*

4.40 Johnny Henderson Grand Annual Hcap Chase ITV/RTV
> 2m ➤ Premier Handicap ➤ £150,000

This hotly contested 2m handicap chase had a significant change four years ago by moving from the New course to the Old. The Old course is slightly sharper and tighter, favouring a quicker, strong-travelling type.

LAST YEAR'S WINNER Unexpected Party scored at 12-1 for Dan Skelton. He was described in the Racing Post comments as "prominent on outer", following on from other recent "prominent" winners Sky Pirate (2021) and Global Citizen (2022) and 2023 scorer Maskada, who was "in touch with leaders".

FORM AND RATINGS Nine of the last 15 British-trained winners had been successful at Cheltenham before. Unexpected Party wasn't one of them but had recorded his best two Racing Post Ratings at the course. The quality has improved year on year and ten of the last 14 winners were rated at least 140.

AGE This has been a good race for novices with 15 winners since 1983. Only three winners have been older than nine since 12-year-old Uncle Ernie in 1997.

BETTING Chosen Mate in 2020 became only the second successful favourite since 2004 and 14 of the last 18 winners were sent off 10-1 or bigger.

ONES TO WATCH Last year's one-two **Unexpected Party** and **Libberty Hunter** (Evan Williams) could be back on higher marks. Skelton also has **Madara**, a Cheltenham winner at around this trip when trained by Sophie Leech. **The King Of Prs**, a Grade 3 handicap chase winner at 2m1f in January, looks an ideal type for Gavin Cromwell.

GRAND ANNUAL HANDICAP CHASE RESULTS AND TRENDS

	FORM WINNER	AGE & WGT	OR	SP	TRAINER	BEST RPR LAST 12 MONTHS (RUNS SINCE)
24	15549 Unexpected Party	9 10-10	138ᵀ	12-1	D Skelton	5th Gd1 Turners novice chase (2m4f) (6)
23	-4F10 Maskada D, BF	7 11-1	142⁻⁹	22-1	H de Bromhead (IRE)	won Limerick hcap chase (2m3½f) (1)
22	92023 Global Citizen D	10 10-6	136⁻⁶	28-1	B Pauling	Seasonal debutant (0)
21	25112 Sky Pirate C, D	8 11-6	152⁻³	14-1	J O'Neill	won Warwick Class 2 hcap chase (2m) (1)
20	60341 Chosen Mate D	7 11-4	147⁻⁸	7-2f	G Elliott (IRE)	won Gowran Park novice chase (2m) (0)
19	835/2 Croco Bay D	12 10-12	139⁻⁵	66-1	B Case	2nd Worcester Class 3 hcap chase (2m½f) (0)
18	P-238 Le Prezien C, D	7 11-8	150⁻²	15-2	P Nicholls	3rd BetVictor Gold Cup hcap chase (2m4½f) (1)
17	63-3P Rock The World C, D	9 11-5	147⁻²	10-1	J Harrington (IRE)	2nd Punchestown hcap chase (2m) (2)
16	63-3P Solar Impulse D	6 11-0	140⁻⁸	28-1	P Nicholls	3rd Haydock Class 2 chase (2m½f) (1)
15	5-604 Next Sensation D	8 11-2	143⁻⁵	16-1	M Scudamore	4th Newbury Class 2 hcap chase (2m½f) (0)

WINS-RUNS: 5yo 0-5, 6yo 1-16, 7yo 3-44, 8yo 2-59, 9yo 2-36, 10yo 1-23, 11yo 0-9, 12yo 1-3, 13yo 0-2 **FAVOURITES:** -£5.50

FATE OF FAVOURITES: 430F01F224 **POSITION OF WINNER IN MARKET:** 7062017007

Key trends
> Distance winner, 9/10
> Carried no more than 11st 6lb, 9/10
> Top-three finish on at least one of last two starts, 8/10
> Aged nine or under, 8/10
> No more than 11 runs over fences, 8/10
> Officially rated 138 to 147, 7/10

> Had run at a previous festival, 7/10
> Yet to win that season, 6/10

Other factors
> Three winners had scored at the course – three of the exceptions had been placed in this race previously
> The record of the previous year's winner is 009090037

5.20 Weatherbys Champion Bumper
> 2m½f > Grade 1 > £80,000   RTV

Entries are made late for this Grade 1, giving as much time as possible for likely contenders to gain vital racecourse experience. Often only one run is deemed necessary, as was the case with last year's one-two Jasmin De Vaux and Romeo Coolio, who came out to win in January and then were put away until the festival. Those two, along with the rest of last year's first seven, were trained by Willie Mullins and Gordon Elliott, who between them have won seven of the last eight runnings. It is not surprising, therefore, that the ante-post betting is dominated again by possibles from Ireland's two biggest stables. Dublin Racing Festival bumper winner Bambino Fever looks set to head the Mullins team along with Copacabana, a later arrival to the racecourse, while Elliott has dual winner Kalypso'chance on his long list. Britain has realistic hopes of success this year, principally with David Pipe's impressive Ascot winner Windbeneathmywings. Further down the betting on the Irish side is Henry de Bromhead's Scope To Improve – probably an apt description of the whole field.

Kalypso'chance
5 ch g; Trainer Gordon Elliott
Bumper form 11, best RPR 130
Left-handed 1, best RPR 130
Right-handed 1, best RPR 126

A 13-length point winner in April who might well be a bargain at £85,000 as he's 2-2 in bumpers and, on RPRs, one of the best in the field this year. He scored by 15 lengths at Punchestown on his debut in November, after which he impressed when quickening up to land a five-runner Listed contest at Navan. Gordon Elliott suggested he might go to the Dublin Racing Festival after that, but he didn't make it. Is one of the favourites in the early lists but is owned by Gigginstown House Stud, who don't have many runners in the Champion Bumper, so it's best to wait and see if he figures when the entries are made.

Bambino Fever
5 ch m; Trainer Willie Mullins
Bumper form 11, best RPR 124
Left-handed 1, best RPR 124
Right-handed 1, best RPR 110

Won a two-finisher point by 40 lengths last May and is 2-2 in bumpers since, and is now apparently Willie Mullins' first-string according to the betting. This mare showed a tidy change of gear when scoring by five lengths at Punchestown on New Year's Eve,

but it wasn't enough to persuade Patrick Mullins to choose her in the Grade 2 bumper at the DRF. He went for 9-4 favourite Future Prospect and could only watch from a distance as Jody Townend steered Bambino Fever to another impressive success, this time by seven and a half lengths. Only 17 fillies or mares have run in this in the past ten years, but two won and two others were third.

Windbeneathmywings
5 ch g; Trainer David Pipe
Bumper form 1211, best RPR 130
Left-handed 1, best RPR 119
Right-handed 121, best RPR 130

One of the more experienced in the field, having run four times in bumpers, and did manage to get beat in one at lowly Ballinrobe. Has won the other three, though, two in Ireland for Patrick Flynn and the latest at Ascot in December after a move to David Pipe. There he looked very useful indeed as he slammed his field by 14 lengths in a Listed contest, returning an RPR of 130, which is one of the best figures on show. He also represents one of the few British yards with a good record in this, Martin Pipe having won it with Liberman in 2003 and David with Moon Racer in 2015.

Copacabana
5 b g; Trainer Willie Mullins
Bumper form (left-handed) 1, best RPR 119

Launched his way into the top end of the betting after an impressive debut for Willie Mullins at Navan in the second week of February, winning by a comfortable five lengths from a couple of rivals who had more experience and had shown reasonable form.

No Drama This End
5 gr g; Trainer Paul Nicholls
Bumper form (left-handed) 1, best RPR 115

Represents Paul Nicholls, who has yet to win this but had Captain Teague finish third two years ago and Al Ferof second in 2010. By superstar jumps sire Walk In The Park and out of a dam who won a 3m Grade 1 hurdle in France, No Drama This End ran out a 23-length point winner in February last year before being sent to Nicholls and he's since bolted up at Warwick, albeit in a race run in a very slow time. Afterwards Nicholls said he'd get a tentative entry and may run at Cheltenham if the ground is soft.

Ksar Fatal
5 br g; Trainer Willie Mullins

Point winner in October who had yet to run in a bumper at the time of writing but

Kalypso'chance: winner of both his bumpers and high up the list on Racing Post Ratings

had evidently attracted some interest from punters. Has had a few entries lately, so we may see him soon.

Jalon D'Oudairies
6 b g; Trainer Gordon Elliott
Bumper form 113, best RPR 134
Left-handed 13, best RPR 134
Right-handed 1, best RPR 117
Cheltenham form 3, best RPR 134
At the festival 13 Mar 2024 Prominent, led narrowly 2f out, headed over 1f out, soon lost second, kept on inside final furlong, finished third, beaten four and a quarter lengths by Jasmin De Vaux in Champion Bumper

Finished third to Jasmin De Vaux in the Champion Bumper last year as the first horse Gigginstown had run in it for four years, and the fact he hasn't been seen since probably hasn't helped to make the race more popular with them. That said, Gordon Elliott has indicated he's on the way back and, as it's too late to go hurdling this term, he might have another crack.

Idaho Sun
5 b g; Trainer Harry Fry
Bumper form (left-handed) 11, best RPR 118

Scrambled home by only a short head on his debut at Newton Abbot in October, but it turned out to be a rather good race for the time of year and track. The second, third and fourth have won bumpers since, one of them in Listed company, and the sixth scored over hurdles. Idaho Sun again showed a good attitude to win at Windsor's Winter Million fixture but he has a bit to find in terms of RPRs.

He Can't Dance
5 gr g; Trainer Gordon Elliott
Bumper form (left-handed) 13, best RPR 123

Out of an unraced half-sister to Master Minded, he won his point in March last year and got off the mark at the first time of asking in bumpers in December, albeit at odds of 2-9 in a seven-runner race at Navan. Defeat followed in the Grade 2 bumper at the DRF, but he wasn't disgraced in finishing just under two-lengths third to the well-supported Colcannon. Another Gigginstown horse, though, and it'll be a departure from the norm if they're mob-handed.

Mossy Fen Road
5 b g; Trainer Harry Derham
Bumper form (left-handed) 1, best RPR 113

Point winner in March last year who subsequently joined Harry Derham but had to wait until this February to make his debut having missed two engagements previously, one in November (vet's advice) and one just before he did turn up (heavy ground) at Wetherby for a five-length success. Was very well backed and won in little more than a canter from his market rival, who had much more experience, so is clearly useful even if an RPR of 113 leaves him way off the principals.

Scope To Improve
5 b g; Trainer Henry de Bromhead
Bumper form 1, best RPR 115

A 12-length point winner in May, this half-brother to a 3m winner won comfortably enough on his debut at Naas in December, but the form has taken its share of knocks since.

Ravendark
4 b g; Trainer Gordon Elliott

In the betting largely because he's a half-brother to Brighterdaysahead, Mighty Potter and French Dynamite, but hadn't seen a racecourse by mid-February and a big surprise if he turns up for Gigginstown, even if he does get to make his debut by early March.

Champagne Jury
6 gr g; Trainer Gavin Cromwell
Bumper form (left-handed) 1, best RPR 118

Pulled up in first point in March last year and was beaten ten lengths into second in another in November, but looked a different proposition when making his debut for Gavin Cromwell in a Naas bumper at the end of January. He ran out a five-length winner that day despite drifting from 11-2 to 8-1 and the runner-up had shown fair form on his debut, albeit had run badly next time.

Kovanis
5 gr g; Trainer Gordon Elliott
Bumper form (left-handed) 1, best RPR 117

Yet another Gordon Elliott-trained, Gigginstown-owned contender who has won a point and a bumper. He faced only four

CHAMPION BUMPER RESULTS AND TRENDS

	FORM WINNER	AGE & WGT	Adj RPR	SP	TRAINER	BEST RPR LAST 12 MONTHS (RUNS SINCE)
24	1 Jasmin De Vaux	5 11-7	135-4	9-2	W Mullins (IRE)	won Naas bumper (2m2½f) (0)
23	111 Dream To Share D	5 11-7	147T	7-2	J Kiely (IRE)	won Leopardstown Gd2 bumper (2m) (0)
22	11 Facile Vega D	5 11-5	145T	15-8f	W Mullins (IRE)	won Leopardstown Gd2 bumper (2m) (0)
21	11 Sir Gerhard D	6 11-5	140-11	85-40	W Mullins (IRE)	won Navan Listed bumper (2m) (0)
20	221 Ferny Hollow D	5 11-5	138-9	11-1	W Mullins (IRE)	won Fairyhouse bumper (2m) (0)
19	1-111 Envoi Allen D	5 11-5	144T	2-1f	G Elliott (IRE)	won Leopardstown Gd2 bumper (2m) (0)
18	11 Relegate D	5 10-12	126-25	25-1	W Mullins (IRE)	won Leopardstown Gd2 bumper (2m) (0)
17	811 Fayonagh D	6 10-12	140T	7-1	G Elliott (IRE)	won Fairyhouse Listed bumper (2m) (0)
16	1121 Ballyandy CD	5 11-5	146T	5-1	N Twiston-Davies	won Newbury Listed bumper (2m½f) (0)
15	-11 Moon Racer CD	6 11-5	140-7	9-2f	D Pipe	won Cheltenham bumper (2m½f) (0)

WINS-RUNS: 4yo 0-21, 5yo 7-134, 6yo 3-47 FAVOURITES: £1.38

TRAINERS IN THIS RACE (w-pl-r): Willie Mullins 5-9-54, Gordon Elliott 2-4-16, David Pipe 1-0-4, Dan Skelton 0-1-4, Stuart Crawford 0-0-1, Paul Nicholls 0-1-6, Nicky Henderson 0-1-3, Henry de Bromhead 0-0-1, Joseph O'Brien 0-0-4

FATE OF FAVOURITES: 1704122123 POSITION OF WINNER IN MARKET: 1230152122

rivals in the latter and won by three-quarters of a length.

OTHERS TO CONSIDER

There's no real point in discussing any others, as with no entries the bookies are clearly simply trying to guess the likely field. At the time of writing there was one horse in the betting, **Kindly Prince**, who had won a point but didn't even have a trainer listed on his Racing Post profile page, and another, **Leader Des Bordes**, who didn't even have a Racing Post profile page.

VERDICT

Not my favourite festival race, to say the least, and I don't really have a clue what's going to happen. Nor do the bookmakers, who have priced up a stack of Gigginstown-owned horses despite the fact they have had just seven runners in this race since 2009. You certainly don't want to be backing any of those until the entries come out, and probably not until the day itself. I get the impression the Irish are not as strong this season as usual, so perhaps the Pipe yard will win it again with WINDBENEATHMYWINGS, who certainly showed a decent engine when winning for the third time, and first for his new yard, at Ascot in December. Let's not pretend it's anything but a guess, though.

Key trends
- Won last time out, 10/10
- Aged five or six, 10/10
- Won a bumper worth at least £4,000 or €4,000 to the winner, 9/10
- Won a bumper with at least 12 runners, 9/10
- Adjusted RPR of at least 138, 8/10
- Off the track for at least 32 days, 8/10 (three not seen since Christmas or earlier)

Other factors
- Ireland has won eight of the last ten and 25 of the 32 runnings.
- Willie Mullins has had the most winners with 13 victories (five in the last ten years) but is often mob-handed. On four of the occasions he won, he saddled just one runner; on the other eight, the winner was not his most fancied in the market on six occasions.
- Gordon Elliott has trained two of the last eight winners.

THURSDAY, MARCH 13 (NEW COURSE)
PAUL KEALY ON THE KEY PLAYERS

1.20 Ryanair Mares' Novices' Hurdle   ITV/RTV
➤2m1f   ➤Grade 2   ➤£105,000

Ireland took the first six runnings after this race was introduced in 2016 but the home side has hit back with consecutive wins for Harry Fry with Love Envoi, Jamie Snowden with You Wear It Well and Jeremy Scott with Golden Ace last year.

The ante-post betting indicates the prize will go back to Ireland this year, with Willie Mullins' Maughreen and the Gavin Cromwell-trained Sixandahalf disputing favouritism. Both have landed their only starts over hurdles having been bumper winners last season, but in between Sixandahalf had a successful Flat campaign last year (rated 94) that ended with third place in the Irish Cesarewitch.

Cromwell's mare was given a Racing Post Rating of 130 for her hurdles win, compared with 120 for Maughreen (the latter had the edge in bumpers at 121 to 119).

Mullins has another good contender in French import Karoline Banbou, who was beaten on her hurdles debut in Ireland by stablemate Baby Kate but won her maiden well next time at Fairyhouse.

The leading British hope could be Paul Nicholls' Jubilee Alpha, who was runner-up in the Grade 2 mares' bumper at Aintree last spring and has plenty of experience over hurdles, having won two out of three to reach an RPR of 125. Nicholls also has Just A Rose, who has the same RPR after her wide-margin debut success at Taunton.

MARES' NOVICES' HURDLE RESULTS

	FORM WINNER	AGE & WGT	Adj RPR	SP	TRAINER	BEST RPR LAST 12 MONTHS (RUNS SINCE)
24	52-11 **Golden Ace** D	6 11-2	142-8	10-1	J Scott	won Taunton Class 3 novice hurdle (2m½f) (0)
23	-1121 **You Wear It Well** D	6 11-7	143-6	16-1	J Snowden	won Sandown Gd2 novice hurdle (2m4f) (0)
22	-1111 **Love Envoi** D	6 11-7	140-8	15-2	H Fry	won Sandown Gd2 novice hurdle (2m4f) (0)
21	13113 **Tellmesomethinggirl** D	6 11-2	149-4	5-1	H de Bromhead (IRE)	3rd Leopardstown hcap hurdle (2m2f) (0)
20	2-433 **Concertista**	6 11-2	154-T	9-2	W Mullins (IRE)	3rd Leopardstown hcap hurdle (2m2f) (0)
19	1-13 **Eglantine Du Seuil** D	5 11-2	135-13	50-1	W Mullins (IRE)	3rd Listowel novice hurdle (2m) (0)
18	F2-11 **Laurina** D	5 11-7	155-T	4-7f	W Mullins (IRE)	won Fairyhouse Gd3 novice hurdle (2m2f) (0)
17	21111 **Let's Dance** D	5 11-7	153-T	11-8f	W Mullins (IRE)	won Leopardstown Gd2 nov hurdle (2m4f) (0)
16	11 **Limini** D	5 11-7	148-4	8-11f	W Mullins (IRE)	won Fairyhouse Gd3 novice hurdle (2m2f) (0)

WINS-RUNS: 4yo 0-8, 5yo 4-58, 6yo 5-63, 7yo 0-19, 8yo 0-5 **FAVOURITES:** -£3.33

TRAINERS IN THIS RACE (w-pl-r): Willie Mullins 5-3-32, Henry de Bromhead 1-3-14, Harry Fry 1-0-2, Jamie Snowden 1-0-1, Gordon Elliott 0-4-11, Nicky Henderson 0-2-14, Dan Skelton 0-0-3, Paul Nicholls 0-0-2, Paul Nolan 0-0-1

FATE OF FAVOURITES: 111900042 **POSITION OF WINNER IN MARKET:** 111032483

Key trends

➤Aged five or six, nine winners in nine runnings

➤Top-three finish last time out, 9/9

➤Top-three finish in a Listed or Graded hurdle, 8/9

➤Rated within 8lb of RPR top-rated, 8/9

➤Adjusted RPR of at least 142, 7/9

➤Two to four hurdle starts, 7/9

Other factors

➤Seven winners had won over further than 2m1f

➤One winner was still a maiden but she had been beaten a short head in the race the previous year

➤Willie Mullins has trained five of the nine winners (the first five) but Britain has landed the last three

2.00 Jack Richards Novices' Handicap Chase ITV/RTV
➤ 2m4½f ➤ Grade 2 limited handicap ➤ £125,000

New for this year is this Grade 2 2m4½f novice limited handicap chase, which takes the place of the Grade 1 Golden Miller Novices' Chase (run most recently under the Turners sponsorship). The aim is to bolster the Grade 1 numbers in the 2m Arkle and 3m Brown Advisory by removing the option for the top novices at the intermediate distance, while adding a competitive handicap in its place.

This is an adaptation of the contest held at the festival from 2006 until 2020, after which it was moved to Sandown. A major difference is that the new race is a limited handicap with a 20lb weight range.

If this race follows a similar pattern to the previous version, there will be an accent on strong recent form (look for winners/runners-up last time out) and that will tend to mean the winner is more likely to come from the top six in the betting.

There might also be a greater spread of winning connections. Fourteen different trainers were successful in the 15 runnings of the previous novice handicap chase and victory went only three times to the trainers who now make up the 'big five'.

ONES TO WATCH JP McManus's **Jagwar** *(below right)* became clear ante-post favourite for Oliver Greenall and Josh Guerriero after his course-and-distance handicap win on Trials day, which took him to a mark of 139. **Springwell Bay** (Jonjo and AJ O'Neill) is another big handicap winner this season over track and trip. **Down Memory Lane** (Gordon Elliott) and **No Flies On Him** (Edward O'Grady) look other likely types for McManus. **Nurburgring** (Joseph O'Brien) could be on a decent mark.

2.40 Pertemps Network Final Handicap Hurdle ITV/RTV
➤3m ➤Premier Handicap ➤£110,000

The race conditions for this 3m handicap hurdle were tightened again in 2023, with horses having to finish in the first four in a qualifier to be eligible for the final. This year there has been another change, guaranteeing a run for all winners of series qualifiers (provided they are within the weights at declaration stage).

LAST YEAR'S WINNER Monmiral scored at 25-1 for Paul Nicholls, becoming only the second British-trained winner in the last nine runnings. He was rated in the golden range from 138 to 142. Six of the last ten winners have been in that bracket.

FORM Over the longer term last-time-out winners have a strong record and, while that has waned somewhat in recent years, a top-four finish at least is preferable.

BETTING Favourites have a poor record. Fingal Bay in 2014 and Sire Du Berlais in 2019 are the only two market leaders to have won in the past 21 runnings.

ONES TO WATCH The Wallpark could be another Sire Du Berlais for Gordon Elliott – one with Stayers' Hurdle potential who could defy a high rating if he runs in this handicap. The Padraig Roche-trained **Win Some Lose Some**, winner of the Leopardstown Christmas qualifier, is another JP McManus possible.

PERTEMPS FINAL RESULTS AND TRENDS

	FORM WINNER	AGE & WGT	OR	SP	TRAINER	BEST RPR LAST 12 MONTHS (RUNS SINCE)
24	7-744 **Monmiral**	7 10-12	138-3	25-1	P Nicholls	4th Chepstow Class 2 hcap hurdle (2m7½f) (0)
23	P4030 **Good Time Jonny** D	8 11-4	142-2	9-1	T Martin (IRE)	3rd Leopardstown hcap hurdle (3m) (1)
22	P-733 **Third Wind** D	8 10-11	141-6	25-1	H Morrison	3rd Warwick Class 2 hcap hurdle (3m1f) (1)
21	1324F **Mrs Milner**	6 10-9	134-7	12-1	P Nolan (IRE)	won Galway hcap hurdle (2m½f) (4)
20	8-494 **Sire Du Berlais** CD	8 11-12	152-3	10-1	G Elliott (IRE)	4th Navan hcap hurdle (3m½f) (2)
19	48-86 **Sire Du Berlais**	7 11-9	145-6	4-1f	G Elliott (IRE)	4th Martin Pipe cond hcap hurdle (2m4½f) (3)
18	33243 **Delta Work**	5 10-10	139-T	6-1	G Elliott (IRE)	4th Leopardstown hcap hurdle (3m) (1)
17	11541 **Presenting Percy**	6 11-11	146-4	11-1	P Kelly (IRE)	won Fairyhouse hcap hurdle (2m4f) (0)
16	31433 **Mall Dini**	6 10-11	139-7	14-1	P Kelly (IRE)	won Thurles maiden hurdle (2m6½f) (3)
15	21-41 **Call The Cops** (5x) D	6 10-12	138-5	9-1	N Henderson	won Doncaster Class 2 hcap hdl (3m½f) (0)

WINS-RUNS: 5yo 1-6, 6yo 4-55, 7yo 2-68, 8yo 3-42, 9yo 0-34, 10yo 0-13, 11yo 0-7, 12yo 0-4, 13yo 0-2 **FAVOURITES:** -£5.00

FATE OF FAVOURITES: 0002122203 **POSITION OF WINNER IN MARKET:** 3652156930

Key trends
➤Aged six to eight, 9/10

➤Top-four finish last completed start, 8/10

➤Winning form between 2m4f and 2m6f, 7/10

➤Officially rated 138-146, 8/10

➤Six to ten runs over hurdles, 7/10

Other factors
➤Six winners had yet to win over 3m

and five winners had run at the festival before

➤In 2018 Delta Work became the first successful five-year-old since Pragada in 1988, while Buena Vista in 2011 was the first aged older than nine to oblige since 1981

➤Four winners were set to carry at least 11st 9lb

➤Lightly raced types are generally favoured, but three of the last five winners had 14 starts over hurdles

3.20 Ryanair Chase — ITV/RTV
➤ 2m4½f ➤ Grade 1 ➤ £375,000

Some of those prominent in the ante-post betting may be diverted to the Gold Cup or the Champion Chase, but this is still shaping up as a cracking contest. Among the probables are three festival scorers, including the last two winners of this race. Having been beaten twice by stablemate Galopin Des Champs over Leopardstown's 3m½f, Willie Mullins' Fact To File may well be best suited by dropping back to this intermediate distance if he is to add to last year's festival success in the Brown Advisory Novices' Chase. He started this season with victory in the John Durkan over a similar mid-range trip, with Galopin Des Champs behind him on that occasion. The old hands are previous winners Protektorat (Dan Skelton) and Envoi Allen (Henry de Bromhead), while the young guns include Venetia Williams' still-improving dual Grade 2 winner Djelo and narrow John Durkan runner-up Spillane's Tower for Jimmy Mangan.

Fact To File

8 b g; Trainer Willie Mullins
Chase form 2111123, best RPR 171
Left-handed 211123, best RPR 171
Right-handed 1, best RPR 169
Cheltenham form (all) 21, best RPR 166
At the festival 15 Mar 2023 Towards rear of midfield, headway on outer from over 3f out, pushed along over 2f out, ridden over 1f out, disputed lead when short of room and unbalanced inside final furlong, kept on but held inside final 110yds, finished second, beaten a length and a quarter by A Dream To Share in Champion Bumper
13 Mar 2024 Jumped right on occasions, took keen hold, towards rear, in touch with leaders 10th, headway 3 out, soon pressed leaders going easily, led 2 out, good jump last, ridden briefly and went clear run-in, readily, won Brown Advisory Novices' Chase by three and three-quarter lengths from Monty's Star

Star novice last season who won the last three of his four chase outings, the final two in Grade 1 company. The first was only a match against a below-par Gaelic Warrior, who unseated when well beaten at the last, but Fact To File oozed class throughout. Connections opted for a first crack at 3m½f at Cheltenham in the Brown Advisory and Fact To File passed the test, never really looking in trouble as he beat Monty's Star by three and three-quarter lengths, although his final 50 yards gave some cause for concern regarding the two furlongs extra in a Gold Cup. Those concerns look justified now as after beating a star-studded field that included Galopin Des Champs in the 2m3½f John Durkan Memorial on his return, he has twice seen the back of the dual Gold Cup winner. Originally made favourite in the run-up to the Savills Chase at Leopardstown over Christmas, Fact To File was displaced by Galopin Des Champs in the market overnight and put in his place in the race itself, with his top-class stablemate powering away after the last to score by seven and a half lengths. Fact To File hadn't helped his cause by racing keenly in a prominent position and the tactics were changed in the Irish Gold Cup, in which he was held up in midfield with a view to making a later challenge. All looked to be going swimmingly enough heading to the second-last but Galopin Des Champs, who admittedly had been given an easy lead, again had too much on the run-in and this time Fact To File lost second place close home to outsider Grangeclare West. He's still second favourite for the Gold Cup with most bookmakers and may yet go there, but on that evidence he's not going to get the trip and this is surely his best chance of gaining back-to-back festival victories. That said, his overall level of form arguably doesn't entitle him to be such a clear favourite in what could end up being the most hotly contested of the three major Grade 1 chases. He's only eight, though, and could improve on what he's done so far over his correct trip.

Going preference No apparent issues
Star rating ⊙⊙⊙⊙⊙

Spillane's Tower
7 b g; Trainer Jimmy Mangan
Chase form 441121125, best RPR 166
Left-handed 42, best RPR 148
Right-handed 4111125, best RPR 166

In the same ownership as Fact To File, but is likely to line up irrespective of where that one goes as this is his only entry despite the fact he has a 3m1f Grade 1 victory to his name from the Champion Novice Chase at Punchestown last season. He beat Monty's Star by three-quarters of a length in that, a month after scoring on his first foray into Grade 1 company in the WillowWarm Gold Cup over 2m4f at Fairyhouse. Spillane's Tower is no stranger to taking on Fact To File as he also reappeared in the John Durkan and he gave his ownermate the most to do, finishing strongly for a half-length second despite being very weak in the market. That promising run led to him being sent off as the 11-4 favourite after being supplemented for the King George at Kempton, but he ultimately proved disappointing and couldn't get into the race from off the pace, finishing fifth, beaten just under 18 lengths by Banbridge. He's better than that and it's quite possible the good ground was against him, with most of his best form coming on a much deeper surface. He needs to improve again to justify his place in the market, though, and he has no experience of Cheltenham, unlike the vast majority who'll line up against him.

Going preference Acts very well on soft
Star rating ⊙⊙⊙

Gaelic Warrior
7 b g; Trainer Willie Mullins
Chase form 11U1223, best RPR 172
Left-handed 1U123, best RPR 172
Right-handed 112, best RPR 159
Cheltenham form (all) 221, best RPR 172
At the festival 15 Mar 2022 Jumped right throughout, led, pushed along home turn, 2 lengths ahead last, soon ridden and faced strong challenge, headed inside final 110yds, kept on well, finished second, beaten a short head by Brazil in Fred Winter Juvenile Handicap Hurdle 15 Mar 2023 Took keen hold, midfield, headway and prominent after 2 out, pushed along and went second 4 lengths down last, soon edged right, kept on final 110yds, no match for winner, finished second, beaten six and a half lengths by Impaire Et Passe in Ballymore Novices' Hurdle 12 Mar 2024 Travelled strongly, prominent, switched right and pressed leaders going easily 2 out, led approaching last, pushed along and went clear run-in, impressive, won Arkle Chase by eight and a half lengths from Found A Fifty

Has been dealt with in more detail for the Champion Chase, but having looked short of pace over 2m at Leopardstown on both outings this season, he could well end up here if the ground isn't soft enough on day one. There's no doubt he stays as he has a ten-length 3m Grade 1 novice hurdle win to his name, while the bare form of his Arkle success 12 months ago is better than a lot of his rivals have ever managed. It's also becoming something of an outlier, though, as the 172 RPR he earned there is 13lb superior to anything else he has done over fences. At least he won't be running at Leopardstown, which he really doesn't seem to like.

Going preference Acts on any but soft preferable
Star rating ⊙⊙⊙

Protektorat
10 b g; Trainer Dan Skelton
Chase form 112212134145432313621, best RPR 172
Left-handed 121213414543231361, best RPR 172
Right-handed 122, best RPR 157
Cheltenham form (all) U513012345316, best RPR 170
At the festival 11 Mar 2020 Midfield, ridden on outer and headway between last 2 to chase leaders, weakened approaching last, finished tenth, beaten 12 lengths by Dame De Compagnie in Coral Cup 18 Mar 2022 Midfield, mistake 4th, headway on outer 4 out, pressed leaders home turn, ridden and disputing second before 2 out, 6 lengths third and staying on when blundered last, no chance but kept on run-in, just held third, beaten 17 and a half lengths in Gold Cup won by A Plus Tard 17 Mar 2023 Prominent, left in second 17th, ridden 3 out, briefly led before 2 out, soon headed and lost second, weakened approaching last, finished fifth, beaten 15 and a quarter lengths by Galopin Des Champs in Gold Cup

14 Mar 2024 Travelled strongly, in touch with leaders, headway and challenging 2 out, disputed lead approaching last, led run-in, soon ridden, kept on well inside final 110yds, won going away, beat Envoi Allen by four lengths in Ryanair Chase

One of the old men of the party now, but hard to argue he's not as good as he was when winning this 12 months ago given the way he thrashed possible rival Djelo at Windsor's Winter Million fixture in January. He had been well held in two previous outings this season, first on good ground when only sixth in the Paddy Power Gold Cup in November and then when having a rare spin around a right-handed course in the Peterborough Chase at Huntingdon, where Djelo was six lengths too good for him. The score is 1-1 between those two then, although it's fair to say neither was on their A-game when beaten. Protektorat does have the advantage of plenty of rock-solid Cheltenham form, though, as he has been third and fifth in a pair of Gold Cups. It's now 14 years since Albertas Run won the second of his Ryanairs at the age of ten, which just goes to show how hard it is to win at the festival at that age, but if the ground is soft we can expect Protektorat to put up a stout defence. If it's quicker, some of his rivals might be as well.

Going preference Acts on any but soft is perfect
Star rating ✪✪✪

Banbridge

9 ch g; Trainer Joseph O'Brien
Chase form 113211914U1, best RPR 174
Left-handed 12194, best RPR 158
Right-handed 1311U1, best RPR 174
Cheltenham form (all) 119, best RPR 158
At the festival 18 Mar 2022 Took keen hold, raced wide early, prominent, went second 7th, joined leader 3 out, led after 2 out, joined but clear with one other before last, soon ridden, kept on strongly final 110yds, won Martin Pipe Conditional Jockeys' Handicap Hurdle by a length and a half from Cobblers Dream
14 Mar 2024 Took keen hold, in touch with leaders, mistake 2nd, not fluent 11th, lost ground when mistake 4 out, weakened after 3 out, finished ninth, beaten 75 lengths by Protektorat in Ryanair Chase

Arguably the coming force in all divisions over the last 12 months as he beat Champion Chase winner Captain Guinness in a Grade 1 over 2m½f last April and then gunned down Il Est Francais under an incredibly confident ride from Paul Townend in the King George at Kempton over Christmas. Before that Kempton success he'd unseated at the last when in the process of giving the returning Energumene a serious race in the 2m½f Hilly Way at Cork despite the fact he was conceding 10lb to the dual Champion Chase winner. When he's good, he's very good indeed, and he has run career bests on four of his last six visits to the track, but all of those have come on ground that was no slower than good to soft. That's the issue for ante-post punters with Banbridge as when the ground is soft his record suggests he won't show up (missed the 2023 Turners because of the ground) or won't perform (beaten 75 lengths when ninth of 11 in last season's Ryanair at odds of 4-1). There's also the possibility, and increased likelihood given the way the race has cut up, that quicker ground will see him have a crack at Galopin Des Champs in the Gold Cup.

Going preference Has won on soft but the quicker the better
Star rating ✪✪✪

Il Est Francais

7 b g; Trainer Noel George & Amanda Zetterholm
Chase form 11151P2, best RPR 173
Left-handed 1151P, best RPR 156
Right-handed 12, best RPR 173

Looked a superstar when slamming his field by 11 lengths in last season's Kauto Star at Kempton, scoring in a quicker time than the King George winner later on the card, but had his problems after that, being well beaten either side of a comfortable Grade 3 win at Auteuil. He was certainly back to his best in the King George, though, going clear from an early stage and only being pegged back by Banbridge at the last. Many originally thought he'd gone much too fast, but the sectionals showed that the end of the race was exceptionally fast, and the chances are he was simply beaten by a better horse. He certainly stayed, given he still beat the rest by ten lengths. Even so, connections have said they're seriously considering dropping right down in distance for the Champion Chase, primarily to avoid Fact To File. For some reason he seems to scare them more than Jonbon, who has considerably better form in the book. Il Est Francais would also have a far better chance of dominating this field from the front given the number of possible pacesetters in the Champion Chase. It's a strange one, for sure, and he's never run on an undulating track.

Going preference Has won on heavy but big figures in Britain have come on good
Star rating ✪✪✪

El Fabiolo
8 b g; Trainer Willie Mullins
Chase form 111111P2F, best RPR 178
Left-handed 111PF, best RPR 178
Right-handed 1112, best RPR 174
Cheltenham form 1P, best RPR 172
At the festival 14 Mar 2023 Prominent, not fluent 1st, led just after 2 out, 3 lengths ahead when not fluent last, soon ridden, kept on strongly and went further clear final 110yds, ridden out, won Arkle Novices' Chase by five and a half lengths from Jonbon
13 Mar 2024 Prominent, lost position when not fluent 1st, dropped to last when bad mistake and almost fell 5th, soon pulled up in Champion Chase won by Captain Guinness

Brilliant Arkle winner who looked to have the 2m division at his mercy last season and started at 2-9 for the Champion Chase only to make a tremendous howler at the fifth fence, which led to him being pulled up quite quickly. Beaten by Jonbon next time at Sandown, he's been hard to train this season and got no further than the second fence in the Dublin Chase on his return in February. The ability is probably still there, but he's never run over this trip and is probably still more likely to run on Wednesday.

Going preference No ground issues
Star rating ✪

Djelo
7 b g; Trainer Venetia Williams
Chase form 111F2382121, best RPR 170
Left-handed 11F3821, best RPR 170
Right-handed 1221, best RPR 165

Cheltenham form 3, best RPR 154
At the festival 14 Mar 2024 Pressed leader, prominent when not fluent 3rd, not fluent 6th, jumped slightly right 9th, challenging before 3 out, weakened gradually before 2 out, finished third, beaten ten lengths by Grey Dawning in Turners Novices' Chase

Djelo won his first three chases as a novice last season and it wasn't his fault that he fell at the first on his fourth attempt as he was badly hampered. However, he did find Grade 1 company a touch too much for him, finishing a seven-length second in the Scilly Isles at Sandown and a ten-length third in the Turners before losing his form completely back at 2m at Aintree. He has been well on the up this year, though, running career-best RPRs on three of his four starts, all of them over different distances. In the first he ran a three-quarter-length second to JPR One in the 2m1½f Haldon Gold Cup, a race in which he was a big eyecatcher, while next time he took his form to a new level when sauntering to a six-length victory over Protektorat in the Peterborough Chase at Huntingdon. The runner-up, who arguably wasn't suited to going right-handed, gained his revenge in no uncertain terms with a 23-length success in a 2m6f race at Windsor next time, but it would be fair to say that, for whatever reason, Djelo wasn't at his best either. He was back on song in the Denman Chase at Newbury, though, finding no problem with the 2m7½f trip under new waiting tactics and having the race in the bag as far as three out, with Hitman, a perennial runner-up (now three times in that race), following him home. That took him up to a heady personal best of 170 on RPRs and the BHA assessor now rates him 166, which is the same rating as the Irish handicapper has for Fact To File. The market clearly doesn't agree, but he's an improving seven-year-old going into the meeting in the form of his life and it's hard to understand why he's on offer at a double-figure price. That ten-length Turners defeat last year might have something to do with it, but he was a 25-1 shot there and actually ran a career best at the time, so it's hard to hold it against him. He's just a better horse now.

Going preference Vast majority of form on soft but can handle quicker
Star rating ○○○○

Envoi Allen

11 b g; Trainer Henry de Bromhead
Chase form 111FP16133171432241U, best RPR 167
Left-handed F13124, best RPR 167
Right-handed 111P163174321U, best RPR 167
Cheltenham form (all) 11F312, best RPR 167
At the festival 13 Mar 2019 Held up, headway 5f out, led over 3f out, ridden over 1f out, strongly pressed inside final furlong, ran on gamely and found extra near finish, won Champion Bumper by three-quarters of a length from Blue Sari
11 Mar 2020 Raced keenly, in touch, chased leaders 2 out, about 6 lengths off the pace home bend, closed quickly to lead just before last, edged left run-in, ran on to draw clear final 100yds, won Ballymore Novices' Hurdle by four and a quarter lengths from Easywork
18 Mar 2021 Prominent, fell 4th in Marsh Novices' Chase won by Chantry House
16 Mar 2022 Disputed lead at good pace, tracked leader from 2nd, disputed lead 3 out, pushed along when mistake 2 out, soon ridden and lost second, weakened gradually from last, finished third, beaten 13 lengths by Energumene in Champion Chase
16 Mar 2023 Took keen hold, jumped right on occasions, prominent, not fluent 4 out, pecked on landing 3 out, disputed lead going easily before 2 out, pushed along and led clearly approaching last, ridden and edged left but kept on well run-in, won Ryanair Chase by two and three-quarter lengths from Shishkin
14 Mar 2024 Travelled strongly but jumped right on occasions, midfield, headway before 3 out, challenging when not fluent 2 out, disputed lead approaching last, not fluent last, lost position run-in, hung left and no extra run-in, finished second, beaten four lengths by Protektorat in Ryanair Chase

Grand veteran who looked like the second coming in Ireland when winning the first 11 starts of his career, including the Champion Bumper and Ballymore Novices' Hurdle. However, he fell when odds-on for a third different race at the festival, the Turners Novices' Chase in 2021, and didn't quite turn out to be the superstar many had hoped for. That said, he has still compiled an impressive body of work since then, winning Grade 1s

from 2m1f to 3m, and he got another festival win when beating Shishkin by two and three-quarter lengths in this race in 2023. Last season he was made 9-4 favourite for a repeat, having run a blinder when second to Gerri Colombe at Down Royal four months earlier, but although travelling very sweetly into the race, he didn't have the legs of Protektorat after the last, going down by four lengths. Envoi Allen resumed his career as enthusiastically as ever in November and he went one better in the Down Royal Champion Chase, beating Hewick by half a length for his fifth win in six visits to that meeting, but he unseated when seemingly going nowhere five out in the King George next time. That's the second time he has run poorly in that race, though, and it didn't stop him from returning to beat Shishkin the first time. His age, 11, is more of a stumbling block this time as there has yet to be a winner so old, and some of the younger guns have superior figures.

Going preference Acts on any ground
Star rating ○

OTHERS TO CONSIDER

Energumene is another top-class two-miler from the Mullins camp to have an entry in this and, while he hasn't run over such a trip for a long time, connections are beginning to believe he's lost that little bit of pace. It's hard to see all of Gaelic Warrior, El Fabiolo and him running in the Champion Chase, but who goes where remains anyone's guess. The Mullins-trained **Grangeclare West** will surely go for the Gold Cup, given the way he stayed on for second behind Galopin Des Champs at Leopardstown last time, although there's always a chance he'll go straight to the Grand National. **Jungle Boogie** is still in all three major Grade 1s, but rarely runs and is 11 anyway. It's possible that the novices **Heart Wood** and **Springwell Bay** will turn up as there's no novice Grade 1 for them. Heart Wood has the best form of the pair as things stand at the moment, but Springwell Bay was seriously impressive in handicap company when last seen over this course and distance and could well develop into a proper Grade 1 performer. Handicaps are an option, though.

RYANAIR CHASE RESULTS AND TRENDS

	FORM WINNER	AGE & WGT	Adj RPR	SP	TRAINER	BEST RPR LAST 12 MONTHS (RUNS SINCE)
24	-4323 **Protektorat** C, D	9 11-10	173-2	17-2	D Skelton	2nd Lingfield Class 2 chase (2m6f) **(1)**
23	3-317 **Envoi Allen** C, D	9 11-10	171-12	13-2	H de Bromhead (IRE)	won Down Royal Gd1 Chase (3m) **(1)**
22	1-211 **Allaho** CD	8 11-10	182^T	4-7f	W Mullins (IRE)	won Gd1 Ryanair Chase (2m4½f) **(3)**
21	3-641 **Allaho** D	7 11-10	171-5	3-1f	W Mullins (IRE)	won Thurles Gd2 chase (2m4f) **(0)**
20	1-212 **Min** D	9 11-10	182^T	2-1	W Mullins (IRE)	won Gd1 Melling Chase (2m4f) **(3)**
19	-1211 **Frodon** CD	7 11-10	180^T	9-2	P Nicholls	won Cheltenham Gd3 hcap chase (2m4½f) **(1)**
18	-1232 **Balko Des Flos** D	7 11-10	172-6	8-1	H de Bromhead (IRE)	2nd Gd1 Christmas Chase (3m) **(0)**
17	-1611 **Un De Sceaux** C, D	9 11-10	178^T	7-4f	W Mullins (IRE)	won Cheltenham Gd1 chase (2m½f) **(0)**
16	11-12 **Vautour** CD	7 11-10	184^T	Evensf	W Mullins (IRE)	2nd Gd1 King George VI Chase (3m) **(0)**
15	-418U **Uxizandre** C	7 11-10	170-5	16-1	A King	Won Cheltenham Listed chase (2m) **(2)**

WINS-RUNS: 6yo 0-6, 7yo 5-23, 8yo 1-35, 9yo 4-22, 10yo 0-10, 11yo 0-3, 12yo 0-2 **FAVOURITES:** £0.32

TRAINERS IN THIS Willie Mullins 5-4-20, Henry de Bromhead 2-3-11, Dan Skelton 1-0-3, Paul Nicholls 1-1-8, Gordon Elliott 0-2-8, Jamie Snowden 0-0-2, Joseph O'Brien 0-1-2, Venetia Williams 0-2-5, Nigel Twiston-Davies 0-0-2, Lucinda Russell 0-0-1

FATE OF FAVOURITES: 3112031122 **POSITION OF WINNER IN MARKET:** 8113221134

VERDICT

I'm kind of hoping *Fact To File* wins as I had a rare moment of clarity and backed him for this about ten minutes before Galopin Des Champs kicked his backside in the Savills Chase at Leopardstown over Christmas. The question is whether I'd back him at 2-1 now, and the answer there has to be a resounding no. It's quite possible he'll improve again for being dropped back in trip, but the form of his John Durkan win is certainly no better than his subsequent two efforts at 3m (you have to accept third-placed Galopin Des Champs wasn't at his best first time out or over the trip) and he'll have to step up on it to win. He might well do, as he has age on his side, but he's priced as though he already has. *Spillane's Tower* needs to find even more to be a player and doesn't make that much appeal as second favourite either, and of the certain runners it's last year's winner *Protektorat* who has the best form. I'll definitely save on him if the ground is soft, but the one who looks way overpriced is *DJELO*, who keeps running career bests. You might think it's nonsense that the handicappers on each side of the Irish Sea have him on the same rating as Fact To File, but what's beyond doubt is that he's improving and is a year younger too.

Key trends

➤ No more than four runs since October, ten winners in last ten runnings

➤ Rated within 6lb of RPR top-rated, 9/10

➤ Top-two finish in at least one of last two starts, 9/10

➤ Adjusted RPR of at least 171, 9/10

➤ No more than 12 runs over fences, 7/10

➤ Course winner, 7/10

Other factors

➤ Six winners had recorded a top-four finish in a Grade 1 or 2 chase over 3m-plus

➤ The first five winners (2005-2009) had either won or been placed in the Paddy Power Gold Cup or December Gold Cup earlier that season. However, 2019 winner Frodon is the only one in the last ten years to have run in those races

4.00 Paddy Power Stayers' Hurdle   ITV/RTV
➤ 3m   ➤ Grade 1   ➤ £325,000

Ireland had a recent dual winner of the Stayers' Hurdle in Flooring Porter and many expect Gordon Elliott's Teahupoo to follow up last year's comfortable victory, which came at the expense of Flooring Porter's hat-trick bid. A stayer in his prime can dominate in this often weak division and arguably that scenario has played out in favour of those two Irish stars in recent years. After Teahupoo was third in his first attempt at the Stayers' Hurdle in 2023, Elliott kept him fresher last year by giving him just one run beforehand in the Hatton's Grace Hurdle and the same formula has been followed again. Just as important to Teahupoo is soft ground, which is something Elliott cannot control, and quicker conditions than last year could bring him back to the pack. Home By The Lee has been in the pack for the past three years, achieving his best Stayers' result when third last year, and Joseph O'Brien's ten-year-old will be back again off a Grade 1 victory at Leopardstown's Christmas meeting. New rivals await too and one on an upward curve is Nicky Henderson's six-year-old Lucky Place, a Grade 2 course winner on New Year's Day in the Relkeel Hurdle. Even younger is the Declan Queally-trained Rocky's Diamond, who was still only four when he was third to Home By The Lee at Christmas and then a month later (after officially turning five) won the Grade 2 Galmoy Hurdle. Elliott also has an up-and-comer of his own in The Wallpark, who would be another interesting new rival for Teahupoo but could go for the Pertemps Final instead.

Teahupoo

8 b g; Trainer Gordon Elliott
Hurdles form 11121119611341112, best RPR 168
Left-handed 11931, best RPR 165
Right-handed 112116114112, best RPR 168
Cheltenham form 931, best RPR 165
At the festival 15 Mar 2022 Midfield, bit short of room 1st, pushed along and dropped to last 3 out, weakened before 2 out, finished ninth, beaten 33 lengths by Honeysuckle in Champion Hurdle
16 Mar 2023 Held up in rear, steady headway from 3 out, not fluent 2 out, switched left then ridden and pressed leader approaching last, switched right final 110yds, kept on well, finished 3rd, placed 2nd, demoted to 3rd after appeal, beaten three-quarters of a length by Sire Du Berlais in Stayers' Hurdle
14 Mar 2024 Raced wide, in touch with leaders, not fluent 7th, pressed leaders on outer when mistake 2 out, went second then switched left before last, soon led and edged right, ridden and kept on well run-in, won Stayers' Hurdle by three and three-quarter lengths from Flooring Porter

Second but demoted to third in the 2023 Stayers', Teahupoo was given a very light campaign last season to take advantage of how well he goes fresh, and that strategy paid dividends. After reappearing to win the Hatton's Grace by a length from Impaire Et Passe at Fairyhouse in December, he wasn't seen again until the Stayers', for which he went off 5-4 favourite and was a commanding three-and-three-quarter-length scorer from dual previous winner Flooring Porter. Just one more run followed, and Teahupoo won that as well, beating Asterion Forlonge in the Champion Stayers Hurdle at Punchestown in May. Gordon Elliott has adopted the same approach with him this season, but Teahupoo was this time made to look pedestrian by Lossiemouth in the Hatton's Grace, running to an RPR of just 149 as the grey mare cruised past him at the last to win by three and three-quarter lengths. That form would give him little chance of making a successful defence, although to be fair the race was run at a crawl over just 2m4f and on yielding ground, neither of which would have suited ideally. There's no real reason to think he's any worse than was a year ago, which is why he remains a very warm favourite for a repeat. The Stayers' will have a considerably different complexion this time, though. Last year's race, run on Teahupoo's favoured bottomless ground, was loaded with fully exposed horses, only three of the 12 runners being less than nine years old. You can never guarantee deep ground at Cheltenham, for all that has been the case for the last couple of seasons, and the field will be almost entirely different this time, with several younger horses among the dangers. That said, they all need to improve a good deal on what they've done so far, which is why the ten-year-old Home By The Lee is second favourite. No doubt Teahupoo's the one to beat assuming he's still capable of the same level.

Going preference Acts on any but the more mud the better

Star rating ✪✪✪✪

Home By The Lee

10 b g; Trainer Joseph O'Brien
Hurdles form 218U226R115P3533611, best RPR 163
Left-handed 286115P353611, best RPR 159
Right-handed 1U22R3, best RPR 154
Cheltenham form 653, best RPR 158
At the festival 17 Mar 2022 Chased winner, lost second but close up 5th, pushed along and lost position after 3 out, not fluent 2 out, ridden and rallied against near rail after last, not reach leaders, finished sixth, beaten seven and a half lengths by Flooring Porter in Stayers' Hurdle 16 Mar 2023 In touch with leaders, bad mistake

Home By The Lee: set for his fourth attempt at the race, having been sixth, fifth and third

and dropped to midfield 6th, pushed along 3 out, headway home turn, ridden and outpaced before last, held but kept on well run-in, finished fifth, beaten three and three-quarter lengths by Sire Du Berlais in Stayers' Hurdle 14 Mar 2024 Jumped right on occasions, towards rear, not fluent 4th, mistake 7th, headway 2 out, went third then not fluent last, kept on run-in, finished third, beaten six lengths by Teahupoo in Stayers' Hurdle

Was a 16-1 shot when finishing a six-length third to Teahupoo 12 months ago and occupied the same spot behind him at Punchestown at a similar distance before finishing sixth in the French Champion Hurdle (3m1½f) in May. He has taken advantage of Teahupoo's absence to win both outings this term, landing the Grade 2 Lismullen Hurdle by three and a half lengths from Bob Olinger in November and then extending his margin of victory to six lengths over the same horse in the Grade 1 Savills Hurdle over Christmas. He'll go into the meeting as second favourite this time, but that's more an indication of the weakness of the division than any notion that he has improved at the age of ten. His best RPR of 163 actually came when he finished fifth in the 2023 Stayers', but the level he has reached this season is still considerably better than anything shown by the up-and-comers (and Teahupoo) in the same period.

Going preference Can handle any ground
Star rating ✪✪✪

Lucky Place
6 b g; Trainer Nicky Henderson
Hurdles form 2122411, best RPR 152
Left-handed 1241, best RPR 152
Right-handed 221, best RPR 144
Cheltenham form 241, best RPR 152
At the festival 13 Mar 2024 Held up in rear, raced wide and headway 2 out, went fourth last, stayed on final 110yds, finished fourth, beaten four and three-quarter lengths by Langer Dan in Coral Cup

The first of the improving young guns, Lucky Place was progressive as a novice last season, and having been one of the few Nicky Henderson-trained runners allowed to take part at the festival, he performed with some credit in his first handicap to finish fourth to Langer Dan in the Coral Cup, staying on

strongly at the end. His improvement has continued apace this term, as like Home By The Lee he's 2-2, in his case winning the Grade 2 Ascot Hurdle over 2m3½f and the Relkeel at the same level over 2m4½f on New Year's Day. Each time he won by a length or less, so it's hard to say the form is outstanding or anywhere near what's required to win this, but he was conceding 6lb to Gowel Road at Cheltenham and that one at least boosted the form when winning the Cleeve on Trials day. On the upside, Lucky Place has improved his RPR every time he has hit the racecourse, shapes as though he's well worth trying at 3m and is only six years old, so it's likely he hasn't stopped improving. One of the more interesting ones.

Going preference Has improved on good and soft this season
Star rating ✪✪✪

The Wallpark
7 b g; Trainer Gordon Elliott
Hurdles form 251130911114, best RPR 152
Left-handed 1191, best RPR 152
Right-handed 25301114, best RPR 152
Cheltenham form 1, best RPR 152

Handicapper who was on a roll for Gordon Elliott in the summer, winning four times. He started in a lowly Kilbeggan contest off a mark of just 129 in July, defied 8lb higher in a valuable handicap at the Galway festival, won a three-runner conditions race and then ran out a commanding winner of a Pertemps qualifier at Cheltenham, giving 4lb and a two-and-a-half-length beating to course regular Gowel Road. Raised to a rating of 152 after that, he dipped his toes into Grade 1 company for the first time and ran with plenty of credit in the Long Walk Hurdle at Ascot, grabbing fourth on the line, three and a half lengths behind winner Crambo in a race that wasn't run at a particularly strong gallop. He's a strong stayer on the up and is entitled to some respect as a second string to Teahupoo assuming he comes here rather than runs under a big weight in the Pertemps Final.

Going preference All of his improvement has come on good, yielding or good to soft, with the fact he was busy in the summer

suggesting he doesn't want it much softer
Star rating ✪✪✪

Rocky's Diamond
5 b g; Trainer Declan Queally
Hurdles form 015131, best RPR 149
Left-handed 53, best RPR 147
Right-handed 0111, best RPR 149

The youngest in the field at the age of five and another who started this season with a low handicap mark, in his case just 123. He scored off that rating at Gowran Park in October, winning by just half a length, after which he was thrown into the deep end by trainer Declan Queally in the Grade 1 Savills Hurdle at Leopardstown. A 66-1 shot outclassed on all known form, he nevertheless ran a blinder to be third, albeit finishing just over nine lengths behind winner Home By The Lee. Having gone up 15lb for that, Rocky's Diamond stayed in decent company next time for the Grade 2 Galmoy Hurdle and rewarded his trainer's faith with a strong staying performance to win going away by a length and a quarter from Thedevilscoachman. Again, with no Teahupoo or Home By The Lee, it was a very weak race for the grade, and his winning RPR was just 149, but he's a horse on the up with very few miles on the clock.

Going preference Seems to act on anything
Star rating ✪✪

Gowel Road
9 bbg; Trainer Nigel Twiston-Davies
Hurdles form 24110613274734622221, best RPR 145
Left-handed 241106132743622221, best RPR 145
Right-handed 74, best RPR 140
Cheltenham form 017622221, best RPR 145
At the festival 19 Mar 2021 Tracked leaders, hit 4th, lost position after 3 out, weakened 2 out, finished 20th, beaten 21 and three-quarter lengths by Belfast Banter in County Hurdle 16 Mar 2022 Tracked leaders, mistake 7th, ridden after 3 out, soon held, stayed on run-in, finished seventh, beaten 22 and a quarter lengths by Commander Of Fleet in Coral Cup 14 Mar 2024 In touch with leaders, lost position after 3 out, rallied on turn before last, weakened gradually final 110yds, finished sixth, beaten eight and a quarter lengths by Monmiral in Pertemps Final

Cheltenham regular who has run in three festival handicaps, finishing a creditable seventh in the Coral Cup and sixth in last season's Pertemps Final. He has finished first or second in his six visits to the course away from the festival, with five of those runs coming this season. Gowel Road has finished runner-up in 3m handicaps in October (won by The Wallpark), November (Doyen Quest) and December (Long Draw), and also finished second in the 2m4½f Relkeel on New Year's Day over a trip that is arguably short of his best. He finally gained the win he deserved when beating last year's Pertemps Final winner Monmiral by two and a quarter lengths in the Grade 2 Cleeve Hurdle, although was getting 4lb. As game as he is, his last four RPRs have been exactly 145 and, while he's now on a career-high mark of 148, that's just 2lb higher than he was rated in October 2022, so it's hard to say he's a massive improver. He always runs his race, but his form says it won't be good enough at this level.

Going preference Ground seems irrelevant
Star rating ✪✪

Hiddenvalley Lake
8 ch g; Trainer Henry de Bromhead
Hurdles form 11281327, best RPR 154
Left-handed 1813, best RPR 154
Right-handed 1227, best RPR 154
Cheltenham form 8, best RPR 120
At the festival 17 Mar 2023 Midfield on outer, pushed along after 2 out, soon weakened, finished eighth, beaten 45 and three-quarter lengths by Stay Away Fay in Albert Bartlett Novices' Hurdle

Fair staying novice a couple of seasons ago despite being beaten a long way when only eighth in the Albert Bartlett. A chase campaign was shelved after just one run last term when he fell on his debut at Navan, but he resumed his progress back over hurdles, beating Beacon Edge in the Grade 2 Boyne Hurdle before swerving Cheltenham and going to Aintree for the Liverpool Hurdle. There he finished a highly respectable third to near five-length winner Strong Leader and he may well have been second but for running short of room at the last. Hiddenvalley Lake resumed from an eight-month break to run a fine second to Crambo in the Long Walk, failing by just a head to get up after being only fifth on the run to the final hurdle, but he took a massive backwards step after that when only seventh of nine, beaten 21 lengths by Rocky's Diamond in the Galmoy. That clearly wasn't his form and came at a time when Henry de Bromhead's team was badly struggling for winners (was just 4-55 in January), so he can be given a pass for that, not least because his trainer's horses usually turn up at Cheltenham in much better nick.

Going preference Has comparable form on good to soft and heavy
Star rating ✪✪

Langer Dan
9 b g; Trainer Dan Skelton
Hurdles form 11226954126B137816P90132355, best RPR 159
Left-handed 126952B13781913355, best RPR 159
Right-handed 124166P02, best RPR 157
Cheltenham form 262B8115, best RPR 148
At the festival 11 Mar 2020 Held up towards rear of midfield, headway after 2 out, switched left after turning in, disputing 6th jumping last, kept on but not pace to get on terms, finished sixth, beaten four and three-quarter lengths by Aramax in Fred Winter Juvenile Handicap Hurdle
19 Mar 2021 Held up in rear, steady headway after 3 out, pushed along and went third approaching last, chased winner when ridden run-in, kept on well but not pace to challenge, finished second, beaten two and a quarter lengths by Galopin Des Champs in Martin Pipe Conditional Jockeys' Handicap Hurdle
18 Mar 2022 Held up in rear, brought down 2nd in Martin Pipe Conditional Jockeys' Handicap Hurdle won by Banbridge
15 Mar 2023 Held up in midfield, steady headway before 3 out, ridden and went third before last, led and hard pressed inside final 110yds, just prevailed, gamely, won Coral Cup by a head from An Epic Song
13 Mar 2024 Travelled strongly, midfield, headway 2 out, led narrowly before last, ridden clear final 110yds, readily, won Coral Cup by three and a half lengths from Ballyadam

Splits opinion among punters given the way he has been campaigned as he always tends to run terribly in the first half of the season but come alive at the spring festivals, most

notably Cheltenham. Trainer Dan Skelton says it's just him, while others point to the fact that he has an uncanny knack of suddenly finding his form when it matters. Other than when being unluckily brought down in 2022, he has finished second in a Martin Pipe to Galopin Des Champs (2021) and won the last two Coral Cups, last year in comfortable fashion by three and a half lengths from Ballyadam from exactly the same mark as he'd scored off the previous season (141). He improved considerably again after that, finishing third in a three-way photo to Impaire Et Passe and Bob Olinger in the Grade 1 Aintree Hurdle and then a two-and-a-quarter-length second to Impaire Et Passe in the Select Hurdle at Sandown. He ended the season on a mark of 160, which meant he was hugely unlikely to get down to anywhere near a workable rating for a handicap this year, while the BHA assessor is not playing ball this time either, having dropped him only 2lb for three awful runs this term, each one considerably worse than the last. It's hardly going to be a great surprise if he bounces back to some form at Cheltenham, and the pick of his is better than some of his shorter-priced rivals, but he's yet to prove he stays 3m, albeit his one attempt came at the wrong time of year.

Going preference Acts on any ground
Star rating ✪✪

Crambo
8 b g; Trainer Fergal O'Brien
Hurdles form 1P1171319815, best RPR 156
Left-handed P1713985, best RPR 150
Right-handed 1111, best RPR 156
Cheltenham form 95, best RPR 150
At the festival 14 Mar 2024 Took keen hold, towards rear on inner, in touch with leaders after 3rd, not fluent 5 out, not fluent 2 out, soon no impression, weakened before last, finished ninth, beaten 14 and a half lengths by Teahupoo in Stayers' Hurdle

Looked the coming force last season, having graduated from handicap company to win the Grade 1 Long Walk Hurdle at Ascot, in which he just got up to deny the evergreen Paisley Park his third win in the race. However, he was given a break after that and seemed to be found out at the spring festivals, beating only three home in the Stayers' at Cheltenham and then coming home last of eight finishers in the Liverpool Hurdle. Looked back to his best at Ascot on his return, just doing enough to hold the finish of Hiddenvalley Lake to land his second Long Walk Hurdle, but he then took another thumping at Cheltenham, finishing only fifth of six to Gowel Road in the Cleeve, having been weak in the market. He'd need to find a bit of improvement on his best form to be a player anyway, but his record strongly points to the course, and left-handed tracks in general, not being in his favour. Crambo is 6-6 on right-handed tracks (two bumpers to go with his four hurdles), but only 2-8 the other way around, with his last success coming in handicap company off a mark of just 133.

Going preference Has won on good and heavy
Star rating ⭘

Gold Tweet

8 b g; Trainer Gabriel Leenders
Hurdles form 148514312181, best RPR 157
Left-handed 48141181, best RPR 157
Right-handed 1532, best RPR 137
Cheltenham form 18, best RPR 157
At the festival 16 Mar 2023 Always towards rear, minor headway after 2 out, weakened before last, finished eighth, beaten 16 lengths by Sire Du Berlais in Stayers' Hurdle

Burst on to the scene from France in January 2023 with a smooth three-length win in the Cleeve Hurdle from Dashel Drasher and was expected to make his presence felt in the Stayers' six weeks later. However, he was a drifter on the day (9-2 to 7-1) and was never a factor. Since then he has mostly been chasing, running ten times in that sphere (two wins) but also landing a Listed hurdle at Compiegne in April. He didn't run that badly on his next visit to Britain when fourth to Royale Pagaille in the Betfair Chase, but has since unseated in a Grade 3 at Pau (rider lost irons after four out, went at next, but seemingly still going okay at the time). His Cleeve form is better than some of those ahead of him in the betting, but whether he can reproduce it after that prep is another matter.

Going preference All form on soft or heavy
Star rating ⭘⭘

OTHERS TO CONSIDER

Strong Leader had looked a potential improver this season following his breakthrough in the Liverpool Hurdle in April, and he started well enough when beating **Monmiral** a shade handily in the Long Distance at Newbury in November, but then finished a tailed-off last in the Long Walk. That was obviously nowhere near his form, and he was sent for a wind operation just six days later, but a returning fourth of six to Gowel Road in the Cleeve is unlikely to change trainer Olly Murphy's mind about him being more of an Aintree horse

Langer Dan: twice a festival winner in the Coral Cup

STAYERS' HURDLE RESULTS AND TRENDS

	FORM	WINNER	AGE & WGT	Adj RPR	SP	TRAINER	BEST RPR LAST 12 MONTHS (RUNS SINCE)
24	134-1	**Teahupoo** D	7 11-10	170ᵀ	5-4f	G Elliott (IRE)	Won Gd1 Hatton's Grace Hurdle (2m4½f) (0)
23	455P4	**Sire Du Berlais** CD	11 11-10	166⁷	33-1	G Elliott (IRE)	Won Gd1 Liverpool Hurdle (3m½f) (5)
22	1-PF2	**Flooring Porter** CD	7 11-10	173²	4-1	G Cromwell (IRE)	Won Gd1 Stayers' Hurdle (3m) (3)
21	13211	**Flooring Porter** D	6 11-10	169⁵	12-1	G Cromwell (IRE)	Won Leopardstown Gd1 hurdle (3m) (0)
20	239F3	**Lisnagar Oscar** D	7 11-10	155²¹	50-1	R Curtis	3rd Gd2 Cleeve Hurdle (3m) (0)
19	-1111	**Paisley Park** CD	7 11-10	176ᵀ	11-8f	E Lavelle	won Gd2 Cleeve Hurdle (3m) (0)
18	4112-	**Penhill** CD, BF	7 11-10	159¹⁰	12-1	W Mullins (IRE)	won Gd1 Albert Bartlett Novices' Hurdle (3m) (1)
17	-312F	**Nichols Canyon** CD	7 11-10	170²	10-1	W Mullins (IRE)	won Punchestown Gd1 hurdle (2m) (2)
16	-2111	**Thistlecrack** CD	8 11-10	176ᵀ	Evensf	C Tizzard	won Gd2 Cleeve Hurdle (3m) (0)
15	-1234	**Cole Harden**	6 11-10	162⁷	14-1	W Greatrex	2nd Newbury Gd2 hurdle (3m½f) (2)

WINS-RUNS: 5yo 0-2, 6yo 2-18, 7yo 6-37, 8yo 1-29, 9yo 0-20, 10yo 0-21, 11yo 1-6, 12yo 0-2, 13yo 0-1 **FAVOURITES:** -£3.38

TRAINERS IN THIS RACE (w-pl-r): Willie Mullins 2-2-21, Gordon Elliott 2-1-6, Fergal O'Brien 0-0-3, Henry de Bromhead 0-0-1, Paul Nicholls 0-2-5, Nicky Henderson 0-1-8, Gabriel Leenders 0-0-1, Joseph O'Brien 0-1-3, Nigel Twiston-Davies 0-1-4

FATE OF FAVOURITES: 2135173531 **POSITION OF WINNER IN MARKET:** 6145197291

than a Cheltenham one. Last year's Pertemps winner **Monmiral** has run solid races on his last two outings, just coming out best at the weights when second in the Cleeve, and could run a fair race if the ground is deep. **Buddy One** was fourth last year and could turn up again having not taken to fences this season, although he ran a shocker returned to hurdles at Gowran in January (said to have made a respiratory noise).

VERDICT

*There's no doubt at all that **Teahupoo** is the one to beat as he goes for a second win. In terms of top-class staying hurdlers, he's hardly a great, but on his best form he's well clear of the others and it's up to them to take a step forward. He did, however, have all his stars aligned last year, as it was the weakest Stayers' Hurdle for a while, and at least this time there are some younger legs to challenge him. They've all got to improve to do so as this division is terribly weak, but some of them are least on the up. I'd be quite interested in Elliott second-string **The Wallpark** if he's allowed to come here rather than run in the Pertemps, but the tentative each-way selection is **LUCKY PLACE**. He's got a fair amount to find but is at least going forwards quite rapidly, having run big career bests on his two outings this season, shapes as though he'll stay 3m and ought to have more to come at the age of six.*

Key trends

➤Ran no more than four times since August, 9/10

➤Aged six to eight, 9/10

➤Won a Graded hurdle over at least 3m, 9/10

➤Top-three finish on last completed start, 8/10

➤Ran between eight and 16 times over hurdles, 8/10

➤Previously ran at the festival, 8/10

➤Adjusted RPR of at least 166, 7/10

➤Finished in first three in all completed hurdle starts that season, 6/10

Other factors

➤Five of the 11 Irish winners since the mid-1980s prepped in the Boyne Hurdle at Navan

➤The record of Cleeve Hurdle winners is 21317387

4.40 TrustATrader Plate Handicap Chase   ITV/RTV
➤2m4½f   ➤Premier Handicap   ➤£150,000

Established in 1951 and traditionally known as the Mildmay of Flete, this is a highly competitive 2m4½f handicap chase that usually attracts a maximum field of 24.

LAST YEAR'S WINNER Shakem Up'Arry scored at 8-1 for Ben Pauling, equalling the score at 5-5 for Britain and Ireland in the past decade.

FORM Shakem Up'Arry was the sixth last-time-out winner to strike in the past nine runnings (one of the other winners had been second the time before).

WEIGHT AND RATINGS The previous trend of winners rated in the 130s has changed now that it is less common to get into the race with that sort of mark. Nine of the last 11 winners were in the 140-145 range and most carried less than 11st.

TRAINERS Gordon Elliott (with The Storyteller in 2018) is the only one of the current big five trainers to have taken the prize in the past 17 years.

BETTING This race has been the biggest graveyard for favourites over the years, although Shakem Up'Arry became the fifth winner in the last seven years below 10-1.

ONES TO WATCH Course-and-distance winner **Jagwar** could be sent here instead of the novice handicap chase by Oliver Greenall and Josh Guerriero. The Dan Skelton-trained **Madara** is also proven over track and trip after his good second in the December Gold Cup. Last year's runner-up **Crebilly** (Jonjo and AJ O'Neill) looks set to return off the same mark.

FESTIVAL PLATE RESULTS AND TRENDS

	FORM WINNER	AGE & WGT	OR	SP	TRAINER	BEST RPR LAST 12 MONTHS (RUNS SINCE)
24	4-P61 **Shakem Up'arry** CD	10 11-5	143-7	8-1	B Pauling	won Cheltenham Gd3 hcap chase (2m4½f) (0)
23	F2311 **Seddon** C, D	10 10-9	143-2	20-1	J McConnell (IRE)	won Leopardstown hcap chase (2m5f) (0)
22	2F187 **Coole Cody** CD	11 11-2	145-2	22-1	E Williams	won Cheltenham Gd3 hcap chase (2m½f) (2)
21	14131 **The Shunter** C, D	8 10-5	140T	9-4f	E Mullins (IRE)	3rd Leopardstown hcp chase (2m1½f) (0)
20	-1121 **Simply The Betts** CD	7 11-4	149T	10-3f	H Whittington	won Cheltenham Class 2 hcap chase (2m4½f) (0)
19	3-111 **Siruh Du Lac** CD	6 10-8	141-6	9-2	N Williams	won Cheltenham Gd3 hcap chase (2m4½f) (0)
18	-2137 **The Storyteller** D	7 11-4	147-7	5-1f	G Elliott (IRE)	7th Leopardstown Gd1 novice chase (2m5f) (0)
17	14322 **Road To Respect**	6 10-13	145-16	14-1	N Meade (IRE)	3rd Leopardstown Gd1 novice chase (2m1f) (2)
16	-F2P1 **Empire Of Dirt** D	9 10-11	142-13	16-1	C Murphy (IRE)	2nd Punchestown hcp chase (2m6f) (2)
15	7/157 **Darna** D	9 10-11	140-6	33-1	K Bailey	won Sedgefield Class 3 hcp chase (2m3½f) (2)

WINS-RUNS: 5yo 0-2, 6yo 2-19, 7yo 2-44, 8yo 1-48, 9yo 2-46, 10yo 2-42, 11yo 1-10, 12yo 0-5 **FAVOURITES:** +£3.58

FATE OF FAVOURITES: 2PP12112PF **POSITION OF WINNER IN MARKET:** 0871211804

Key trends

➤Won between 2m3f and 2m5f, 10/10

➤No more than 12 runs over fences, 9/10

➤Won a Class 3 or higher, 8/10

➤Officially rated 140 to 145, 8/10

➤Carried no more than 11st 2lb, 7/10

Other factors

➤Three of the last ten winners won or placed in one of the big 2m4f-2m5f handicaps at Cheltenham that season

➤Irish trainers have won five of the last nine runnings (their last winner before them was Doubleuagain in 1982)

➤Six winners scored last time out but three of the other four failed to place

5.20 Fulke Walwyn Kim Muir Handicap Chase RTV
➤3m2f   ➤Amateur riders   ➤£75,000

This 3m2f handicap chase is now one of two festival races left open only to amateur riders (the other is the hunter chase) and typically attracts a full field of 24.

LAST YEAR'S WINNER Hot favourite Inothewayurthinkin (13-8) made it five wins in six years for Ireland, giving trainer Gavin Cromwell his first handicap success at the festival.

FORM There is a trend of Kim Muir winners bouncing back from disappointing efforts (15 of the last 24 winners had been unplaced on their previous run). Inothewayurthinkin had been ninth in Leopardstown's 2m5½f handicap chase at the Dublin Racing Festival.

WEIGHT AND RATINGS With little between most of the runners nowadays, the higher-rated runners have started to do well and 12 of the last 16 winners carried 11st 4lb or more (including topweights Character Building in 2009, Ballabriggs in 2010, Mount Ida in 2021 and Inothewayurthinkin last year). Most recent winners were rated in the 140s (Inothewayurthinkin was 145).

AGE Only four horses aged older than nine have won in the last 30 runnings and horses aged seven or eight have won ten of the last 14.

TRAINERS This tends to get shared around and Cromwell was the 12th different winning trainer in the last 13 runnings. Only Gordon Elliott has doubled up in that time (2021 winner Mount Ida also came from his stable, officially under Denise Foster's name). Elliott has become the most powerful force with two winners, two seconds, two thirds and three fourths from 21 runners.

BETTING Inothewayurthinkin was only the second winning favourite in the past decade but continued the trend of most recent winners coming from the top six in the market.

ONES TO WATCH Gavin Cromwell has options with his strong squad of handicap chasers and this is a possibility for **Now Is The Hour**. **Hasthing** could be well suited by this test having won over 2m6f on soft ground at Windsor and his trainers Jonjo and AJ O'Neill also have smart novice **Johnnywho** for JP McManus.

KIM MUIR HANDICAP CHASE RESULTS AND TRENDS

	FORM	WINNER	AGE & WGT	OR	SP	TRAINER	BEST RPR LAST 12 MONTHS (RUNS SINCE)
24	-2239	Inothewayurthinkin	6 12-0	145-9	13-8f	G Cromwell (IRE)	3rd Limerick Gd1 novice chase (2m3½f) (1)
23	8421U	Angels Dawn BF	8 11-0	131-9	10-1	S Curling (IRE)	Unseated Punchestown hcap chase (3m4f) (0)
22	12211	Chambard (5x)	10 10-12	134-10	40-1	V Williams	won Hunt Class 3 nov hcap chase (2m7½f) (0)
21	0-312	Mount Ida	7 11-9	142-10	3-1f	D Foster (IRE)	2nd Thurles Gd2 novice chase (2m4f) (0)
20	52422	Milan Native	7 11-1	141-2	9-1	G Elliott (IRE)	2nd Thurles novice chase (2m2f) (3)
19	-5253	Any Second Now	7 11-11	143-4	6-1	T Walsh (IRE)	5th Leopardstown hcap chase (3m½f) (1)
18	-P632	Missed Apporach	8 11-5	138-2	8-1	W Greatrex	8th Scottish Grand National (4m1f) (4)
17	45683	Domesday Book	7 11-4	137-6	40-1	S Edmunds	3rd Leicester Class 3 hcap chase (2m4f) (0)
16	8-005	Cause Of Causes C	8 11-9	142-6	9-2	G Elliott (IRE)	5th Naas Gd2 chase (2m) (0)
15	30-6P	The Package CD	12 11-4	137T	9-1	D Pipe	6th Cheltenham Gd3 hcap chase (3m3½f) (1)

WINS-RUNS: 6yo 1-11, 7yo 4-46, 8yo 3-62, 9yo 0-55, 10yo 1-26, 11yo 0-15, 12yo 1-7 **FAVOURITES:** -£3.38

FATE OF FAVOURITES: 0UU2871221 **POSITION OF WINNER IN MARKET:** 3203261051

Key trends

> Officially rated 134 to 143, 8/10

> No more than ten runs over fences, 8/10

> Finished in first three in either or both of last two starts, 8/10

> Aged seven or eight, 7/10

> Ran at a previous festival, 7/10

> Winning for the first time that season, 7/10

Johnnywho (white cap): one of the possibles in the JP McManus colours

Other factors

> Irish trainers have won six of the last ten runnings – the last Irish-trained winner before them was Greasepaint in 1983

> Four winners had yet to win over three miles or beyond

FRIDAY, MARCH 14
(NEW COURSE)

PAUL KEALY
ON THE KEY
PLAYERS

1.20 JCB Triumph Hurdle ITV/RTV
➤ 2m1f ➤ Grade 1 ➤ £150,000

If the home team have struggled to make a telling impact on the first three days, the juvenile hurdling championship contest promises a strong start to the final card. Britain has the top two in the ante-post betting, and they present quite a contrast. Lulamba is favourite for Nicky Henderson (who has won the Triumph a record seven times) and has come from traditional jumping roots in France with a big reputation. The hype was justified to some extent by his hurdles debut win at Ascot but arguably he has still to prove he has as much substance as style. That is not the case for Flat recruit East India Dock, who has a much superior Racing Post Rating from his course-and-distance victory on Trials day. His trainer James Owen is at the opposite end of the experience scale to Henderson, having yet to taste festival success. Ireland's best chance appears to be the Gavin Cromwell-trained Hello Neighbour, winner of the often significant Grade 1 juvenile hurdle at the Dublin Racing Festival.

Lulamba
4 b g; Trainer Nicky Henderson
Hurdles form 11, best RPR 132
Left-handed 1, best RPR 103
Right-handed 1, best RPR 132

Impressive five-length winner on his hurdles debut at Auteuil in October, after which he was purchased by the Donnellys and sent to Nicky Henderson. The dogs were barking his name long before his intended stable debut at Ascot in January and it's fair to say he didn't let his connections down by romping to another impressive victory, this time by three and a half lengths from high-class Flat performer Mondo Man, after which Henderson had to pooh-pooh rumours he'd been kicking Jonbon out of the way on the gallops. There's no doubt he was very impressive, but what he actually achieved has to be open to question. While Mondo Man, who was receiving 10lb, was very useful on the Flat, having been fifth in the French Derby and fourth in the King Edward VII at Royal Ascot, he pulled his jockey's arms out for at least a mile and cannot possibly have run to his full potential. A better guide may be the third, Viyanni, who was beaten just over six lengths in receipt of 4lb and has subsequently made a meal out of winning at odds of 2-7 at Ludlow. Racing Post Ratings awarded Lulamba a figure of 132, which is very respectable for a horse having

his second start, but no more than that. To put it into perspective, the 15-year-average RPR recorded by a favourite going into the Triumph is a tad over 143, while it's 150 for a winner (although I added 7lb for when a mare was favourite or won). It will surprise no-one if Lulamba turns out to be everything people expect him to be as Henderson is the master when it comes to the Triumph, having won it no fewer than seven times. At the moment, however, he's just over 10lb short of an average favourite for the race, yet priced up like a superior favourite. That will have something to do with the absence of many really strong contenders, but there is one with considerably better form.

Going preference Wins have come on good and heavy
Star rating ✪✪✪✪

East India Dock
4 b g; Trainer James Owen
Hurdles form 111, best RPR 143
Left-handed 11, best RPR 143
Right-handed 1, best RPR 114
Cheltenham form 11, best RPR 143

A half-brother to Burdett Road, who was favourite for the Triumph early last season until getting thumped ten lengths by Sir Gino on Trials day but has improved massively this term, winning the Greatwood, and is on target to run in the Champion Hurdle. With a rating of 89 on the Flat, East India Dock was some way behind his sibling in that sphere (Burdett Road was 101 when switched to hurdles) but the signs are good that he's going to prove the better of the two over hurdles. For a start, unlike Burdett Road, he settles well, while his jumping is about as slick as you'd like for an ex-Flat performer. He has won all three starts over hurdles, beginning with a comfortable four-length success from Hot Fuss (similarly rated on the Flat) when made a 1-2 shot at Wincanton. He was odds-on again in November's Triumph Trial at Cheltenham and didn't give his supporters any worries, travelling strongly, taking it up two out and strolling home by 18 lengths. It was then on to Trials day and the Triumph course and distance, over which he shrugged off a 5lb Grade 2 penalty by making all and hitting the line hard without being unduly pressed to win by ten lengths. He clearly stays very well (best form on the Flat over 2m at Goodwood), while he doesn't waste any time in the air at his hurdles, even when he gets in close. With an RPR of 143, he's bang on the 15-year average for a favourite and, given he's 11lb clear of Lulamba on the RPR figures, he surely should be heading the market.

Going preference Has won on good and soft ground
Star rating ✪✪✪✪✪

Hello Neighbour
4 b g; Trainer Gavin Cromwell
Hurdles form (left-handed) 11, best RPR 132

Didn't make his Flat debut until September but won both starts in that sphere and an Irish rating of 97 makes him better than East India Dock already. It's hurdles that count, of course, and Hello Neighbour has won both outings in that sphere as well, even though he went straight into Graded company. On his Grade 2 debut at Leopardstown over Christmas he took a keen enough hold, but took it up approaching the last and looked set to win easily, only to tie up close home and hang on by a short head from the strong-finishing Lady Vega Allen. Next time it was the Grade 1 at the Dublin Racing Festival, and there Hello Neighbour extended his winning margin over

Lady Vega Allen, beating that one a length and a half into third, with the filly Galileo Dame taking second spot. As an unbeaten and lightly raced horse, he deserves plenty of respect, but he has given the impression on both starts that he was desperate for the line, and he's going to have to run a furlong further at Cheltenham.

Going preference Has won on anything from good to soft
Star rating ✪✪✪

Lady Vega Allen
4 b f; Trainer Willie Mullins
Hurdles form 123, best RPR 122
Left-handed 23, best RPR 122
Right-handed 1

Won a hurdle at Moulins in September before joining Willie Mullins and has run with credit in a pair of Graded races behind Hello Neighbour since, going down by a short head on the first occasion and a length and a half the next time. There's no obvious reason why she should turn the tables as the winner looked to be running all over her heading to the last, but she'll stay the extra furlong well. Wasn't given an entry in the mares' novice, so this is where she'll go unless the Fred Winter is considered an option.

Going preference Not enough to go on
Star rating ✪

Galileo Dame
4 ch f; Trainer Joseph O'Brien
Hurdles form (left-handed) 22, best RPR 125

Decent filly on the Flat last season with two Listed seconds to her name over 1m4f at Naas and the Curragh, and has continued her penchant for taking the runner-up spot (six times in ten races overall) by doing so in both outings over hurdles. On the first occasion she was a little bit disappointing to be beaten two lengths at Leopardstown when favourite, and only just held on to second, but she left that form well behind when splitting Hello Neighbour and Lady Vega Allen in Grade 1 company at the DRF, and this time she was strong at the finish. Is a bigger price than those two, but with good reason as she's also in the mares' novice on Thursday.

Going preference Seems versatile
Star rating ✪

Palladium
4 b c; Trainer Nicky Henderson
Hurdles form (right-handed) 1, best RPR 110

It's not often a Group 1 winner is sent hurdling, but Palladium won the German Derby in July. That's obviously not a high-quality Group 1, but he still returned an RPR of 112, and new owner Lady Bamford shelled out €1.4m for him at the Arqana sale in October. Much was expected from him on his hurdles debut at Huntingdon, but it was underwhelming as he had to work hard enough for a two-length win from a 50-1 shot making its rules debut. He's going to need to show a lot more than that (RPR just 110) to justify his place in the Triumph, but was reportedly on target for another try in the Adonis at Kempton at the end of February. Whatever happens there, this colt will be going back on the Flat.

Going preference Acts on good to soft and heavy
Star rating ✪

Charlus
4 b g; Trainer Willie Mullins
Hurdles form (left-handed) 1, best RPR 117

Won first three of four Flat starts for Jean-Claude Rouget, finishing second in Listed company in the other, and earned a top RPR of 96. Has since joined Willie Mullins and made a good start to hurdling career at the end of January, scoring at odds of 10-11 at Naas. However, he was pretty much all out to score by a length and a quarter and the runner-up has since been a well-beaten favourite back at the same track.

Going preference Not enough evidence
Star rating ✪

Live Conti
4 b g; Trainer Dan Skelton
Hurdles form (left-handed) 11, best RPR 102

A short-head winner at Auteuil for Noel George and Amanda Zetterholm in October, Live Conti has joined Dan Skelton in a syndicate that includes Sir Alex Ferguson, and he made it 2-2 with the minimum of fuss

at Wetherby in February, scoring by three lengths. However, he was a 1-9 shot in what was a dreadful race by any standards, with the runner-up, who was second favourite, having posted a top hurdles RPR of just 81 in two previous efforts, so we still have no idea how good he really is.

Going preference Has run only on soft or heavy
Star rating ✪

Mondo Man
4 ch g; Trainer Gary and Josh Moore
Hurdles form (right-handed) 2, best RPR 114

Another high-class Flat performer, Mondo Man was fifth in Look De Vega's French Derby (beaten only four lengths) and fourth in the King Edward VII Stakes at Royal Ascot to Calandagan. Bought by new connections for €520,000 at the Arqana sale in October, he was immediately gelded and sent to Gary and Josh Moore, and he ran well enough all things considered when second to Lulamba at Ascot. An RPR of just 114 tells you how much he must find even to hit the frame in a Triumph, but that was his first run for six months and he was incredibly keen, pulling for at least a mile. Will doubtless do better when he settles and is another who was reportedly set to continue his education in the Adonis at Kempton.

Going preference Handled heavy and good to firm on the Flat
Star rating ✪

OTHERS TO CONSIDER
That's all the horses who were quoted at under 33-1 and, with a few of those next in the lists being Flat horses who at the time of writing had yet to run over hurdles (**Pappano**, **Spaceport**, **Too Bossy For Us**), it's hard to see where any further dangers are going to come from at this late stage. Considerably more was expected from the Susannah Ricci-owned **Sainte Lucie** at the DRF as she was backed into favouritism for Hello Neighbour's race, but she ran way too free in the early stages and finished a distant last of eight. She has it to prove after that and, while she hasn't got an entry in the mares' novice, three runs

over hurdles opens up the option of the Fred Winter. That said, the same owner's **Willy De Houelle**, quite an eyecatcher when fourth from way off the pace in the same Leopardstown race, is likely to go for that too.

VERDICT

*The Irish have taken the last five runnings of this, with Willie Mullins bagging four, but their challenge this year is underwhelming and it's hard to argue with a pair of British-trained runners heading the market. It's easier to argue with their respective market positions, though, as **EAST INDIA DOCK** is*

the one who is 11lb clear of the field on RPRs after his two runaway Grade 2 wins. It would, of course, be no surprise at all if Lulamba, called "the next Sir Gino" even before he'd made his British debut, is everything the gossip says he is because when a horse from the Henderson yard is so well backed they're rarely far away. Henderson certainly knows how to win a Triumph, although he'll be hoping this one has more luck in getting to the festival than Sir Gino. All that said, there's so much to like about the way East India Dock goes about hurdling and he boasts far and away the best form.

TRIUMPH HURDLE RESULTS AND TRENDS

	FORM	WINNER	AGE & WGT	Adj RPR	SP	TRAINER	BEST RPR LAST 12 MONTHS (RUNS SINCE)
24	1-3	Majborough	4 11-2	150-5	6-1	W Mullins (IRE)	3rd Gd1 Leopardstown novice hurdle (2m) (0)
23	1-112	Lossiemouth D, BF	4 10-9	161T	11-8f	W Mullins (IRE)	won Leopardstown Gd2 hurdle (2m) (1)
22	21	Vauban D	4 11-0	158T	6-4f	W Mullins (IRE)	won Gd1 Leopardstown novice hurdle (2m) (0)
21	1-111	Quilixios D	4 11-0	158-4	2-1	H de Bromhead (IRE)	won Down Royal hurdle (2m½f) (1)
20	1	Burning Victory D	4 10-7	139-21	12-1	W Mullins (IRE)	won Gd3 Fairyhouse novice hurdle (2m) (0)
19	1	Pentland Hills D	4 11-0	139-21	20-1	N Henderson	won Plumpton Class 4 novice hurdle (2m) (0)
18	22	Farclas	4 11-0	155-3	9-1	G Elliott (IRE)	2nd Gd1 Leopardstown novice hurdle (2m) (0)
17	11111	Defi Du Seuil CD	4 11-0	164T	5-2f	P Hobbs	won Gd1 Finale Hurdle (2m) (1)
16	14	Ivanovich Gorbatov D, BF	4 11-0	149-5	9-2f	A O'Brien (IRE)	won Leopardstown maiden hurdle (2m) (1)
15	111	Peace And Co CD	4 11-0	159T	2-1f	N Henderson	2nd Doncaster Gd2 hurdle (2m½f) (1)

FAVOURITES: £6.88

TRAINERS IN THIS RACE (w-pl-r): Willie Mullins 4-9-36, Nicky Henderson 2-2-9, Gordon Elliott 1-4-7, Henry de Bromhead 1-1-3, Alan King 0-0-10, Dan Skelton 0-1-2, David Pipe 0-1-5, Joseph O'Brien 0-1-6, Paul Nicholls 0-0-11, Ben Pauling 0-0-2

FATE OF FAVOURITES: 1114PU4115 **POSITION OF WINNER IN MARKET:** 1115752114

Key trends

➤Last ran between 18 and 55 days ago, ten winners in the last ten runnings

➤Won at least 50 per cent of hurdle races, 9/10 (exception still a maiden)

➤Top-two finish last time out, 8/10 (six won)

➤Adjusted RPR of at least 150, 7/10

➤By a Group 1-winning sire, 7/10

➤Ran no more than three times over hurdles, 7/10

Other factors

➤Five of the last ten winners were undefeated over hurdles (two had run only once)

➤Six winners had landed Graded events

➤Since the introduction of the Fred Winter Hurdle in 2005, 17 of the 20 winners have had an SP of 10-1 or shorter

➤The two winners to have finished outside the first two on their most recent start were both owned by JP McManus

East India Dock: Racing Post Rating of 143 puts him 11lb clear of Lulamba

2.00 William Hill County Handicap Hurdle ITV/RTV
➤2m1f ➤Premier Handicap ➤£110,000

This ultra-competitive 2m1f handicap hurdle can have up to 26 runners and being in the right ratings bracket has become a virtual prerequisite.

LAST YEAR'S WINNER Absurde scored at 12-1 for Willie Mullins, who has now won seven of the 15 runnings since his first success in 2010.

FORM The William Hill Hurdle (formerly Betfair) at Newbury and the Liffey Handicap Hurdle at the Dublin Racing Festival have been key pointers – ten of the last 24 winners had run in one of those.

RATINGS All bar four winners since 2006 were rated in the 130s with five of the last ten having run off 137-139.

AGE Only five horses older than six have won in the last 21 runnings. Second-season hurdlers have won 16 of the last 24 runnings.

TRAINERS Ireland has accounted for 12 of the last 17 winners, with nine of them trained by a Mullins. Dan Skelton (four wins) has become the British trainer to watch.

ONES TO WATCH McLaurey (Emmet Mullins) took the Liffey at the DRF. Runner-up **Storm Heart** will be a threat again for Willie Mullins, whose options also include Grade 1 runner-up **Karniquet**. **Valgrand** could get in on a decent mark for Skelton.

COUNTY HURDLE RESULTS AND TRENDS

	FORM	WINNER	AGE & WGT	OR	SP	TRAINER	BEST RPR LAST 12 MONTHS (RUNS SINCE)
24	16P4	Absurde	6 10-10	138-7	12-1	W Mullins (IRE)	4th Gd1 Leopardstown novice hurdle (2mf) (0)
23	05-4P	Faivoir C, D	8 10-7	134T	33-1	D Skelton	5th Aintree cond/am hcap hurdle (2m½f) (2)
22	2-F1	State Man D	5 11-1	141-9	11-4f	W Mullins (IRE)	won Limerick maiden hurdle (2m) (0)
21	12562	Belfast Banter D	6 10-0	129-8	33-1	P Fahey (IRE)	2nd Naas Gd2 novice hurdle (1m7½f) (0)
20	3-51	Saint Roi D	5 10-13	137-8	11-2f	W Mullins (IRE)	won Tramore maiden hurdle (2m) (0)
19	-5692	Ch'Tibello D	8 11-5	146-3	12-1	D Skelton	2nd Aintree class 2 hcap hurdle (2m4f) (0)
18	-1023	Mohaayed D	6 10-8	139-4	33-1	D Skelton	3rd Gd1 Christmas Hurdle (0)
17	1142-	Arctic Fire D	8 11-12	158-4	20-1	W Mullins (IRE)	Seasonal debutant (0)
16	44-12	Superb Story D	5 10-12	138T	8-1	D Skelton	2nd Cheltenham Gd3 hcap hurdle (2m½f) (0)
15	F580P	Wicklow Brave D	6 11-4	138-1	25-1	W Mullins (IRE)	11th Newbury Gd3 hcap hurdle (2m½f) (1)

WINS-RUNS: 5yo 3-72, 6yo 4-70, 7yo 0-53, 8yo 3-23, 9yo 0-13, 10yo 0-7, 11yo 0-1 **FAVOURITES:** +£0.25

FATE OF FAVOURITES: 0460410102 **POSITION OF WINNER IN MARKET:** 0300610107

Key trends
➤No previous festival form, 8/10
➤At least one top-three finish in last two starts, 7/10
➤Aged five or six, 7/10
➤Officially rated 134-141, 7/10
➤Carried no more than 11st 1lb, 7/10 (two of the exceptions trained by Willie Mullins)

➤Ran no more than nine times over hurdles, 6/10

Other factors
➤There have been nine winning novices since 1996
➤Ireland has won six of the last ten runnings, including five for Willie Mullins. Dan Skelton accounts for the last four British-trained winners

2.40 Mrs Paddy Power Mares' Chase — ITV/RTV
> 2m4½f > Grade 2 > £130,000

Willie Mullins won the first two runnings but has had to settle for second in the next two, first with Allegorie De Vassy and then with Dinoblue.

That pair remain the top two hopes for Closutton and are set to line up again after their tight battle in the Opera Hat Mares Chase at Naas in February. Dinoblue just edged that 2m contest by a neck but this step up to 2m4½f will be more in favour of Allegorie De Vassy, although she was beaten by her stablemate when fourth in this race last year.

Gavin Cromwell could send Limerick Lace for a repeat bid after last year's three-quarters-of-a-length success, but on this season's form he may have better chances with up-and-coming novices Bioluminescence and Only By Night (below). Bioluminescence has been disputing ante-post favouritism with Dinoblue.

It is worth noting that the four winners have been prominent in the betting (no bigger than 3-1) but the favourites (all saddled by Mullins) have been beaten.

PADDY POWER MARES' CHASE

FORM	WINNER	AGE & WGT	OR	SP	TRAINER	BEST RPR LAST 12 MONTHS (RUNS SINCE)
24	3-121 Limerick Lace D	7 11-2	165-4	3-1	G Cromwell (IRE)	won Clonmel chase (2m2½f)(2)
23	5-111 Impervious D	7 11-5	168-3	15-8	C Murphy (IRE)	won Punchestown Gd3 nov chase (2m3½f)(0)
22	1-321 Elimay D	8 11-2	171T	9-4	W Mullins (IRE)	2nd Mares' Chase Gd2 (2m4½f) (4)
21	5-111 Colreevy D	8 11-7	166-2	9-4	W Mullins (IRE)	won Thurles Gd2 nov chase (2m4f) (0)

WINS-RUNS: 6yo 0-4, 7yo 2-11, 8yo 2-11, 9yo 0-7, 10yo 0-4 **FAVOURITES:** -£4.00

TRAINERS IN THIS RACE (w-pl-r): Willie Mullins 2-3-12, Colm Murphy 1-0-1, Gavin Cromwell 1-0-2, Henry de Bromhead 0-0-1, Venetia Williams 0-2-3, Gordon Elliott 0-0-4, Stuart Edmunds 0-1-1

FATE OF FAVOURITES: 2522 **POSITION OF WINNER IN MARKET:** 2223

3.20 Albert Bartlett Novices' Hurdle ITV/RTV
➤ 3m ➤ Grade 1 ➤ £150,000

The hardest of the Grade 1s to solve for punters, with ten of the last 11 winners priced in double figures and four of them coming in at 33-1 or 50-1. The possibly poisoned chalice of favouritism has been held recently by Gordon Elliott's The Yellow Clay, who has clear form claims after numbering a Grade 1 success in his 4-4 record over hurdles. Others in the reckoning include The Big Westerner (Henry de Bromhead), France's Jet Blue (David Cottin) and Jasmin De Vaux (Willie Mullins), last year's Champion Bumper winner. A couple of British contenders who might catch the eye further down the list are Wendigo (Jamie Snowden) and Derryhassen Paddy (Lucinda Russell). Mullins' Final Demand would be top-rated if he came here but the Turners looks his likely destination.

The Yellow Clay
6 b g; Trainer Gordon Elliott
Hurdles form 1111, best RPR 148
Left-handed 111, best RPR 148
Right-handed 1, best RPR 116
Cheltenham form (bumper) 6, best RPR 125
At the festival 13 Mar 2024 Prominent, weakened from over 1f out, finished sixth, beaten 12 lengths by Jasmin De Vaux in Champion Bumper

Has racked up plenty of experience in bumpers, which is no bad thing for this race, and wasn't far off top class in that sphere, finishing sixth at Cheltenham and second at Punchestown. He has left even that form well behind since going up in trip over hurdles, though, and is 4-4. His opening nine-length success was nothing special, but then it was never likely to be given he was 4-11 in a Down Royal maiden in November, but just 16 days later he won by ten lengths in Grade 3 company at Navan. Kept busy, he went back there for the Grade 2 Navan Novice Hurdle, but may have been feeling the effects of his previous outing as this time he only just managed to get up to beat Fleur In The Park (beaten more than 12 lengths behind him the time before) by a neck. Better was to come after he'd been fully rested, though, and he ran out a comfortable eight-length winner of the Grade 1 Lawlor's of Naas Novice Hurdle from Supersundae, with Wingmen three lengths further back in third and Champion Bumper winner and 11-8 favourite Jasmin De Vaux beaten another 11 lengths. Afterwards

trainer Gordon Elliott said The Yellow Clay would more than likely go for the Turners, but he'd likely have Final Demand and The New Lion to deal with there, and the market has been anticipating him coming here instead for quite a while. He'd be the clear form pick of those likely to run and there isn't much doubt that he'll stay.

Going preference Has won on anything from good to yielding to soft

Star rating ✪✪✪✪✪

Final Demand
6 b g; Trainer Willie Mullins
Hurdles form 11, best RPR 154
Left-handed 1, best RPR 154
Right-handed 1, best RPR 134

Considered more likely to run in the Turners on Wednesday, so is dealt with in more detail in that section, but would be favourite for this as well, and was going further and further clear at the line over 2m6f at the Dublin Racing Festival.

Going preference Has won on soft and yielding/soft

Star rating ✪

The Big Westerner
6 b m; Trainer Henry de Bromhead
Hurdles form (right-handed) 11, best RPR 130

Point winner last March who is 2-2 over hurdles for Henry de Bromhead since, winning her maiden hurdle over 2m5½f at Punchestown in November and then picking up well to take the Grade 2 Land Rover Novice Hurdle at Limerick by just over four lengths from Mozzies Sister (Fleur In The Park beaten ten lengths into fourth). Her trainer says she has gears and would have no problem coming back down in trip, but she's a considerably bigger price for the Turners and she's a half-sister to Stay Away Fay, who won this two years ago. Doesn't have the level of experience often associated with a winner of this, but De Bromhead's Minella Indo was similarly lightly raced (one extra run in bumper), although he was 50-1.

Going preference Yet to race on quicker than yielding to soft

Star rating ✪✪✪

Jet Blue
6 b g; Trainer David Cottin
Hurdles form U3121, best RPR 141
Left-handed 3121, best RPR 141
Right-handed U
Cheltenham form 1, best RPR 141

Has certainly packed in the experience because he ran, ridiculously, in no fewer than ten bumpers in France, winning three of them. Went back to bumpers last spring after two uninspiring first efforts over hurdles but has got his act together this season, winning two of his three hurdles outings since October. The first two runs came over just 2m2f at Auteuil (runner-up in the second of them) but he then showed massive improvement when sent to Cheltenham and upped to 3m for an Albert Bartlett trial in December, powering away to win by six and a half lengths under James Reveley and on his debut for David Cottin. That form isn't particularly strong, but there was a lot to like about the way he went about it, not least the fact that he ran arrow-straight after the last. A lot of inexperienced horses tend to wander all over the place in this race, but he's had more than enough practice to know what to do when asked. The French won the very first running of this with Moulin Riche (Francois Doumen) in 2005, and he had 15 runs under his belt, having won over both hurdles and fences.

Going preference Cheltenham win on good

to soft and has won on heavy in France
Star rating ✪✪✪✪

Wingmen
7 b g; Trainer Gordon Elliott
Hurdles form (left-handed) 1232, best RPR 138
Cheltenham form 2, best RPR 125

Point and dual bumper winner who won his opening novice hurdle at Navan in November but has been found wanting since, including at Cheltenham on his second outing when made to look pedestrian by the Dan Skelton-trained Country Mile. He still went up to Grade 1 company on his next two starts, performing with some credit when an 11-length third to stablemate The Yellow Clay in the Lawlor's of Naas and a 12-length runner-up to Final Demand at the DRF, but that obviously leaves him with a fair bit to find. A clear second string behind The Yellow Clay, but last year's winning stablemate Stellar Story lost his next three runs in Graded company after a debut win, including when putting up a similar effort at the DRF, and he bounced back to win this at 33-1. It's that type of race.

Going preference Best form on soft but has won on quicker
Star rating ✪

Jasmin De Vaux
6 b g; Trainer Willie Mullins
Hurdles form (left-handed) 144, best RPR 135
Cheltenham form (bumper) 1, best RPR 137
At the festival 13 Mar 2024 Held up in rear, steady headway on outer from 7f out, pressed leaders 2f out, ridden over 1f out, led inside final furlong, soon edged right, kept on well, won Champion Bumper by a length and three-quarters from Romeo Coolio

Top-class bumper horse last season who was the choice of Patrick Mullins at Cheltenham following a 15-length debut win at Naas and duly did the business with a length-and-three-quarters success from Romeo Coolio in the big one. A well-beaten eighth when attempting to follow up at Punchestown in May, he made a good start to his hurdling career by winning a 25-runner maiden at Navan in December, but since then has been found wanting, albeit in Grade 1 company. Beaten 22 lengths when fourth to The Yellow Clay in the Lawlor's of Naas, he occupied the same spot behind Final Demand at the DRF at a distance of 17 and a half lengths, although he kept on again on the run-in and could do better stepped up another couple of furlongs (has a half-brother who won over 3m1½f, albeit in weak company). He needs to step up quite a lot to take a hand, and definitely needs to improve his jumping, but he has festival-winning form to his name, which must count for something. A Champion Bumper winner has yet to win this.

Going preference Acts very well on soft, below-par on one run on quicker
Star rating ✪

Wendigo
6 br g; Trainer Jamie Snowden
Hurdles form 2121, best RPR 139
Left-handed 221, best RPR 139
Right-handed 1, best RPR 123

Point and dual bumper winner who has yet to finish outside the first two in four outings over hurdles and showed quite useful form in one of them. A beaten favourite at lowly Hexham on his debut in October, he then took a quite valuable novice at Ludlow by five lengths, although only four turned up, one of them was 200-1 and it was a Class 2 in name only. Still, trainer Jamie Snowden had seen enough to give him a shot at the Grade 1 Challow Hurdle at Newbury and he was certainly vindicated when Wendigo took second place behind The New Lion, although he was beaten nearly five lengths by a horse who barely came off the bridle. He made it 2-4 over hurdles in mid-February a Wetherby, but that was in one of a couple of races at the track that day that were a bad advertisement for British racing as he went off at odds of 1-11 and beat a second favourite who had no better than an RPR of 89 to his name. It told us nothing. Yet to try 3m, but this is his only entry.

Going preference Winning form on all surfaces
Star rating ✪

Ballybow
6 b g; Trainer Gordon Elliott
Hurdles form 0211, best RPR 132
Left-handed 1, best RPR 127

The Yellow Clay: clear form choice after winning all four starts over hurdles

Right-handed 021, best RPR 132

Second in a couple of points and won on his bumper debut for Gordon Elliott, but has been a slower learner over hurdles. Could manage no better than 15th of 25 on his debut at Fairyhouse in November, but improved to take second over 2m4f at Down Royal the

Derryhassen Paddy
6 b g; Trainer Lucinda Russell
Hurdles form (left-handed) 11, best RPR 134

Point winner in December 2023 who was quite impressive when making all on his bumper debut for Lucinda Russell the following February, albeit in a weak enough race. He's gone 2-2 over hurdles since, winning his maiden at Uttoxeter in November, then battling well for a short-head victory over Honky Tonk Highway at Windsor's Winter Million fixture.

Going preference Has won on soft and heavy
Star rating ✪

Flicker Of Hope
6 bb g; Trainer Mark Fahey
Hurdles form 0094118113, best RPR 134
Left-handed 113, best RPR 134
Right-handed 0094181, best RPR 118

Has packed in plenty of experience over hurdles, running ten times since his debut in November 2023, and it's fair to say he's been a bit of a slow-burner. Didn't bust an RPR of 100 until winning a handicap off a mark of 99 in May last year, but he's won two more handicaps since, including a valuable Listed one at Navan over 3m1f in December. Arguably improved again when a two-length third to Perceval Legallois in another big handicap at the DRF and is certainly well worth his Irish handicap mark of 132. However, despite winning three handicaps at 3m-plus, he hasn't run in a Pertemps qualifier, so if he's going over 3m at Cheltenham it'll have to be in this.

Going preference Best form on soft
Star rating ✪

Fishery Lane
6 gr g; Trainer Willie Mullins
Hurdles form (right-handed) 31, best RPR 116
Cheltenham form (bumper) 5, best RPR 131
At the festival 13 Mar 2024 Held up in rear, headway on outer over 3f out, outpaced 2f out, stayed on inside final furlong, finished fifth, beaten six lengths by Jasmin De Vaux in Champion Bumper

Didn't manage to win in three bumper outings for Willie Mullins but showed considerably

following month and made further progress with a maiden win back down to 2m2½f in January. He completed his prep with a game half-length win in a Grade 3 over 3m at Clonmel, but it was only a three-runner race.

Going preference Seems versatile
Star rating ✪

better form than some who did because he was a 66-1 fifth on his second outing in the Champion Bumper and was staying on strongly at the line. Finishing tailed off at Punchestown next time was a big backward step, however, and he has been kept very low key over hurdles since, running a ten-length third in a 2m7f Fairyhouse maiden in December and then winning one over 2m4f at the same track in January. Bumper run suggests there's loads of ability, but he has tons to find on hurdles form.

Going preference Acts well on soft
Star rating ✪

Moon Rocket
5 br g; Trainer Kim Bailey and Mat Nicholls
Hurdles form (left-handed) 1122, best RPR 131

Won the second of his two points in April last year and started well over hurdles for Kim Bailey and Mat Nicholls, running away with a Doncaster maiden by 12 lengths in November and defying a penalty with an eight-length romp at Southwell on New Year's Day, albeit from a 66-1 shot with little worthwhile form. A step up in grade followed in the River Don back at Doncaster at the end of that month and he progressed again to go down by just a neck to Yellow Car, rallying well after a less than fluent jump at the last and just failing to get up. He appeared to be put well in his place by Battle Born Lad in the Albert Bartlett Trial at Haydock, though, going down by five and a half lengths to a horse not even entered for this.

Going preference Acts on good to soft and soft
Star rating ✪

Sounds Victorius
6 br g; Trainer Willie Mullins
Hurdles form 215, best RPR 128
Left-handed 5, best RPR 128
Right-handed 21, best RPR 122
Cheltenham form (bumper) 4, best RPR 132
At the festival 13 Mar 2024 In touch with leaders, outpaced over 2f out, went fourth over 1f out, stayed on, finished fourth, beaten five and a half lengths by Jasmin De Vaux in Champion Bumper

Won only one of four bumpers for Willie Mullins but stayed on strongly for fourth in the Champion Bumper and occupied the same spot at the Punchestown festival afterwards. Beaten at odds of 2-5 in a seven-runner good-ground maiden hurdle back at Punchestown in November, he got the job done next time on New Year's Day in another one at Fairyhouse, albeit at odds of 4-11 this time. After that he made the big jump up to Grade 1 company and wasn't altogether disgraced despite finishing a 22-length fifth to Final Demand at Leopardstown. He was noted keeping on again after the last and is the sort who looks like he'll stay forever, so if we get deep ground and a real test on the final day he might outrun his odds.

Going preference Seems best on soft/heavy
Star rating ✪✪

Yellow Car
7 br g; Trainer David Killahena and Graeme McPherson
Hurdles form (left-handed) 121531, best RPR 130
Cheltenham form 3, best RPR 126

Won one of three points in May last year and won two of first three outings over hurdles, albeit in small races at Newton Abbot in July and Fontwell in September. He looked to have been found out when well beaten on his handicap debut at Doncaster in November, but that was over just 2m3½f and he improved again when stepped up to 3m afterwards, first when beaten just under ten lengths into third by Jet Blue in an Albert Bartlett trial at Cheltenham in December and then when just holding off Moon Rocket in the River Don at Doncaster. Clearly stays well but plenty to find.

Going preference Has yet to race on anything worse than good to soft
Star rating ✪

OTHERS TO CONSIDER
You could probably name another half a dozen 40-1 shots and not find the winner, such has been the nature of this race in the last ten years (Stellar Story just crept into the 'others' section a year ago). **Intense Approach** is a second-season hurdler with loads of experience

ALBERT BARTLETT NOVICES' HURDLE RESULTS AND TRENDS

	FORM	WINNER	AGE & WGT	Adj RPR	SP	TRAINER	BEST RPR LAST 12 MONTHS (RUNS SINCE)
24	-1324	Stellar Story	7 11-7	146-13	33-1	G Elliott (IRE)	4th Gd1 Leopardstown nov hurdle (2m6½f) (0)
23	12	Stay Away Fay BF	6 11-7	144-15	18-1	P Nicholls	2nd Doncaster Gd2 novice hurdle (3m½f) (0)
22	111	The Nice Guy	7 11-8	147-10	18-1	W Mullins (IRE)	won Naas maiden hurdle (2m3f) (0)
21	2120	Vanillier	6 11-5	153-3	14-1	G Cromwell (IRE)	2nd Limerick Gd2 novice hurdle (2m7f) (1)
20	2211	Monkfish D	6 11-5	159-2	5-1	W Mullins (IRE)	won Thurles novice hurdle (2m6½f) (0)
19	3-32	Minella Indo	6 11-5	147-13	50-1	H de Bromhead (IRE)	2nd Clonmel Gd3 novice hurdle (3m) (0)
18	3113	Kilbricken Storm CD	7 11-5	152-11	33-1	C Tizzard	won Cheltenham Gd2 novice hurdle (3m) (1)
17	11141	Penhill D	6 11-5	157-2	16-1	W Mullins (IRE)	won Limerick Gd2 novice hurdle (3m) (0)
16	-1111	Unowhatimeanharry CD	8 11-5	154-9	11-1	H Fry	won Exeter class 2 hcap hurdle (2m7f) (0)
15	11F12	Martello Tower D	7 11-7	151-6	14-1	M Mullins (IRE)	2nd Leopardstown Gd2 novice hurdle (2m4f) (0)

WINS-RUNS: 5yo 0-24, 6yo 5-108, 7yo 4-38, 8yo 1-7 **FAVOURITES:** -£10.00

TRAINERS IN THIS RACE (w-pl-r): Willie Mullins 3-4-39, Gavin Cromwell 1-1-3, Henry de Bromhead 1-1-8, Paul Nicholls 1-0-5, Gordon Elliott 1-4-14, Margaret Mullins 1-0-1, Dan Skelton 0-0-4, Alan King 0-0-2, Ben Pauling 0-1-4, John McConnell 0-2-4, Lucy Wadham 0-0-1, Nicky Henderson 0-2-11, Emma Lavelle 0-0-2, Rebecca Curtis 0-0-6, Olly Murphy 0-0-2

FATE OF FAVOURITES: 0PU3244POP **POSITION OF WINNER IN MARKET:** 7670039680

and on the up judging by his Musselburgh win, **Mozzies Sister** is consistent and **Ma Shantou** shaped as though he wants a strong test when third in the River Don. He's only tiny, though, and may get lost in this. **Battle Born Lad**, quite an impressive winner of the Albert Bartlett Trial at Haydock in the middle of February, wasn't entered and, while there is a supplementary stage, his winning jockey appeared to think this race would come too soon, so Aintree is his likely next port of call.

VERDICT

The Yellow Clay is the clear pick of those who are likely to run, and one day this race will again go to form, but this contest often leaves you wanting to tear up the form book and the history of long-priced winners makes him easy enough to leave alone. Of course, SP stats are usually totally meaningless, but in the case of this race you can find a reason for its unpredictability. Most of the runners are backward, long-term chasing types with any amount of improvement in them, but they lack the nous to deal with a strongly run race run under championship conditions. Some will thrive and some will fold (the best four horses to emerge from the 2023 running were Monty's Pass, Corbetts Cross, Chianti Classico and Embassy Gardens and they all failed to finish) and it's so very hard to bet with confidence. I normally have a stab

Key trends

➤Aged six or seven, 9/10

➤Adjusted RPR of at least 146, 9/10

➤Top-three finish last time out, 8/10

➤No more than four hurdle runs, 7/10 (the last seven)

➤Won over at least 2m4f, 7/10

Other factors

➤Only four winners had won a Graded hurdle

➤None of the last ten winners was RPR top-rated and five of the last seven winners were rated 10lb-15lb off top

➤Nine winners had an SP in double figures (from 11-1 to 50-1)

*at an outsider or two on the day (without any success, to be fair) and the pick for the moment is **SOUNDS VICTORIUS**. He'll probably need an absolute bog to be a factor, but he gives the impression he'll stay forever and he might be able to surprise a few of those with better form.*

4.00 Boodles Cheltenham Gold Cup — ITV/RTV
➤ 3m2½f ➤ Grade 1 ➤ £625,000

Galopin Des Champs landed his third consecutive Irish Gold Cup in February and has an outstanding chance of doing the same at Cheltenham to become the first to complete a Gold Cup hat-trick since Best Mate in 2004. The last before that was the mighty Arkle in the 1960s, showing what a rare and coveted feat Galopin Des Champs stands on the verge of completing. Willie Mullins' superstar chaser has recorded a Racing Post Rating in the 180s for the third consecutive season, which again puts him head and shoulders above the opposition. The King George VI Chase, a championship contest in its own right, is always a place to look for a serious challenger (Bravemansgame, that season's winner, was runner-up in Galopin Des Champs' first Gold Cup) and Banbridge is firmly in the picture after his Kempton triumph. Joseph O'Brien's highly versatile nine-year-old took his RPR to a career-best 174 there and would be a threat if he gets decent ground. There are plenty of high-class chasers around, mostly among the second-season group (Fact To File, Corbetts Cross, Monty's Star), but none is yet to touch the exceptional quality of Galopin Des Champs.

Galopin Des Champs

9 bl g; Trainer Willie Mullins
Chase form 11F1111231112311, best RPR 184
Left-handed 11F1111111, best RPR 184
Right-handed 112323, best RPR 177
Cheltenham form (all) 1F11, best RPR 184
At the festival 19 Mar 2021 Led, tracked leaders when headed after 2nd, led approaching last, ridden and kept on strongly run-in, readily, won Martin Pipe Conditional Jockeys' Handicap Hurdle by two and a quarter lengths from Langer Dan
17 Mar 2022 Led, 5 lengths ahead 2nd, not fluent 6th, mistake 9th, going easily 3 out, pushed along and went clear when good jump 2 out, 12 lengths ahead when fell last in Turners Novices' Chase won by Bob Olinger
17 Mar 2023 Held up in rear, not fluent 5th, headway 16th, in touch with leaders 17th, mistake 3 out, going easily when switched right before 2 out, soon went second, led last, ridden and kept on strongly run-in, won going away by seven lengths from Bravemansgame in Gold Cup
15 Mar 2024 Prominent, disputing second going easily 3 out, pushed along to lead 2 out, 3 lengths ahead last, ridden run-in, kept on well, won Gold Cup by three and a half lengths from Gerri Colombe

The superstar staying chaser of his generation and bang on target to join Arkle and Best Mate as the most recent three-time winners of the Gold Cup. When suffering defeat at Punchestown after his first Gold Cup, and then again at the same track in the John Durkan Memorial first time out the next season, there were those keen to suggest that the Gold Cup "breaks horses" and that he wouldn't be the same again, but he made those assertions look laughable by then winning the Savills, Irish Gold Cup and Gold

Galopin Des Champs wins his second Gold Cup from Gerri Colombe

Cup in commanding fashion and confirming himself head and shoulders the best staying chaser in training. It has been a similar story since then as he again lost to Fastorslow (sadly now out for this season) at Punchestown in May and then found young guns Fact To File and Spillane's Tower too quick for him in the John Durkan, going down by two and three-quarter lengths to the pair who were split by only half a length. While nobody suggested he was finished then, it was Fact To File who was made ante-post favourite for the Savills over Christmas. However, Galopin Des Champs had assumed the mantle of favouritism by the off, made all the running and powered away to score by seven and a half lengths from Fact To File, who briefly looked a threat going to the last but didn't have the winner's staying power. A third Irish Gold Cup couldn't have gone any better for him and trainer Willie Mullins as Galopin Des Champs was again allowed to set his own pace, went steady and can't have had that hard a race in beating stablemate Grangeclare West by just under five lengths, with Fact To File losing second on the run-in. His only defeat in ten chase outings on a left-handed track came when he fell with a 12-length advantage at the last in the 2022 Turners, and all looks set fair for him to join the greats. Indeed, with his main market rivals not even guaranteed to line up, it's hard to see what's going to beat him.

Going preference Has won on anything from good to yielding to soft
Star rating ✪✪✪✪✪

Fact To File
8 b g; Trainer Willie Mullins
Chase form 2111123, best RPR 171
Left-handed 211123, best RPR 171
Right-handed 1, best RPR 169
Cheltenham form (all) 21, best RPR 166
At the festival 15 Mar 2023 Towards rear of midfield, headway on outer from over 3f out, pushed along over 2f out, ridden over 1f out, disputed lead when short of room and unbalanced inside final furlong, kept on but held inside final 110yds, finished second, beaten a length and a quarter by A Dream To Share in Champion Bumper
13 Mar 2024 Jumped right on occasions, took keen hold, towards rear, in touch with leaders

10th, headway 3 out, soon pressed leaders going easily, led 2 out, good jump last, ridden briefly and went clear run-in, readily, won Brown Advisory Novices' Chase by three and three-quarter lengths from Monty's Star

Is now a short-priced favourite for the Ryanair on Thursday, so is dealt with in more detail in that section, but remains clear second favourite for this despite all the evidence suggesting he's going to have a real struggle with the Gold Cup distance, which is two furlongs further than he ran over in the Savills and Irish Gold Cup and in which he looked to be running out of puff both times. Unless his trainer thinks he can find some way of getting him to last the extra distance or owner JP McManus puts his foot down – and he may end up with the second favourite in Corbetts Cross anyway – it's hard to see him lining up, and it's hard to see him being a threat anyway.

Going preference Acts on any, zero chance of staying if it's very soft
Star rating ✪

Banbridge
9 ch g; Trainer Joseph O'Brien
Chase form 113211914U1, best RPR 174
Left-handed 12194, best RPR 158
Right-handed 1311U1, best RPR 174
Cheltenham form (all) 119, best RPR 158
At the festival 18 Mar 2022 Took keen hold, raced wide early, prominent, went second 7th, joined leader 3 out, led after 2 out, joined but clear with one other before last, soon ridden, kept on strongly final 110yds, won Martin Pipe Conditional Jockeys' Handicap Hurdle by a length and a half from Cobblers Dream
14 Mar 2024 Took keen hold, in touch with leaders, mistake 2nd, not fluent 11th, lost ground when mistake 4 out, weakened after 3 out, finished ninth, beaten 75 lengths by Protektorat in Ryanair Chase

Another who could well go elsewhere, although in his case it's more up in the air as he's a similar price for this and the Ryanair (and was even left in the Champion Chase at the latest scratchings stage). Although already nine, he could be the coming force at any distance as he has bagged Grade 1 victories from 2m to 3m in the past 12 months. On the first occasion he beat Champion Chase winner Captain Guinness in the Punchestown version in May, just getting up to win by a neck in first-time cheekpieces. While he didn't show much at all in the Grade 2 Fortria on his return at Navan, he looked to be in the process of giving dual Champion Chase winner Energumene a real fright the following month in the Hilly Way at Cork, but unseated at the last when closing. He was conceding 10lb to the winner, who was admittedly returning from a long absence, so that had to go down as a top-class effort, and he bettered that when stepping up to 3m for the first time over fences in the King George at Kempton, with the cheekpieces back on for the first time since Punchestown. There he was given a patient ride and, despite the sectionals suggesting runaway leader Il Est Francais hadn't gone overly fast, he managed to turn a ten-length deficit turning for home into a length-and-three-quarters victory, nabbing the runner-up just after the last. The question, of course, is whether he'll be able to see out 3m2½f, as even on good ground the Gold Cup will take a good 40 seconds more to run, while it'll be an extra minute and more on soft. The ground is an issue, as Banbridge doesn't want it soft. A non-runner in the Turners because of soft ground in 2023, he did show up on bad ground in last season's Ryanair but finished a tailed-off last of nine finishers, 40 lengths behind the eighth.

Going preference Doesn't want it worse than good to soft
Star rating ✪✪✪

Corbetts Cross
8 ch g; Trainer Emmet Mullins
Chase form 312F13262, best RPR 169
Left-handed 32132, best RPR 169
Right-handed 1F62, best RPR 157
Cheltenham form (all) RO1, best RPR 163
At the festival 17 Mar 2023 Raced freely, towards rear, headway and midfield after halfway, switched right and prominent on outer when not fluent 2 out, pushed along and made strong challenge approaching last, ridden and 1 length down when jinked right and ran out last in Albert Bartlett Novices' Hurdle won by Stay Away Fay
12 Mar 2024 Held up in rear, in touch with leaders on outer 10th, pressed leaders going easily after 3 out, good jump to lead 2 out, soon went clear, readily, won National Hunt Chase by

17 lengths from Embassy Gardens

Took time to reveal his true talents as a chaser, running to a peak RPR of just 149 in his first four starts and falling in one of them, but that all changed at last year's festival when he ran to 163 after being well backed for the 3m6f National Hunt Chase and romping home by 17 lengths from Embassy Gardens. He then proved he had the potential to be a player in the big league when he stepped out of novice company to run a two-and-three-quarter-length third to Gold Cup runner-up Gerri Colombe, upping his personal best to 169. However, he didn't fare so well in his first two runs this season, although the market suggested he badly needed the run when a seven-length second to Heart Wood and he was conceding plenty of weight to the winner. However, it was a backward step in the King George as he could never get into it from the back, finishing a 21-length sixth to Banbridge. Warmed up for the Gold Cup in the Ascot Chase in February, finishing ten-length runner-up to Pic D'Orhy over a way-too-short 2m5f. It wasn't a bad run at all considering he clearly wants further, but he's not the quickest jumper at times and that may hold him back when it matters.

Going preference Has won on yielding, best form on soft or heavy
Star rating ✪✪

Monty's Star
8 b g; Trainer Henry de Bromhead
Chase form 312225, best RPR 162
Left-handed 25, best RPR 162
Right-handed 3122, best RPR 155
Cheltenham form (all) P2, best RPR 156
At the festival 17 Mar 2023 Towards rear, not fluent 7th, pushed along after 3 out, soon weakened and behind, pulled up before 2 out in Albert Bartlett Novices' Hurdle won by Stay Away Fay
13 Mar 2024 Pressed leader, briefly led 7th, challenging 2 out, kept on run-in, no match for winner, finished second, beaten three and three-quarter lengths by Fact To File

Shapes like a very strong stayer and plugged on best of the rest to be second to Fact To File in last season's Brown Advisory. While he never laid a glove on the winner, he was beaten only three and three-quarter lengths. Went that little bit closer to a maiden Grade 1 success after that at Punchestown, but this time had no answer to the finish of Spillane's Tower, who headed him at the last. He's another who has been slow to get going this term, as he went down by five lengths to Embassy Gardens in the Grade 3 New Year's Day Chase at Tramore despite being in receipt of 6lb, but he stepped up a fair bit on that when fifth to Galopin Des Champs in the Irish Gold Cup (got a little closer to Fact To File than he had in the Brown Advisory) and his whole season has been geared around the spring. The extra two furlongs of the Gold Cup at Cheltenham look sure to suit and, with potential runners dropping like flies, it won't be a surprise if he can get in the frame. A peak RPR of just 162 tells you he has a mountain to climb to beat the favourite, however.

Going preference Seems to act on most surfaces
Star rating ✪✪✪

Grangeclare West
9 b g; Trainer Willie Mullins
Chase form 11P62, best RPR 165
Left-handed 1162, best RPR 165
Right-handed P

Fragile nine-year-old who has managed just ten career runs over four seasons but has occasionally looked as though he could be top class if he could ever stay sound. His promise as a chaser was undeniable in his first two novice outings last term as he won both, beating the talented Heart Wood on his debut at Naas in November and then running out an easy winner of the Grade 1 Neville Hotels Novice Chase at Leopardstown over Christmas, being eased down to beat Corbetts Cross by six lengths. Unfortunately disaster then struck as he was cast in his box when due to challenge for the Ladbrokes Novice Chase at the DRF and he wasn't seen again until November, when he shared the early lead in the John Durkan Memorial at Punchestown but weakened quickly after the fourth-last and was pulled up before the last. He at least finished his race next time, taking a distant sixth (23 lengths) to Galopin Des Champs

in the Savills, and he was better still when a 66-1 runner-up to the same horse in the Irish Gold Cup last time, nabbing Fact To File for that spot on the run to the line. As usual for a top Willie Mullins-trained horse, he's being primed to hit top form in the spring, so it won't be a surprise if he can step up on that performance at Cheltenham – if he can get there in one piece.

Going preference Seems to act on any ground
Star rating ✪✪

L'Homme Presse
10 b g; Trainer Venetia Williams
Chase form 1111131U12431P, best RPR 172
Left-handed 1131141, best RPR 172
Right-handed 111U23P, best RPR 170
Cheltenham form 1141, best RPR 166
At the festival 16 Mar 2022 Travelled strongly, jumped well, tracked leader, led and made rest from 7th, 3 lengths ahead 2 out, ridden after last, kept on well, won Brown Advisory Novices' Chase by three and a half lengths from Ahoy Senor
15 Mar 2024 Raced in second, not fluent 5th, disputed lead 12th, led clearly 4 out, headed 2 out, weakened and lost two places approaching last, finished fourth, beaten 15 and a half lengths by Galopin Des Champs in Gold Cup

Possibly Britain's only realistic contender for the Gold Cup, L'Homme Presse has given every indication he's just as good as he was this season. The Venetia Williams-trained ten-year-old, who finished fourth to Galopin Des Champs in last year's Gold Cup and won the Brown Advisory two years earlier, was a perfectly respectable 12-length third in the King George on his return despite jumping left on occasions. That was a fine effort after nearly 300 days off the track and he built on it with a three-quarter-length victory over Stage Star in the Cotswold Chase at Cheltenham. While the runner-up came out best at the weights as he was receiving 4lb, L'Homme Presse was always going to hold him after the last. For the second year running he had his warm-up in the Ascot Chase in mid-February but was pulled up after the seventh.

Going preference Acts on any ground, most effective on soft
Star rating ✪

L'Homme Presse (left): Cheltenham winner in January in the Cotswold

Grey Dawning
8 gr g; Trainer Dan Skelton
Chase form 3121132P, best RPR 168
Left-handed 121132, best RPR 168
Right-handed 3P, best RPR 134
Cheltenham form 21, best RPR 165
At the festival 14 Mar 2024 In touch with leaders, going easily when challenging before 3 out, jumped slightly left and led 2 out, edged left approaching last, ridden run-in, soon idled, kept on towards finish, won Turners Novices' Chase by two lengths from Ginny's Destiny

Had an excellent year as a novice over fences, winning three times from 2m4f to 3m, including landing the Turners at the festival by two lengths from Ginny's Destiny. Took his form to a new level on his return, though, when possibly a shade unlucky not to beat Royale Pagaille in the Grade 1 Betfair Chase at Haydock. He had assumed command heading to the last but got in too close, gave it a whack and was headed by the rallying course specialist, who went on to win by two lengths. Some saw it as evidence that he didn't

really stay, but he looked like he was edging clear until the mistake and it isn't possible to be too sure what would have happened. The ground was very testing, as it often is at Haydock, and he had the rest well beaten off. Things didn't go to plan for him in the King George next time, though, as he jumped too high at the first fence and dragged his hind legs through, which took him to the back of the field. He was always on the back foot after that and was beaten halfway down the back straight, being pulled up after the third-last. That clearly wasn't his form, and perhaps good ground on that track as well as the mistake contributed. He's worth another chance, but whether trainer Dan Skelton lets him take in the Gold Cup this year is another matter as he was leaning towards sending him to Kelso for an easy assignment in February and then on to the Bowl at Aintree. When it dawns on him how weak the challenge to Galopin Des Champs is going to be, he may yet change his mind as there's plenty of place money even

GOLD CUP RESULTS AND TRENDS

	FORM WINNER	AGE & WGT	Adj RPR	SP	TRAINER	BEST RPR LAST 12 MONTHS (RUNS SINCE)
24	2-311 **Galopin Des Champs** CD	8 11-10	188^T	10-11f	W Mullins (IRE)	won Gd1 Irish Gold Cup (3m½f) **(0)**
23	F1-11 **Galopin Des Champs** C	7 11-10	181^{-6}	7-5f	W Mullins (IRE)	won Gd1 Fairyhouse novice chase (2m4f) **(2)**
22	12-12 **A Plus Tard** C, D, BF	8 11-10	184^T	3-1f	H de Bromhead (IRE)	won Gd1 Betfair Chase (3m1½f) **(1)**
21	-11F4 **Minella Indo** C, BF	8 11-10	174^{-8}	9-1	H de Bromhead (IRE)	won Wexford Gd3 chase (2m7f) **(3)**
20	11-21 **Al Boum Photo** CD	8 11-10	182^{-1}	10-3f	W Mullins (IRE)	won Gd1 Cheltenham Gold Cup (3m2½f) **(2)**
19	F10-1 **Al Boum Photo**	7 11-10	173^{-9}	12-1	W Mullins (IRE)	won Tramore Listed chase (2m5½f) **(0)**
18	113-1 **Native River** D	8 11-10	177^T	5-1	C Tizzard	won Newbury Gd2 chase (2m7f) **(0)**
17	-3211 **Sizing John**	7 11-10	172^{-12}	7-1	J Harrington (IRE)	won Gd1 Irish Gold Cup (3m½f) **(0)**
16	111F1 **Don Cossack**	9 11-10	185^T	9-4f	G Elliott (IRE)	won Gd1 Punchestown Gold Cup (3m1f) **(4)**
15	3/111 **Coneygree** C	8 11-10	173^{-9}	7-1	M Bradstock	won Newbury Gd2 chase (2m7½f) **(0)**

WINS-RUNS: 6yo 0-2, 7yo 3-19, 8yo 6-45, 9yo 1-40, 10yo 0-16, 11yo 0-5, 12yo 0-1 **FAVOURITES:** £5.89

TRAINERS IN THIS RACE (w-pl-r): Willie Mullins 4-4-27, Henry de Bromhead 2-2-11, Gordon Elliott 1-2-8, Emmet Mullins 0-0-1, Dan Skelton 0-1-2, Patrick Neville 0-0-1, Venetia Williams 0-0-7, Joseph O'Brien 0-0-1, Lucinda Russell 0-1-2

FATE OF FAVOURITES: 0142013111 **POSITION OF WINNER IN MARKET:** 2143614111

if Grey Dawning doesn't win, but he's hardly an ante-post proposition.

Going preference Best form is on soft
Star rating ✪✪✪

OTHERS TO CONSIDER

That's the top eight in the betting discussed, three of whom might not even turn up, and the other seven are 40-1 or considerably bigger. **Jungle Boogie** is the shortest-priced of them, but he's 11, hardly ever runs and all he did last time at Ascot was beat Fil Dor, who has done nothing to justify the €620,000 paid for him at the Caldwell dispersal sale. **Gentlemansgame** doesn't stay, **Hewick** and **Ahoy Senor** have lost their form, **Royale Pagaille** shouldn't go anywhere near the place again, **The Real Whacker** is patently not good enough and **Conflated** went off at 150-1 for the Irish Gold Cup and is massively on the downgrade.

VERDICT

*All roads surely lead to **GALOPIN DES CHAMPS**, who is going to face much his easiest test in a Gold Cup unless the ground is quick and Banbridge runs. Who comes second is going to be more open and my suggestion would be **Monty's Star**, who stayed on up the hill in the Brown Advisory last year, will appreciate the extra distance and might come alive at the festival again, as Henry de Bromhead's horses tend to*

Key trends

➤ Aged between seven and nine, 10/10
➤ Adjusted RPR of at least 172, 10/10
➤ Grade 1 chase winner, 9/10
➤ No more than 13 starts over fences, 9/10
➤ Won over at least 3m, 9/10
➤ Ran no more than four times that season, 9/10
➤ Within 9lb of RPR top-rated, 9/10
➤ Won a Graded chase that season, 9/10
➤ Won or placed previously at the festival, 8/10

Other factors

➤ In 2015, Coneygree became the first winner not to have run at a previous festival since Imperial Call in 1996. He was also the first novice to win since Captain Christy in 1974
➤ Four of the last ten winners had run in the King George or Savills Chase (formerly Lexus) that season

*do. I also think **Grey Dawning** is capable of running a very big race, but Dan Skelton appears less keen to run him after his flop in the King George, at least this year.*

4.40 St James's Place Festival Hunters' Chase   ITV/RTV
➤ 3m2½f   ➤ Amateur riders   ➤ £50,000

Sine Nomine's 8-1 success for Fiona Needham last year made it six British winners in the last eight years and the nine year-old mare looks set to return, albeit after an unseating and a fall this season on her steps out of hunter chase company.

Nine horses since 1956 have won the race twice – three of them (Salsify, On The Fringe and Pacha Du Polder) in recent years.

Sine Nomine became the first winner in ten years not aged in double figures. Before the recent trend towards success for those aged ten or 11, 14 of the previous 19 winners had been nine or younger.

ONES TO WATCH Its On The Line, beaten three-quarters of a length last year as 11-8 favourite, is set to bid to go one better for Emmet Mullins. **Angels Dawn**, the 2023 Kim Muir winner, has moved smoothly into point-to-pointing for Sam Curling this season. Ross O'Sullivan's **Ryehill**, runner-up to Angels Dawn just after Christmas, then had Its On The Line back in third in a classy contest in February. **Willitgoahead** is an up-and-coming Irish seven-year-old for Sean Doyle.

HUNTERS' CHASE RESULTS AND TRENDS

FORM WINNER	AGE & WGT	Adj RPR	SP	TRAINER	BEST RPR LAST 12 MONTHS (RUNS SINCE)
24 -2121 **Sine Nomine**	8 11-7	135-17	8-1	F Needham	won Wetherby Class 5 hunter chase (3m) **(0)**
23 P1-11 **Premier Magic**	10 12-0	129-18	66-1	B Gibbs	Pulled up Festival Hunters' Chase (3m2½f) **(0)**
22 5-211 **Billaway**	10 12-0	147T	13-8f	W Mullins (IRE)	2nd Festival Hunters' Chase (3m2½f) **(4)**
21 21-12 **Porlock Bay**	10 12-0	135-20	16-1	W Biddick	2nd Wincanton Class 6 hunter chase (3m1f) **(0)**
20 -U117 **It Came To Pass**	10 12-0	126-29	66-1	E O'Sullivan (IRE)	won Cork hunter chase (3m) **(2)**
19 12-11 **Hazel Hill**	11 12-0	151-4	7-2f	P Rowley	won Warwick Class 6 hunter chase (3m) **(0)**
18 114-3 **Pacha Du Polder** CD, BF	11 12-0	145-5	25-1	P Nicholls	won Festival Hunters' Chase (3m2½f) **(2)**
17 -3341 **Pacha Du Polder** CD	10 12-0	143-8	16-1	P Nicholls	3rd Uttoxeter Listed hcap chase (3m2f) **(2)**
16 11-17 **On The Fringe** CD, BF	11 12-0	148T	13-8f	E Bolger (IRE)	won Aintree Fox Hunters' Chase (2m5f) **(2)**
15 -1122 **On The Fringe**	10 12-0	144T	6-1	E Bolger (IRE)	won Punchestown hunter chase (2m7f) **(4)**

WINS-RUNS: 6yo 0-4, 7yo 0-16, 8yo 1-22, 9yo 0-35, 10yo 6-44, 11yo 3-46, 12yo 0-32, 13yo 0-10, 14yo 0-3 **FAVOURITES:** -£0.25

TRAINERS IN THIS RACE (w-pl-r): Paul Nicholls 2-1-14, Willie Mullins 1-2-4, Bradley Gibbs 1-0-3, Fiona Needham 1-0-1, Philip Rowley 1-2-5, Emmet Mullins 0-2-2, David Christie 0-1-5, Sam Curling 0-0-1, Declan Queally 0-0-4, Chris Barber 0-0-1

FATE OF FAVOURITES: 3148122102 **POSITION OF WINNER IN MARKET:** 2160109105

Key trends
➤ Aged ten or 11, 9/10

➤ Won over at least 3m, 8/10

➤ Top-three finish last time out, 8/10

➤ Adjusted RPR of at least 135, 8/10

➤ Rated within 8lb of RPR top-rated, 6/10 (exceptions 17lb to 29lb off top)

Other factors
➤ The record of the previous year's winner is 141P7FP

➤ There have been three back-to-back winners since 2012 – Salsify (2012-13), On The Fringe (2015-16) and Pacha Du Polder (2017-18). The last one before them was Double Silk in 1993-94

➤ Five winners had competed at a previous festival

➤ Those aged 12 or older are winless in the last ten years. The 13-year-old Earthmover (2004) is the only winner from this category since 1990

5.20 Martin Pipe Conditional Jockeys' Hcap Hurdle   RTV
➤2m4½f   ➤£75,000

This 2m4½f handicap hurdle for conditional riders, first run in 2009, is not an easy 'getting out stakes' for punters at the end of the festival.

LAST YEAR'S WINNER Better Days Ahead struck at 5-1 for Gordon Elliott ahead of 100-30 favourite Waterford Whispers, with Irish raiders taking the first six places.

FORM Six of the last ten winners ran in Graded company on their previous outing.

WEIGHT AND RATINGS Runners rated between 133 and 139 have won nine of the 16 runnings but four of the last seven winners were rated 142-145.

AGE Five- and six-year-olds have won 14 of the 16 runnings.

TRAINERS Eleven of the last 14 runnings were won by Elliott, Willie Mullins, Paul Nicholls or Joseph O'Brien.

BETTING Ten of the 16 winners have been sent off at double-figure odds and Sir Des Champs in 2011 is the only successful favourite.

ONES TO WATCH Lark In The Mornin, last year's Fred Winter winner for Joseph O'Brien, is ante-post favourite even though he is yet to be tried at the trip. Among the more proven is **Wodhooh** (Gordon Elliott), whose course-and-distance win in December was boosted when runner-up Joyeuse ran away with the William Hill Hurdle at Newbury. **Karafon**, a winner at 2m3½f, is a likely type for Willie Mullins.

MARTIN PIPE HANDICAP HURDLE RESULTS AND TRENDS

	FORM	WINNER	AGE & WGT	OR	SP	TRAINER	BEST RPR LAST 12 MONTHS (RUNS SINCE)
24	-F142	**Better Days Ahead**	6 11-7	140-6	5-1	G Elliott (IRE)	2nd Navan novice hurdle (2m) (0)
23	44-11	**Iroko** D	5 11-5	138T	6-1	O Greenall/J Guerriero won Wetherby Class 3 hcap hurdle (2m3½f) (0)
22	11471	**Banbridge** D	6 11-3	137-7	12-1	J O'Brien (IRE)	won Navan novice hurdle (2m) (0)
21	12P6	**Galopin Des Champs**	5 11-9	142-8	8-1	W Mullins (IRE)	6th Leopardstown Gd1 novice hurdle (2m) (0)
20	52231	**Indefatigable** CD	7 11-9	145-3	25-1	P Webber	won Warwick Listed hurdle (2m5f) (0)
19	30-52	**Early Doors**	6 11-10	145-3	5-1	J O'Brien (IRE)	2nd Leopardstown Gd1 hurdle (3m) (0)
18	32161	**Blow By Blow** D	7 11-10	144-1	11-1	G Elliott (IRE)	won Thurles Gd3 novice hurdle (2m4f) (0)
17	23213	**Champagne Classic** D	6 11-3	138-9	12-1	G Elliott (IRE)	won Thurles maiden hurdle (2m6½f) (1)
16	4-235	**Ibis Du Rheu**	5 11-7	139-4	14-1	P Nicholls	3rd Lanzarote Handicap Hurdle (2m5f) (1)
15	-5123	**Killultagh Vic** D	6 11-1	135-5	7-1	W Mullins (IRE)	3rd Leopardstown Gd2 nov hurdle (2m4f) (0)

WINS-RUNS: 5yo 3-55, 6yo 5-85, 7yo 2-39, 8yo 0-28, 9yo 0-10, 10yo 0-7, 11yo 0-1 **FAVOURITES:** -£10.00

FATE OF FAVOURITES: 3000200B52 **POSITION OF WINNER IN MARKET:** 2676205633

Key trends
➤Top-three finish in at least one of last two starts, 9/10

➤No more than eight hurdle runs, 9/10

➤Aged five or six, 8/10

➤Had won that season, 8/10

➤Officially rated 137-144, 7/10

➤Rated within 6lb of RPR top-rated, 7/10

Other factors
➤Gordon Elliott (three), Willie Mullins and Joseph O'Brien (two each) account for the seven Irish-trained winners

➤The six winners from 2012 to 2017 carried 11st 1lb to 11st 7lb. Four of the last seven had 11st 9lb or 11st 10lb

➤Willie Mullins trained the last two winners rated lower than 137